101 Ready-to-Use
Excel® Macros

by Michael Alexander and John Walkenbach

WILEY

John Wiley & Sons, Inc.

101 Ready-to-Use Excel® Macros

Published by
John Wiley & Sons, Inc.
111 River Street
Hoboken, NJ 07030-5774
www.wiley.com

For general information on our other products and services, please contact our Customer Care Department within the U.S. at 877-762-2974, outside the U.S. at 317-572-3993, or fax 317-572-4002.

For technical support, please visit www.wiley.com/techsupport.

Wiley publishes in a variety of print and electronic formats and by print-on-demand. Some material included with standard print versions of this book may not be included in e-books or in print-on-demand. If this book refers to media such as a CD or DVD that is not included in the version you purchased, you may download this material at http://booksupport.wiley.com. For more information about Wiley products, visit www.wiley.com.

Library of Congress Control Number is available from the Publisher.

ISBN 978-1-118-28121-5 (pbk); 978-1-118-33068-5 (ebk); 978-1-118-33353-2 (ebk); 978-1-118-33466-9 (ebk)

Manufactured in the United States of America

10 9 8 7 6 5 4 3 2 1

WILEY

About the Authors

Mike Alexander is a Microsoft Certified Application Developer (MCAD) and author of several books on advanced business analysis with Microsoft Access and Excel. He has more than 15 years of experience consulting and developing Office solutions. Michael has been named a Microsoft MVP for his ongoing contributions to the Excel community. In his spare time, he runs a free tutorial site, www.datapigtechnologies.com, where he shares Excel and Access tips.

John Walkenbach is author of more than 50 spreadsheet books and lives in southern Arizona. Visit his website at http://spreadsheetpage.com.

Dedication

To Mary

— Mike Alexander

Authors' Acknowledgments

Our deepest thanks to the brilliant team of professionals who helped bring this book to fruition.

Publisher's Acknowledgments

We're proud of this book; please send us your comments at http://dummies.custhelp.com. For other comments, please contact our Customer Care Department within the U.S. at 877-762-2974, outside the U.S. at 317-572-3993, or fax 317-572-4002.

Some of the people who helped bring this book to market include the following:

Acquisitions and Editorial

Project Editor: Linda Morris

Senior Acquisitions Editor: Katie Feltman

Copy Editor: Linda Morris

Technical Editor: John Walkenbach

Editorial Manager: Jodi Jensen

Editorial Assistant: Leslie Saxman

Sr. Editorial Assistant: Cherie Case

Composition Services

Project Coordinator: Sheree Montgomery

Layout and Graphics: Carrie A. Cesavice, Andrea Hornberger

Indexer: BIM Indexing & Proofreading Services

Publishing and Editorial for Technology Dummies

Richard Swadley, Vice President and Executive Group Publisher

Andy Cummings, Vice President and Publisher

Mary Bednarek, Executive Acquisitions Director

Mary C. Corder, Editorial Director

Publishing for Consumer Dummies

Kathleen Nebenhaus, Vice President and Executive Publisher

Composition Services

Debbie Stailey, Director of Composition Services

Contents at a Glance

▶ Table of Contents

Part III: Automating Worksheet Tasks with Macros....................71

Part V: Working with Data 137

Part VI: Working with PivotTables 187

Part VII: Manipulating Charts with Macros 233

Introduction

In its broadest sense, an Excel macro is a sequence of instructions that automates some aspect of Excel so that you can work more efficiently and with fewer errors. You may create a macro, for example, to format and print your month-end sales report. After the macro is developed, you can then execute the macro to perform many time-consuming procedures automatically.

Macros are written in VBA, which stands for Visual Basic for Applications. VBA is actually a programming language developed by Microsoft, and is a tool used to develop programs that control Excel.

Excel programming terminology can be a bit confusing. For example, VBA is a programming language, but it also serves as a macro language. What do you call something written in VBA and executed in Excel? Is it a macro or is it a program? Excel's Help system often refers to VBA procedures as macros, so this is the terminology used in this book. But you can also call VBA code a program.

You'll also see the term *automate* throughout this book. This term means that a series of steps are completed automatically. For example, if you write a macro that adds color to some cells, prints the worksheet, and then removes the color, you have automated those three steps.

People use Excel for thousands of different tasks. Here are just a few examples:

> ➤ Keeping lists of things such as customer names and transactions
> ➤ Budgeting and forecasting
> ➤ Analyzing scientific data
> ➤ Creating invoices and other forms
> ➤ Developing charts from data

The list could go on and on. The point is simply that Excel is used for a wide variety of tasks, and everyone reading this book has different needs and expectations regarding Excel. One thing virtually every reader has in common is the need to automate some aspect of Excel. That is what VBA (and this book) is all about.

Topics Covered

This book approaches the topic of Excel Macros with the recognition that programming with VBA takes time and practice — time that you may not have right now. In fact, many analysts don't have the luxury of taking a few weeks off to become an expert on VBA. So Instead of the same general overview of VBA topics, this book provides 101 of the most commonly used real-world Excel Macros.

Each segment of the book outlines a common problem that needs to be solved and provides the actual Excel macro to solve the problem, along with detailed explanations of how the macro works and where to use the macro.

What You Need to Know

In order to get the most out of this book, we assume you have a certain set of skills. The ideal candidate for this book has experience working with data in Excel, along with familiarity with the basic concepts of data analysis such as working with tables, aggregating data, performing calculations, and creating charts.

What You Need to Have

You will need the following in order to download and use the examples highlighted in this book.

➤ A licensed copy of Excel 2007 or Excel 2010

➤ An internet connection in order to download the sample files

How This Book Is Organized

The style of this book is in the format of the Tips and Tricks books, where each segment shows how to perform a common task via Excel Macros. This lets you, our esteemed reader, use the book as a handy reference for finding a macro that solves a common problem.

Each segment of the book follows this simple construct:

➤ The problem

➤ The macro solution

➤ How it works

After reading each segment of this book, you should be able to

➤ Immediately implement the required Excel macro

➤ Understand how the given macro works

➤ Reuse the given macro in other workbooks or in conjunction with other macros

The chapters of this book are grouped into nine main parts.

Part I: Getting Started with Excel Macros

Part I serves as an introduction to Excel Macros and VBA in general. Here, you gain a concise summary of how VBA works with Excel, giving you the basic foundation you need to work with the 101 macros in this book.

Part II: Working with Workbooks

In Part II you discover how to reference Workbooks through VBA to do cool things like automatically create new workbooks, prevent users from closing workbooks, automatically backing up workbooks, and much more.

Part III: Automating Worksheet Tasks with Macros

Part III focuses on the automation tasks related to worksheets. Whether it is unhiding all sheets in a workbook, or printing all sheets at the same time, many tasks can be automated to save time and gain efficiencies. In this part we cover some of the more useful macros related to worksheets.

Part IV: Selecting and Modifying Ranges

When you're attempting to automate your work through VBA, you'll find that navigating your spreadsheet remains an important part of the automation process. In many cases, you need to dynamically navigate and manipulate Excel ranges, just as you would manually — only through VBA code. Part IV provides some of the most commonly used macros in terms of navigating and working with ranges.

Part V: Working with Data

Part V shows you some of the more useful macros you can use to dynamically transform the data in your workbooks. The idea is that you can run several of these macros in a sequence that essentially automates the scrubbing and shaping of your data.

Part VI: Working with PivotTables

Some PivotTable-related tasks are not easily handled with the macro recorder. This is where Part VI focuses its attention. Here, we cover the most common scenarios where macros help you gain efficiencies when working with PivotTables.

Part VII: Manipulating Charts with Macros

In Part VII you discover how VBA can help you save time and work with charts more efficiently. Here you tackle aspects of charting that lend themselves to a bit of automation.

Part VIII: E-Mailing from Excel

In Part VIII you discover a few examples of how you can integrate Excel and Outlook. Here you see examples of macros that send e-mails, send attachments, and pull files right out of Outlook.

Part IX: Integrating Excel and Other Office Applications

Excel data is often used in other Office applications: Microsoft Access, Microsoft Word, and Microsoft PowerPoint. In Part IX we look at some of the useful macros you can implement to have Excel integrate with some other Office applications.

Conventions in This Book

Menu commands in this book are separated by an arrow (→). For example, File→Open means go to the File menu, click it, and select Open from the list that appears.

All code in this book appears in a `monospaced` font, as do methods, properties, values, and arguments.

Text the reader types appears in **bold**.

Placeholder text that should be replaced with information specific to your needs appears in *italics*.

What the icons mean

Tip

We use Tip icons to indicate a pointer you should file away for future reference. Tips usually make your life easier.

Note

The Note icon indicates you should pay special attention to this.

Caution

We use Caution icons to indicate things that can cause you trouble.

About the Companion Website

Each macro in this book has an associated sample file. These sample files let you see the macro in action, as well as giving you the ability to review the code. The sample files can be downloaded from this book's companion website at www.wiley.com/go/101excelmacros.

PART I

Getting Started with Excel Macros

This Part is a primer on Excel macros, covering everything you need to know about Excel macros and VBA to get started with the 101 macros throughout the rest of this book.

In This Part

Getting Started with Excel Macros

You need not be a power user to create and use simple VBA macros. Even casual users can simply turn on Excel's macro recorder.

Recording a macro is like programming a phone number into your cell phone. You first manually dial and save a number. Then when you want, you can redial those numbers with the touch of a button. Just as with numbers on a cell phone, you can record your actions in Excel while you perform them. While you record, Excel gets busy in the background, translating your keystrokes and mouse clicks to written VBA code. After you've recorded a macro, you can play back those actions anytime you wish.

This Part serves as an introduction to Excel Macros and VBA in general. Here, we give you a concise summary of how VBA works with Excel, giving you the basic foundation you need to work with the 101 macros listed in this book.

Becoming Familiar with Macro Recording Basics

To start recording your first macro, you need to first find the Macro Recorder, which is on the Developer tab. Unfortunately, Excel comes out of the box with the Developer tab hidden — you may not see it on your version of Excel at first. If you plan to work with VBA macros, you'll want to make sure that the Developer tab is visible. To display this tab

1. Choose Office➜Excel Options.
2. In the Excel Options dialog box, select Customize Ribbon.
3. In the list box on the right, place a check mark next to Developer.
4. Click OK to return to Excel.

Now that you have the Developer tab showing in the Excel Ribbon, you can start up the Macro Recorder by selecting Record Macro from the Developer tab. This activates the Record Macro dialog box, as shown in Figure 1-1.

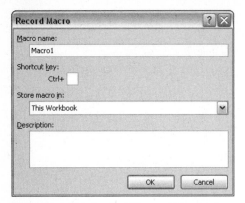

Figure 1-1: The Record Macro dialog box.

Here are the four parts of the Record Macro dialog box:

> **Macro Name:** This should be self-explanatory. Excel gives a default name to your macro, such as Macro1, but you should give your macro a name more descriptive of what it actually does. For example, you might name a macro that formats a generic table as FormatTable.

> **Shortcut Key:** Every macro needs an *event,* or something to happen, for it to run. This event can be a button press, a workbook opening, or in this case, a keystroke combination. When you assign a shortcut key to your macro, entering that combination of keys triggers your macro to run. This is an optional field.

> **Store Macro In:** This Workbook is the default option. Storing your macro in This Workbook simply means that the macro is stored along with the active Excel file. The next time you open that particular workbook, the macro is available to run. Similarly, if you send the workbook to another user, that user can run the macro as well (provided the macro security is properly set by your user — more on that later in this Part, in the section titled "Looking at Other Macro Recording Concepts").

> **Description:** This is an optional field, but it can come in handy if you have numerous macros in a spreadsheet or if you need to give a user a more detailed description about what the macro does.

With the Record Macro dialog box open, follow these steps to create a simple macro that enters your name into a worksheet cell:

1. Enter a new single-word name for the macro to replace the default `Macro1` name. A good name for this example is MyName.

2. Assign this macro to the shortcut key Ctrl+Shift+N by entering uppercase N in the edit box labeled Shortcut Key.

3. Click OK to close the Record Macro dialog box and begin recording your actions.

4. Select any cell on your Excel spreadsheet, type your name into the selected cell, and then press Enter.

5. Choose Developer➔Code➔Stop Recording (or click the Stop Recording button in the status bar).

Examining the macro

The macro was recorded in a new module named Module1. To view the code in this module, you must activate the Visual Basic Editor. You can activate the VB Editor in either of two ways:

➤ Press Alt+F11.

➤ Choose Developer➔Code➔Visual Basic.

In the VB Editor, the Project window displays a list of all open workbooks and add-ins. This list is displayed as a tree diagram, which you can expand or collapse. The code that you recorded previously is stored in Module1 in the current workbook. When you double-click Module1, the code in the module appears in the Code window.

The macro should look something like this:

```
Sub MyName()
'
' MyName Macro
'
' Keyboard Shortcut: Ctrl+Shift+N
'
    ActiveCell.FormulaR1C1 = "Michael Alexander"
End Sub
```

The macro recorded is a Sub procedure that is named MyName. The statements tell Excel what to do when the macro is executed.

Notice that Excel inserted some comments at the top of the procedure. These comments are some of the information that appeared in the Record Macro dialog box. These comment lines (which begin with an apostrophe) aren't really necessary, and deleting them has no effect on how the macro runs. If you ignore the comments, you'll see that this procedure has only one VBA statement:

```
ActiveCell.FormulaR1C1 = "Michael Alexander"
```

This single statement causes the name you typed while recording to be inserted into the active cell.

Testing the macro

Before you recorded this macro, you set an option that assigned the macro to the Ctrl+Shift+N shortcut key combination. To test the macro, return to Excel by using either of the following methods:

> ➤ Press Alt+F11.
> ➤ Click the View Microsoft Excel button on the VB Editor toolbar.

When Excel is active, activate a worksheet. (It can be in the workbook that contains the VBA module or in any other workbook.) Select a cell and press Ctrl+Shift+N. The macro immediately enters your name into the cell.

Note

In the preceding example, notice that you selected the cell to be formatted *before* you started recording your macro. This step is important. If you select a cell while the macro recorder is turned on, the actual cell that you selected will be recorded into the macro. In such a case, the macro would always format that particular cell, and it would not be a general-purpose macro.

Editing the macro

After you record a macro, you can make changes to it (although you must know what you're doing). For example, assume that you want your name to be bold. You could re-record the macro, but this modification is simple, so editing the code is more efficient. Press Alt+F11 to activate the VB Editor window. Then activate Module1 and insert the following statement before the End Sub statement:

```
ActiveCell.Font.Bold = True
```

The edited macro appears as follows:

```
Sub MyName()
'
' MyName Macro
'
' Keyboard Shortcut: Ctrl+Shift+N
'
    ActiveCell.Font.Bold = True
    ActiveCell.FormulaR1C1 = "Michael Alexander"
End Sub
```

Test this new macro, and you see that it performs as it should.

Comparing Absolute and Relative Macro Recording

Now that you've read about the basics of the Macro Recorder interface, it's time to go deeper and begin recording macros. The first thing you need to understand before you begin is that Excel has two modes for recording — absolute reference and relative reference.

Recording macros with absolute references

Excel's default recording mode is in absolute reference. As you may know, the term *absolute reference* is often used in the context of cell references found in formulas. When a cell reference in a formula is an absolute reference, it does not automatically adjust when the formula is pasted to a new location.

The best way to understand how this concept applies to macros is to try it out. Open the Chapter 1 Sample File.xlsx file and record a macro that counts the rows in the Branch list worksheet. (See Figure 1-2.)

▲	A	B	C	D	E	F	G	H	I
1		Region	Market	Branch			Region	Market	Branch
2		NORTH	BUFFALO	601419			SOUTH	CHARLOTTE	173901
3		NORTH	BUFFALO	701407			SOUTH	CHARLOTTE	301301
4		NORTH	BUFFALO	802202			SOUTH	CHARLOTTE	302301
5		NORTH	CANADA	910181			SOUTH	CHARLOTTE	601306
6		NORTH	CANADA	920681			SOUTH	DALLAS	202600
7		NORTH	MICHIGAN	101419			SOUTH	DALLAS	490260
8		NORTH	MICHIGAN	501405			SOUTH	DALLAS	490360
9		NORTH	MICHIGAN	503405			SOUTH	DALLAS	490460
10		NORTH	MICHIGAN	590140			SOUTH	FLORIDA	301316
11		NORTH	NEWYORK	801211			SOUTH	FLORIDA	701309
12		NORTH	NEWYORK	802211			SOUTH	FLORIDA	702309
13		NORTH	NEWYORK	804211			SOUTH	NEWORLEANS	601310
14		NORTH	NEWYORK	805211			SOUTH	NEWORLEANS	602310
15		NORTH	NEWYORK	806211			SOUTH	NEWORLEANS	801607

Figure 1-2: Your pre-totaled worksheet containing two tables.

Tip

The sample dataset used in this Part can be found on this book's companion website. See this book's Introduction for more on the companion website.

Follow these steps to record the macro:

1. Before recording, make sure cell A1 is selected.

2. Select Record Macro from the Developer tab.

3. Name the macro **AddTotal**.

4. Choose This Workbook for the save location.

5. Click OK to start recording.

    At this point, Excel is recording your actions. While Excel is recording, perform the following steps:

6. Select cell A16 and type **Total** in the cell.

7. Select the first empty cell in Column D (D16) and type **= COUNTA(D2:D15)**. This gives a count of branch numbers at the bottom of column D. You need to use the COUNTA function because the branch numbers are stored as text.

8. Click Stop Recording on the Developer tab to stop recording the macro.

The formatted worksheet should look something like the one in Figure 1-3.

	A	B	C	D	E	F	G	H	I
1		Region	Market	Branch			Region	Market	Branch
2		NORTH	BUFFALO	601419			SOUTH	CHARLOTTE	173901
3		NORTH	BUFFALO	701407			SOUTH	CHARLOTTE	301301
4		NORTH	BUFFALO	802202			SOUTH	CHARLOTTE	302301
5		NORTH	CANADA	910181			SOUTH	CHARLOTTE	601306
6		NORTH	CANADA	920681			SOUTH	DALLAS	202600
7		NORTH	MICHIGAN	101419			SOUTH	DALLAS	490260
8		NORTH	MICHIGAN	501405			SOUTH	DALLAS	490360
9		NORTH	MICHIGAN	503405			SOUTH	DALLAS	490460
10		NORTH	MICHIGAN	590140			SOUTH	FLORIDA	301316
11		NORTH	NEWYORK	801211			SOUTH	FLORIDA	701309
12		NORTH	NEWYORK	802211			SOUTH	FLORIDA	702309
13		NORTH	NEWYORK	804211			SOUTH	NEWORLEANS	601310
14		NORTH	NEWYORK	805211			SOUTH	NEWORLEANS	602310
15		NORTH	NEWYORK	806211			SOUTH	NEWORLEANS	801607
16	Total			14					

Figure 1-3: Your post-totaled worksheet.

To see your macro in action, delete the total row you just added and play back your macro by following these steps:

1. Select Macros from the Developer tab.

2. Find and select the AddTotal macro you just recorded.

3. Click the Run button.

If all goes well, the macro plays back your actions to a T and gives your table a total. Now here's the thing. No matter how hard you try, you can't make the AddTotal macro work on the second table. Why? Because you recorded it as an absolute macro.

To understand what this means, examine the underlying code. To examine the code, select Macros from the Developer tab to get the Macro dialog box you see in Figure 1-4.

Figure 1-4: The Excel Macro dialog box.

Select the AddTotal macro and click the Edit button. This opens the Visual Basic Editor to show you the code that was written when you recorded your macro:

```
Sub AddTotal()
  Range("A16").Select
  ActiveCell.FormulaR1C1 = "Total"
  Range("D16").Select
  ActiveCell.FormulaR1C1 = "=COUNTA(R[-14]C:R[-1]C)"
End Sub
```

Pay particular attention to lines two and four of the macro. When you asked Excel to select cell range A16 and then D16, those cells are exactly what it selected. Because the macro was recorded in absolute reference mode, Excel interpreted your range selection as absolute. In other words, if you select cell A16, that cell is what Excel gives you. In the next section, you take a look at what the same macro looks like when recorded in relative reference mode.

Recording macros with relative references

In the context of Excel macros, *relative* means relative to the currently active cell. So you should use caution with your active cell choice — both when you record the relative reference macro and when you run it.

First, make sure the Chapter 1 Sample File.xlsx file is open. (This file is available on this book's companion website.) Then, use the following steps to record a relative reference macro:

1. Select the Use Relative References option from the Developer tab, as shown in Figure 1-5.

2. Before recording, make sure cell A1 is selected.

3. Select Record Macro from the Developer tab.

4. Name the macro **AddTotalRelative**.

5. Choose This Workbook for the save location.

6. Click OK to start recording.

7. Select cell A16 and type **Total** in the cell.

8. Select the first empty cell in Column D (D16) and type **= COUNTA(D2:D15)**.

9. Click Stop Recording on the Developer tab to stop recording the macro.

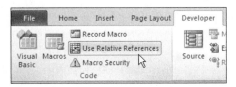

Figure 1-5: Recording a macro with relative references.

At this point, you have recorded two macros. Take a moment to examine the code for your newly-created macro.

Select Macros from the Developer tab to open the Macro dialog box. Here, choose the AddTotalRelative macro and click Edit.

Again, this opens the Visual Basic Editor to show you the code that was written when you recorded your macro. This time, your code looks something like the following:

```
Sub AddTotalRelative()
    ActiveCell.Offset(15, 0).Range("A1").Select
    ActiveCell.FormulaR1C1 = "Total"
    ActiveCell.Offset(0, 3).Range("A1").Select
    ActiveCell.FormulaR1C1 = "=COUNTA(R[-14]C:R[-1]C)"
End Sub
```

Notice that there are no references to any specific cell ranges at all (other than the starting point "A1"). Let's take a moment to take a quick look at what the relevant parts of this VBA code really mean.

Notice that in line 2, Excel uses the Offset property of the active cell. This property tells the cursor to move a certain number of cells up or down and a certain number of cells left or right.

The Offset property code tells Excel to move 15 rows down and 0 columns across from the active cell (in this case, A1). There's no need for Excel to explicitly select a cell as it did when recording an absolute reference macro.

To see this macro in action, delete the total row for both tables and do the following:

1. Select cell A1.

2. Select Macros from the Developer tab.

3. Find and select the AddTotalRelative macro.

4. Click the Run button.

5. Now select cell F1.

6. Select Macros from the Developer tab.

7. Find and select the AddTotalRelative macro.

8. Click the Run button.

Notice that this macro, unlike your previous macro, works on both sets of data. Because the macro applies the totals *relative* to the currently active cell, the totals are applied correctly.

For this macro to work, you simply need to ensure that

➤ You've selected the correct starting cell before running the macro.

➤ The block of data has the same number of rows and columns as the data on which you recorded the macro.

Hopefully, this simple example has given you a firm grasp of macro recording with both absolute and relative references.

Looking at Other Macro Recording Concepts

At this point, you should feel comfortable recording your own Excel Macros. Now here are some of the other important concepts you'll need to keep in mind when working with macros.

Macro-enabled file extensions

Beginning with Excel 2007, Excel has a separate file extension for workbooks that contain macros.

You see, Excel 2010 workbooks have the standard file extension .xlsx. Files with the .xlsx extension cannot contain macros. If your workbook contains macros and you then save that workbook as an .xlsx file, your macros are removed automatically. Excel warns you that macro content will be disabled when saving a workbook with macros as an .xlsx file.

If you want to retain the macros, you must save your file as an *Excel Macro-Enabled Workbook*. This gives your file an .xlsm extension. The idea is that all workbooks with an .xlsx file extension are automatically known to be safe, whereas you can recognize .xlsm files as a potential threat.

Macro security in Excel 2010

With the release of Office 2010, Microsoft introduced significant changes to its Office security model. One of the most significant changes is the concept of trusted documents. Without getting into the technical minutia, a *trusted document* is essentially a workbook you have deemed safe by enabling macros.

If you open a workbook that contains macros in Excel 2010, you see a yellow bar message under the Ribbon stating that macros (active content) have in effect, been disabled.

If you click Enable, it automatically becomes a trusted document. This means you no longer are prompted to enable the content as long as you open that file on your computer. The basic idea is that if you told Excel that you "trust" a particular workbook by enabling macros, it is highly likely that you will enable macros each time you open it. Thus, Excel remembers that you've enabled macros before and inhibits any further messages about macros for that workbook.

This is great news for you and your clients. After enabling your macros just one time, they won't be annoyed at the constant messages about macros, and you won't have to worry that your macro-enabled dashboard will fall flat because macros have been disabled.

Trusted locations

If the thought of any macro message coming up (even one time) unnerves you, you can set up a trusted location for your files. A *trusted location* is a directory that is deemed a safe zone where only trusted workbooks are placed. A trusted location allows you and your clients to run a macro-enabled workbook with no security restrictions as long as the workbook is in that location.

To set up a trusted location, follow these steps:

1. Select the Macro Security button on the Developer tab.

   This activates the Trust Center dialog box.

2. Click the Trusted Locations button. This opens the Trusted Locations menu (see Figure 1-6), which shows you all the directories that are considered trusted.

3. Click the Add New Location button.

4. Click Browse to find and specify the directory that will be considered a trusted location.

After you specify a trusted location, any Excel file that is opened from this location will have macros automatically enabled.

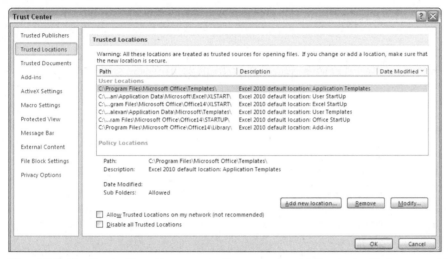

Figure 1-6: The Trusted Locations menu allows you to add directories that are considered trusted.

Storing macros in your Personal Macro Workbook

Most user-created macros are designed for use in a specific workbook, but you may want to use some macros in all your work. You can store these general-purpose macros in the Personal Macro Workbook so that they're always available to you. The Personal Macro Workbook is loaded whenever you start Excel. This file, named personal.xlsb, doesn't exist until you record a macro using Personal Macro Workbook as the destination.

Note

> The Personal Macro Workbook normally is in a hidden window to keep it out of the way.

To record the macro in your Personal Macro Workbook, select the Personal Macro Workbook option in the Record Macro dialog box before you start recording. This option is in the Store Macro In drop-down list.

If you store macros in the Personal Macro Workbook, you don't have to remember to open the Personal Macro Workbook when you load a workbook that uses macros. When you want to exit, Excel asks whether you want to save changes to the Personal Macro Workbook.

Assigning a macro to a button and other form controls

When you create macros, you may want to have a clear and easy way to run each macro. A basic button can provide a simple but effective user interface.

As luck would have it, Excel offers a set of *form controls* designed specifically for creating user interfaces directly on spreadsheets. There are several different types of form controls, from buttons (the most commonly used control) to scrollbars.

The idea behind using a form control is simple. You place a form control on a spreadsheet and then assign a macro to it — that is, a macro you've already recorded. When a macro is assigned to the control, that macro is executed, or *played,* when the control is clicked.

Take a moment to create a button for the AddTotalRelative macro you created earlier. Here's how:

1. Click the Insert button under the Developer tab. (See Figure 1-7.)

2. Select the Button Form Control from the drop-down list that appears.

3. Click the location where you want to place your button. When you drop the button control onto your spreadsheet, the Assign Macro dialog box, as shown in Figure 1-8, activates and asks you to assign a macro to this button.

4. Select the macro you want to assign to the button and then click OK.

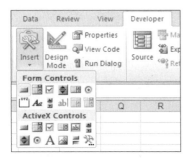

Figure 1-7: You can find the form controls in the Developer tab.

Figure 1-8: Assign a macro to the newly-added button.

Form controls versus ActiveX controls

Notice the form controls and ActiveX controls in Figure 1-7. Although they look similar, they're quite different. Form controls are designed specifically for use on a spreadsheet, and ActiveX controls are typically used on Excel user forms. As a general rule, you should always use form controls when working on a spreadsheet. Why? Form controls need less overhead, so they perform better, and configuring form controls is far easier than configuring their ActiveX counterparts.

At this point, you have a button that runs your macro when you click it! Keep in mind that all the controls in the Form Controls group (shown in Figure 1-7) work in the same way as the command button, in that you assign a macro to run when the control is selected.

Placing a macro on the Quick Access toolbar

You can also assign a macro to a button in Excel's Quick Access toolbar:

1. Right-click your Quick Access toolbar and select Customize Quick Access Toolbar.

2. Click the Quick Access Toolbar button on the left of the Excel Options dialog box.

3. Select Macros from the drop-down list on the left.

4. Select the macro you want to add and click the Add button.

5. Change the icon by clicking the Modify button.

Working in the Visual Basic Editor

The Visual Basic Editor (VBE) is a separate application where you write and edit your VBA macros. You can't run the VBE separately; Excel must be running in order for the VBE to run.

Activating the VBE

The quickest way to activate the VBE is to press Alt+F11 when Excel is active. To return to Excel, press Alt+F11 again.

You can also activate the VBE by using the Developer➜Code➜Visual Basic command.

Understanding VBE components

Figure 1-9 shows the VBE program with some of the key parts identified. Because so much is going on in the VBE, I like to maximize the window to see as much as possible.

Chances are your VBE program window won't look exactly like what you see in Figure 1-9. The VBE contains several windows and is highly customizable. You can hide windows, rearrange windows, dock windows, and so on.

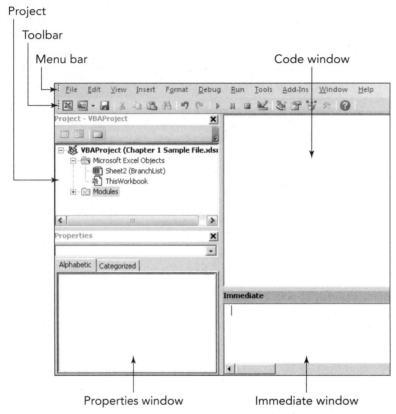

Project

Toolbar

Menu bar

Code window

Properties window

Immediate window

Figure 1-9: The VBE with significant elements identified.

Menu bar

The VBE menu bar works just like every other menu bar you've encountered. It contains commands that you use to do things with the various components in the VBE. You will also find that many of the menu commands have shortcut keys associated with them.

The VBE also features shortcut menus. You can right-click virtually anything in the VBE and get a shortcut menu of common commands.

Toolbar

The Standard toolbar, which is directly under the menu bar by default, is one of four VBE toolbars available. You can customize the toolbars, move them around, display other toolbars, and so on. If you're so inclined, use the View➜Toolbars command to work with VBE toolbars. Most people just leave them as they are.

Project window

The Project window displays a tree diagram that shows every workbook currently open in Excel (including add-ins and hidden workbooks). Double-click items to expand or contract them. We discuss this window in more detail in the "Working with the Project Window" section later in this Part.

If the Project window is not visible, press Ctrl+R or use the View➜Project Explorer command. To hide the Project window, click the Close button in its title bar. Alternatively, right-click anywhere in the Project window and select Hide from the shortcut menu.

Code window

A Code window contains VBA code. Every object in a project has an associated Code window. To view an object's Code window, double-click the object in the Project window. For example, to view the Code window for the Sheet1 object, double-click Sheet1 in the Project window. Unless you've added some VBA code, the Code window will be empty.

You find out more about Code windows later in this Part's "Working with a Code Window" section.

Immediate window

The Immediate window may or may not be visible. If it isn't visible, press Ctrl+G or use the View➜ Immediate Window command. To close the Immediate window, click the Close button in its title bar (or right-click anywhere in the Immediate window and select Hide from the shortcut menu).

The Immediate window is most useful for executing VBA statements directly and for debugging your code. If you're just starting out with VBA, this window won't be all that useful, so feel free to hide it and free up some screen space for other things.

Working with the Project window

When you're working in the VBE, each Excel workbook and add-in that's open is a project. You can think of a *project* as a collection of objects arranged as an outline. You can expand a project by clicking the plus sign (+) at the left of the project's name in the Project window. Contract a project by clicking the minus sign (-) to the left of a project's name. Or, you can double-click the items to expand and contract them.

Figure 1-10 shows a Project window with two projects listed: a workbook named Book1 and a workbook named Book2.

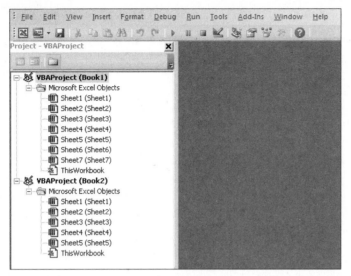

Figure 1-10: This Project window lists two projects. They are expanded to show their objects.

Every project expands to show at least one *node* called Microsoft Excel Objects. This node expands to show an item for each sheet in the workbook (each sheet is considered an object), and another object called `ThisWorkbook` (which represents the Workbook object). If the project has any VBA modules, the project listing also shows a Modules node.

Adding a new VBA module

When you record a macro, Excel automatically inserts a VBA module to hold the recorded code. The workbook that holds the module for the recorded macro depends on where you chose to store the recorded macro, just before you started recording.

In general, a VBA module can hold three types of code:

> **Declarations:** One or more information statements that you provide to VBA. For example, you can declare the data type for variables you plan to use, or set some other module-wide options.

> **Sub procedures:** A set of programming instructions that performs some action. All recorded macros will be `Sub` procedures.

> **Function procedures:** A set of programming instructions that returns a single value (similar in concept to a worksheet function, such as `Sum`).

A single VBA module can store any number of `Sub` procedures, `Function` procedures, and declarations. How you organize a VBA module is completely up to you. Some people prefer to keep all their VBA code for an application in a single VBA module; others like to split up the code into several different modules. It's a personal choice, just like arranging furniture.

Follow these steps to manually add a new VBA module to a project:

1. Select the project's name in the Project window.

2. Choose Insert➡Module.

Or you can

1. Right-click the project's name.

2. Choose Insert➡Module from the shortcut menu.

The new module is added to a Modules folder in the Project window (see Figure 1-11). Any modules you create in a given workbook are placed in this Modules folder.

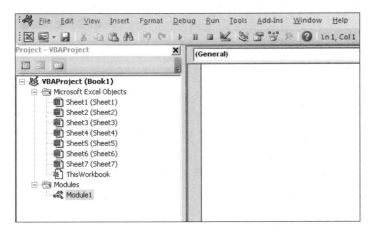

Figure 1-11: Code modules are visible in the Project window in a folder called Modules.

Removing a VBA module

You may want to remove a code module that is no longer needed. To do so, follow these steps:

1. Select the module's name in the Project window.

2. Choose File➡Remove *xxx,* where *xxx* is the module name.

Or

1. Right-click the module's name.

2. Choose Remove *xxx* from the shortcut menu.

Note

Excel, always trying to keep you from doing something you'll regret, asks if you want to export the code in the module before you delete it. Almost always, you don't. (If you do want to export the module, see the next section, "Working with a Code Window.")

You can remove VBA modules, but there is no way to remove the other code modules — those for the Sheet objects or ThisWorkbook.

Working with a Code Window

As you become proficient with VBA, you spend lots of time working in Code windows. Macros that you record are stored in a module, and you can type VBA code directly into a VBA module.

Minimizing and maximizing windows

Code windows are much like workbook windows in Excel. You can minimize them, maximize them, resize them, hide them, rearrange them, and so on. Most people find it much easier to maximize the Code window that they're working on. Doing so lets you see more code and keeps you from getting distracted.

To maximize a Code window, click the maximize button in its title bar (right next to the X). Or, just double-click its title bar to maximize it. To restore a Code window to its original size, click the Restore button. When a window is maximized, its title bar isn't really visible, so you'll find the Restore button to the right of the Type a Question for Help box.

Sometimes, you may want to have two or more Code windows visible. For example, you may want to compare the code in two modules or copy code from one module to another. You can arrange the windows manually, or use the Window➜Tile Horizontally or Window➜Tile Vertically commands to arrange them automatically.

You can quickly switch among code windows by pressing Ctrl+Tab. If you repeat that key combination, you keep cycling through all the open code windows. Pressing Ctrl+Shift+Tab cycles through the windows in reverse order.

Minimizing a Code window gets it out of the way. You can also click the window's Close button in a Code window's title bar to close the window completely. (Closing a window just hides it; you won't lose anything.) To open it again, just double-click the appropriate object in the Project window. Working with these Code windows *sounds* more difficult than it really is.

Getting VBA code into a module

Before you can do anything meaningful, you must have some VBA code in the VBA module. You can get VBA code into a VBA module in three ways:

> ➤ Use the Excel macro recorder to record your actions and convert them to VBA code
>
> ➤ Enter the code directly
>
> ➤ Copy the code from one module and paste it into another

You have discovered the excellent method for creating code by using the Excel Macro recorder. However, not all tasks can be translated to VBA by recording a macro. You often have to enter your code directly into the module. Entering code directly basically means either typing the code yourself or copying and pasting code you have found somewhere else.

Entering and editing text in a VBA module works as you might expect. You can select, copy, cut, paste, and do other things to the text.

A single line of VBA code can be as long as you like. However, you may want to use the line-continuation character to break up lengthy lines of code. To continue a single line of code (also known as a *statement*) from one line to the next, end the first line with a space followed by an underscore (_). Then continue the statement on the next line. Here's an example of a single statement split into three lines:

```
Selection.Sort Key1:=Range("A1"), _
    Order1:=xlAscending, Header:=xlGuess, _
    Orientation:=xlTopToBottom
```

This statement would perform exactly the same way if it were entered in a single line (with no line-continuation characters). Notice that the second and third lines of this statement are indented. Indenting is optional, but it helps clarify the fact that these lines are not separate statements.

The VBE has multiple levels of undo and redo. If you deleted a statement that you shouldn't have, use the Undo button on the toolbar (or press Ctrl+Z) until the statement appears again. After undoing, you can use the Redo button to perform the changes you've undone.

Ready to enter some real, live code? Try the following steps:

1. Create a new workbook in Excel.

2. Press Alt+F11 to activate the VBE.

3. Click the new workbook's name in the Project window.

4. Choose Insert➜Module to insert a VBA module into the project.

5. Type the following code into the module:

```
Sub GuessName()
    Dim Msg as String
    Dim Ans As Long
    Msg = "Is your name " & Application.UserName & "?"
    Ans = MsgBox(Msg, vbYesNo)
    If Ans = vbNo Then MsgBox "Oh, never mind."
    If Ans = vbYes Then MsgBox "I must be clairvoyant!"
End Sub
```

6. Make sure the cursor is located anywhere within the text you typed and press F5 to execute the procedure.

Tip

F5 is a shortcut for the Run➡Run Sub/UserForm command.

When you enter the code listed in Step 5, you might notice that the VBE makes some adjustments to the text you enter. For example, after you type the `Sub` statement, the VBE automatically inserts the `End Sub` statement. And if you omit the space before or after an equal sign, the VBE inserts the space for you. Also, the VBE changes the color and capitalization of some text. This is all perfectly normal. It's just the VBE's way of keeping things neat and readable.

If you followed the previous steps, you just created a VBA `Sub` procedure, also known as a *macro.* When you press F5, Excel executes the code and follows the instructions. In other words, Excel evaluates each statement and does what you told it to do. You can execute this macro any number of times — although it tends to lose its appeal after a few dozen executions.

This simple macro uses the following concepts:

➤ Defining a `Sub` procedure (the first line)

➤ Declaring variables (the `Dim` statements)

➤ Assigning values to variables (`Msg` and `Ans`)

➤ *Concatenating* (joining) a string (using the `&` operator)

➤ Using a built-in VBA function (`MsgBox`)

➤ Using built-in VBA constants (`vbYesNo`, `vbNo`, and `vbYes`)

➤ Using an `If-Then` construct (twice)

➤ Ending a `Sub` procedure (the last line)

As we mentioned previously, you can copy and paste code into a VBA module. For example, a `Sub` or `Function` procedure that you write for one project might also be useful in another project. Instead of wasting time reentering the code, you can activate the module and use the normal copy-and-paste procedures (Ctrl+C to copy and Ctrl+V to paste). After pasting it into a VBA module, you can modify the code as necessary.

Customizing the VBA Environment

If you're serious about becoming an Excel programmer, you'll spend a lot of time with VBA modules on your screen. To help make things as comfortable as possible, the VBE provides quite a few customization options.

When the VBE is active, choose Tools➜Options. You'll see a dialog box with four tabs: Editor, Editor Format, General, and Docking. Take a moment to explore some of the options found on each tab.

The Editor tab

Figure 1-12 shows the options accessed by clicking the Editor tab of the Options dialog box. Use the option in the Editor tab to control how certain things work in the VBE.

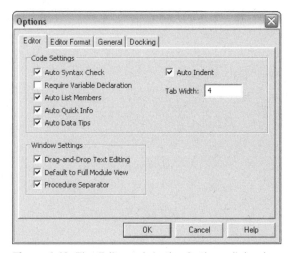

Figure 1-12: The Editor tab in the Options dialog box.

The Auto Syntax Check option

The Auto Syntax Check setting determines whether the VBE pops up a dialog box if it discovers a syntax error while you're entering your VBA code. The dialog box tells roughly what the problem is. If you don't choose this setting, VBE flags syntax errors by displaying them in a different color from the rest of the code, and you don't have to deal with any dialog boxes popping up on your screen.

> **I usually keep this setting turned off because I think the dialog boxes are annoying and I can usually figure out what's wrong with a statement. Before I was a VBA veteran, I found this setting quite helpful.**

Tip

The Require Variable Declaration option

If the Require Variable Declaration option is set, VBE inserts the following statement at the beginning of each new VBA module you insert:

```
Option Explicit
```

Changing this setting affects only new modules, not existing modules. If this statement appears in your module, you must explicitly define each variable you use. Using a `Dim` statement is one way to declare variables.

The Auto List Members option

If the Auto List Members option is set, VBE provides some help when you're entering your VBA code. It displays a list that would logically complete the statement you're typing. This is one of the best features of the VBE.

The Auto Quick Info option

If the Auto Quick Info option is selected, VBE displays information about functions and their arguments as you type. This is similar to the way Excel lists the arguments for a function as you start typing a new formula.

The Auto Data Tips option

If the Auto Data Tips option is set, VBE displays the value of the variable over which your cursor is placed when you're debugging code. This is turned on by default and often quite useful. You have no reason to turn this option off.

The Auto Indent setting

The Auto Indent setting determines whether VBE automatically indents each new line of code the same as the previous line. I'm big on using indentations in my code, so I keep this option on.

> **By the way, you should use the Tab key to indent your code, not the spacebar. Also, you can use Shift+Tab to "unindent" a line of code. If you want to indent more than just one line, select all lines you want to indent and then press the Tab key.**

Tip

The VBE's Edit toolbar (which is hidden by default) contains two useful buttons: Indent and Outdent. These buttons let you quickly indent or "unindent" a block of code. Select the code and click one of these buttons to change the block's indenting.

The Drag-and-Drop Text Editing option

The Drag-and-Drop Text Editing option, when enabled, lets you copy and move text by dragging and dropping with your mouse. I keep this option turned on, but I never use it. I prefer to copy and move by using the keyboard.

The Default to Full Module View option

The Default to Full Module View option sets the default state for new modules. (It doesn't affect existing modules.) If set, procedures in the Code window appear as a single scrollable list. If this option is turned off, you can see only one procedure at a time. I keep this option turned on.

The Procedure Separator option

When the Procedure Separator option is turned on, separator bars appear at the end of each procedure in a Code window. I like the idea of separator bars, so I keep this option turned on.

The Editor Format tab

Figure 1-13 shows the Editor Format tab of the Options dialog box. With this tab, you can customize the way the VBE looks.

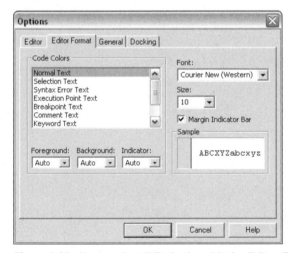

Figure 1-13: Change the VBE's looks with the Editor Format tab.

The Code Colors option

The Code Colors option lets you set the text color and background color displayed for various elements of VBA code. This is largely a matter of personal preference. Personally, I find the default colors to be just fine. But for a change of scenery, I occasionally play around with these settings.

The Font option

The Font option lets you select the font that's used in your VBA modules. For best results, stick with a fixed-width font such as Courier New. In a *fixed-width font,* all characters are exactly the same width. This makes your code more readable because the characters are nicely aligned vertically and you can easily distinguish multiple spaces (which is sometimes useful).

The Size setting

The Size setting specifies the point size of the font in the VBA modules. This setting is a matter of personal preference determined by your video display resolution and how good your eyesight is.

The Margin Indicator Bar option

This option controls the display of the vertical margin indicator bar in your modules. You should keep this turned on; otherwise, you won't be able to see the helpful graphical indicators when you're debugging your code.

The General tab

Figure 1-14 shows the options available under the General tab in the Options dialog box. In almost every case, the default settings are just fine.

The most important setting on the General tab is Error Trapping. We strongly suggest that you use the Break on Unhandled Errors setting. This ensures Excel can identify errors as you type your code.

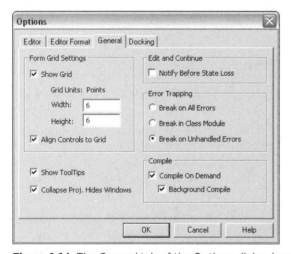

Figure 1-14: The General tab of the Options dialog box.

The Docking tab

Figure 1-15 shows the Docking tab. These options determine how the various windows in the VBE behave. When a window is *docked,* it is fixed in place along one of the edges of the VBE program window. This makes it much easier to identify and locate a particular window. If you turn off all docking, you have a big, confusing mess of windows. Generally, the default settings work fine.

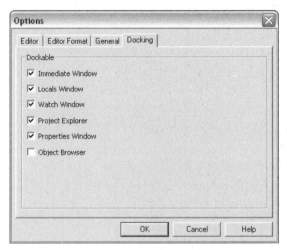

Figure 1-15: The Docking tab of the Options dialog box.

Discovering the Excel Object Model

In Excel, you deal with workbooks, worksheets, and ranges on a daily basis. You likely think of each of these "objects" as all part of Excel, not really separating them in your mind. However, Excel thinks about these internally as all part of a hierarchical model called the *Excel object model*. The Excel object model is a clearly defined set of objects that are structured according to the relationships between them.

In this section, we give you a brief overview of the object model, as well as some of the other terminology and concepts you will encounter in the upcoming 101 macros.

Understanding objects

In the real world, you can describe everything you see as an object. When you look at your house, it is an object. Your house has rooms; those rooms are also separate objects. Those rooms may have closets. Those closets are likewise objects. As you think about your house, the rooms, and the closets, you may see a hierarchical relationship between them. Excel works in the same way.

In Excel, the `Application` object is the all-encompassing object — similar to your house. Inside the `Application` object, Excel has a workbook. Inside a workbook is a worksheet. Inside that is a range. These are all objects that live in a hierarchical structure.

To point to a specific object in VBA, you can traverse the object model. For example, to get to cell A1 on Sheet 1, you can enter this code:

```
Application.Activeworbook.Sheets("Sheet1").Range("A1").Select
```

In most cases, the object model hierarchy is understood, so you don't have to type every level. Entering this code also gets you to cell A1 because Excel infers that you mean the active workbook, and the active sheet:

```
Range("A1").Select
```

Indeed, if you have you cursor already in cell A1, you can simply use the `ActiveCell` object, negating the need to actually spell out the range.

```
Activecell.Select
```

Understanding collections

Many of Excel's objects belong to collections. Your house sits within a neighborhood, for example, which is a collection of houses called a neighborhood. Each neighborhood sits in a collection of neighborhoods called a city. Excel considers collections to be objects themselves.

In each `Workbook` object, you have a collection of `Worksheets`. The `Worksheets` collection is an object that you can call upon through VBA. Each worksheet in your workbook lives in the `Worksheets` collection.

If you want to refer to a worksheet in the `Worksheets` collection, you can refer to it by its position in the collection, as an index number starting with 1, or by its name, as quoted text. If you run these two lines of code in a workbook that has only one worksheet called MySheet, they both do the same thing:

```
Worksheets(1).Select
Worksheets("MySheet").Select
```

If you have two worksheets in the active workbook that have the names MySheet and YourSheet, in that order, you can refer to the second worksheet by typing either of these statements:

```
Worksheets(2).Select
Worksheets("YourSheet").Select
```

If you want to refer to a worksheet in a workbook called MySheet in a particular workbook that is not active, you must qualify the worksheet reference and the workbook reference, as follows:

```
Workbooks("MyData.xls").Worksheets("MySheet").Select
```

Understanding properties

Properties are essentially the characteristics of an object. Your house has a color, a square footage, an age, and so on. Some properties can be changed — like the color of your house. Other properties can't be changed — like the age of your house.

Likewise, an object in Excel like the `Worksheet` object has a sheet name property that can be changed, and a `Rows.Count` row property that cannot.

You refer to the property of an object by referring to the object, and then the property. For instance, you can change the name of your worksheet by changing its `Name` property.

In this example, you are renaming Sheet1 to MySheet:

```
Sheets("Sheet1").Name = "MySheet"
```

Some properties are read-only, which means that you can't assign a value to them directly — for instance, the `Text` property of cell. The `Text` property gives you the formatted appearance of value in a cell, but you cannot overwrite or change it.

Understanding methods

Methods are the actions that can be performed against an object. It helps to think of methods as verbs. You can paint your house, so in VBA, that translates to something like

```
house.paint
```

A simple example of an Excel method is the `Select` method of the `Range` object:

```
Range("A1").Select
```

Another is the `Copy` method of the `Range` object:

```
Range("A1").Copy
```

Some methods have parameters that can dictate how it is applied. For instance, the `Paste` method can be used more effectively by explicitly defining the `Destination` parameter.

```
ActiveSheet.Paste Destination:=Range("B1")
```

Taking a Brief Look at Variables

Another concept you will see throughout the macros in this book is the concept of variables. We need to dedicate a few words to this concept because it plays a big part in most of the macros you will encounter here.

You can think of variables as memory containers that you can use in your procedures. There are different types of variables, each tasked with holding a specific type of data.

Some of the common types of variables you will see in this book are

> **String:** Holds textual data

> **Integer:** Holds numeric data ranging from –32,768 to 32,767

> **Long:** Holds numeric data ranging from –2,147,483,648 to 2,147,483,647

> **Double:** Holds floating point numeric data

> **Variant:** Holds any kind of data

> **Boolean:** Holds binary data that returns `True` or `False`

> **Object:** Holds an actual object from the Excel object model

The term used for creating a variable in a macro is *declaring* a variable. You do so by entering `Dim` (an abbreviation for dimension), the name of your variable, and then the type. For instance:

```
Dim MyText as String
Dim MyNumber as Integer
Dim MyWorksheet as Worksheet
```

After you create your variable, you can fill it with data. Here are a few simple examples of how you would create a variable and assign a value to it:

```
Dim MyText as String
Mytext = Range("A1").Value
```

```
Dim MyNumber as Integer
MyNumber = Range("B1").Value * 25
```

```
Dim MyObject as Worksheet
Set MyWorksheet = Sheets("Sheet1")
```

The values you assign to your variables often come from data stored in your cells. However, the values may also be information that you yourself create. It all depends on the task at hand. This notion becomes clearer as you go through the macros in the book.

About the Macros in This Book

As we mention in the Introduction, the macros in this book are designed to get you up and running with VBA in the quickest way possible. Each macro tackles a common task that benefits from automation. The idea here is learning through application. This book is designed so that you can implement the macro, while getting a clear understanding of what the macro does and how it works.

Getting the sample files

Each macro in this book has an associated sample file. These sample files give you the ability to see the macro working, as well as the ability to review the code. You can also use the sample files to copy and paste the code into your environment (as opposed to typing each macro in from scratch). See the "About the Companion Website" section in this book's Introduction for complete instructions on how to download the sample code.

Using the sample files

Each macro in this book has detailed instructions on where to copy and paste the code. You should open the sample file associated with the macro, go to the Visual Basic Editor (by pressing Alt+F11), and then copy the code. After you've copied the code, you can go to your workbook, go into the Visual Basic Editor, and paste the code into the appropriate location.

Note that in some of the Macro examples in this book, you need to change some aspect of the macro to suit your situation. For instance, Macro 12 in Part II demonstrates how to open all the

Excel files in a directory. In that example, we point to the `C:\Temp\` directory. Before you use this particular macro, you need to edit that portion of the macro to point to *your* target directory.

If a macro is not working for you, it's probably because you need to change some component of the macro. Pay special attention to Range addresses, directory names, and any other hard-coded names. We built these hard-coded values into the macro for demonstration purposes; with the full intent that you, the reader, would edit the macro to alter these hard-coded names to fit your scenario.

Things to keep in mind

Here are some final things to keep in mind while working with the macros in this book:

➤ **Macro-enabled file extensions:** Remember that any file that contains a macro must have the .xlsm file extenstion. See the section called "Macro-enabled file extensions" in this Part for more details.

➤ **Macro security:** Keep in mind that Excel will not run macros until they are Enabled. As you implement these macros, it's important to understand the steps that you and your customers will need to take to comply with Excel's macro security measures. The section in this Part called "Macro security in Excel 2010" highlights these steps.

➤ **You cannot undo macro actions:** When working in Excel, you can often undo the actions you have taken. This is because Excel keeps a log (called the *undo stack*) that records the last 100 actions you have taken. However, running a macro automatically destroys the undo stack, clearing the log of the actions you have taken. You must keep this in mind as you start writing and running your own macros. You cannot undo the action you take in a macro.

➤ **Where to go from here:** As mentioned before, these macros were designed to get you started with VBA. If you find a developing passion for Excel VBA, you may want to know where to get a more detailed reference on Excel VBA in general. Allow us to recommend *Excel 2010 Power Programming with VBA* by John Walkenbach (Wiley) as the next step in your learning. This reference is a comprehensive guide to VBA, diving deeper into the Excel Object model.

PART II

Working with Workbooks

This Part covers macros related to workbooks: opening them, closing them, protecting them, and many other actions.

In This Part

A workbook is not just an Excel file; it's also an object in Excel's Object model (a programming hierarchy that exposes parts of Excel to VBA). This means that you can reference workbooks through VBA to do cool things like automatically create new workbooks, prevent users from closing workbooks, automatically back up workbooks, and much more. We start our list of 101 macros here with a list of the most useful workbook macros.

If you're brand-new to Excel VBA, we highly recommend that you first take a quick look at Part I. There, you will find the basic foundation you'll need to understand many of the concepts found in the macros in this Part.

The code for this Part can be found on this book's companion website. See this book's Introduction for more on the companion website.

Macro 1: Creating a New Workbook from Scratch

You may sometimes want or need to create a new workbook in an automated way. For instance, you may need to copy data from a table and paste it into a newly created workbook. The following macro copies a range of cells from the active sheet and pastes the data into a new workbook.

How it works

This macro is relatively intuitive as you read through the lines of the code.

```
Sub Macro1()

'Step 1 Copy the data
    Sheets("Example 1").Range("B4:C15").Copy

'Step 2 Create a new workbook
    Workbooks.Add

'Step 3 Paste the data
    ActiveSheet.Paste Destination:=Range("A1")

'Step 4 Turn off application alerts
    Application.DisplayAlerts = False

'Step 5 Save the newly created workbook
    ActiveWorkbook.SaveAs _
    Filename:="C:\Temp\MyNewBook.xlsx"

'Step 6 Turn application alerts back on
    Application.DisplayAlerts = True

End Sub
```

Here's how this macro works:

1. In Step 1, we simply copy the data that ranges from cells B4 to C15.

   The thing to note here is that you are specifying both the sheet and the range by name. This is a best practice when you are working with multiple workbooks open at one time.

2. We are using the `Add` method of the Workbook object to create a new workbook. This is equivalent to manually clicking File➜New➜Blank Document in the Excel Ribbon.

3. In this step, you use the `Paste` method to send the data you copied to cell A1 of the new workbook.

   Pay attention to the fact that the code refers to the `ActiveSheet` object. When you add a workbook, the new workbook immediately gains focus, becoming the active workbook. This is the same behavior you would see if you were to add a workbook manually.

4. In Step 4 of the code, we set the `DisplayAlerts` method to `False`, effectively turning off Excel's warnings. We do this because in the next step of the code, we save the newly created workbook. We may run this macro multiple times, in which case Excel attempts to save the file multiple times.

   What happens when you try to save a workbook multiple times? That's right — Excel warns you that there is already a file out there with that name and then asks if you want to overwrite the previously existing file. Because your goal is to automate the creation of the new workbook, you want to suppress that warning.

5. In Step 5, we save the file by using the `SaveAs` method. Note that we are entering the full path of the save location, including the final filename.

6. Because we turned application alters off in Step 4, we need to turn them back on. If we don't, Excel continues to suppress all warnings for the life of the current session.

How to use it

To implement this macro, you can copy and paste it into a standard module:

1. Activate the Visual Basic Editor by pressing ALT+F11.

2. Right-click the project/workbook name in the Project window.

3. Choose Insert➜Module.

4. Type or paste the code in the newly created module. You will probably need to change the sheet name, the range address, and the save location.

Macro 2: Saving a Workbook When a Particular Cell Is Changed

Sometimes, you may be working on data that is so sensitive that you'll want to save every time a particular cell or range of cells is changed. This macro allows you to define the range of cells that, when changed, forces the workbook to save.

How it works

The secret to this code is the Intersect method. Because we don't want to save the worksheet when any old cell changes, we use the Intersect method to determine if the target cell (the cell that changed) intersects with the range we have specified to be the trigger range (C5:C16 in this case).

The Intersect method returns one of two things: either a Range object that defines the intersection between the two given ranges, or nothing. So in essence, we need to throw the target cell against the Intersect method to check for a value of Nothing. At that point, we can make the decision whether to save the workbook.

```
Private Sub Worksheet_Change(ByVal Target As Range)

'Step 1:  Does the changed range intersect specified range?
    If Intersect(Target, Range("C5:C16")) Is Nothing Then

'Step 2: If there is no intersection, exit procedure
    Exit Sub

'Step 3: If there is an intersection, save the workbook
    Else
    ActiveWorkbook.Save

'Close out the If statement
    End If

End Sub
```

1. In Step 1, we are simply checking to see if the target cell (the cell that has changed) is in the range specified by the Intersect method. A value of Nothing means the target cell falls outside the range specified.

2. Step 2 forces the macro to stop and exit the procedure if there is no intersection between the target cell and the specified range.

3. If there is an intersection, Step 3 fires the `Save` method of the active workbook, overwriting the previous version.

4. In Step 4, we simply close out the `If` statement. Every time you instantiate an `If...Then...Else` check, you must close it out with a corresponding `End If`.

How to use it

To implement this macro, you need to copy and paste it into the `Worksheet_Change` event code window. Placing the macro here allows it to run each time you make any change to the sheet.

1. Activate the Visual Basic Editor by pressing ALT+F11.

2. In the Project window, find your project/workbook name and click the plus sign next to it in order to see all the sheets.

3. Click in the sheet from which you want to trigger the code.

4. Select the `Change` event from the Event drop-down list (see Figure 2-1).

5. Type or paste the code in the newly created module, changing the range address to suit your needs.

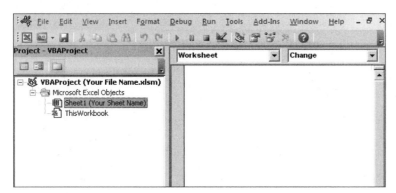

Figure 2-1: Enter or Paste your code in the Worksheet_Change event code window.

Macro 3: Saving a Workbook Before Closing

This macro is an excellent way to protect users from inadvertently closing their file before saving. When implemented, this macro ensures that Excel automatically saves before closing the workbook.

Note

Excel normally warns users who are attempting to close an unsaved workbook, giving them an option to save before closing. However, many users may blow past the warning and inadvertently click No, telling Excel to close without saving. With this macro, you are protecting against this by automatically saving before close.

How it works

This code is triggered by the workbook's `BeforeClose` event. When you try to close the workbook, this event fires, running the code within. The crux of the code is simple — it asks the user whether he really wants to close the workbook (see Figure 2-2). The macro then evaluates whether the user clicked OK or Cancel.

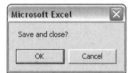

Figure 2-2: A message box activates when you attempt to close the workbook.

The evaluation is done with a `Select Case` statement. The `Select Case` statement is an alternative to the `If...Then...Else` statement, allowing you to perform condition checks in your macros. The basic construct of a `Select Case` statement is simple.

```
Select Case <some expression to check>
Case Is = <some value>
      <do something>
Case Is=<some other value>
      <do something else>
Case Is=<some 3rd value>
      <do some 3rd thing>
End Select
```

With a `Select Case` statement, you can perform many conditional checks. In this case, we are simply checking for OK or Cancel. Take a look at the code.

```vba
Private Sub Workbook_BeforeClose(Cancel As Boolean)

'Step 1:  Activate the message box and start the check
    Select Case MsgBox("Save and close?", vbOKCancel)

'Step 2: Cancel button pressed, cancel the close
    Case Is = vbCancel
    Cancel = True

'Step 3: OK button pressed, save the workbook and close
    Case Is = vbOK
    ActiveWorkbook.Save

'Step 4: Close your Select Case statement
End Select

End Sub
```

1. In Step 1, we activate the message box as the condition check for the `Select Case` statement. Here, we use the `vbOKCancel` argument to ensure that the OK and Cancel buttons are presented as choices.

2. If the user clicked Cancel in the message box, the macro tells Excel to cancel the `Workbook_Close` event. This is done by passing `True` to the Cancel Boolean.

3. If the user clicked OK in the message box, Step 3 takes effect. Here, we tell Excel to save the workbook. And because we did not set the Cancel Boolean to `True`, Excel continues with the close.

4. In Step 4, we simply close out the `Select Case` statement. Every time you instantiate a `Select Case`, you must close it out with a corresponding `End Select`.

How to use it

To implement this macro, you need to copy and paste it into the `Workbook_BeforeClose` event code window. Placing the macro there allows it to run each time you try to close the workbook.

1. Activate the Visual Basic Editor by pressing ALT+F11 on your keyboard.

2. In the Project window, find your project/workbook name and click the plus sign next to it in order to see all the sheets.

3. Click ThisWorkbook.

4. Select the `BeforeClose` event in the Event drop-down list (see Figure 2-3).

5. Type or paste the code in the newly created module.

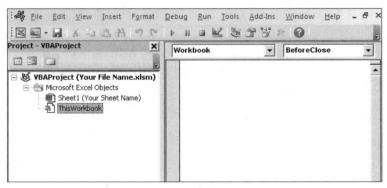

Figure 2-3: Type or paste your code in the Workbook_BeforeClose event code window.

Macro 4: Protect a Worksheet on Workbook Close

Sometimes you need to send your workbook out into the world with specific worksheets protected. If you find that you're constantly protecting and unprotecting sheets before distributing your workbooks, this macro can help you.

How it works

This code is triggered by the workbook's `BeforeClose` event. When you try to close the workbook, this event fires, running the code within. The macro automatically protects the specified sheet with the given password, and then saves the workbook.

```
Private Sub Workbook_BeforeClose(Cancel As Boolean)

'Step 1: Protect the sheet with a password
      Sheets("Sheet1").Protect Password:="RED"

'Step 2: Save the workbook
      ActiveWorkbook.Save

End Sub
```

1. In Step 1, we are explicitly specifying which sheet we want to protect — Sheet1, in this case. We are also providing the password argument, `Password:=RED`. This defines the password needed to remove the protection.

   This password argument is completely optional. If you omit this altogether, the sheet will still be protected, but you won't need a password to unprotect it. Also, be aware that Excel passwords are case-sensitive, so you'll want pay attention to the exact password and capitalization that you are using.

2. Step 2 tells Excel to save the workbook. If we don't save the workbook, the sheet protection we just applied won't be in effect the next time the workbook is opened.

How to use it

To implement this macro, you need to copy and paste it into the `Workbook_BeforeClose` event code window. Placing the macro here allows it to run each time you try to close the workbook.

1. Activate the Visual Basic Editor by pressing ALT+F11.

2. In the Project window, find your project/workbook name and click the plus sign next to it in order to see all the sheets.

3. Click ThisWorkbook.

4. Select the `BeforeClose` event in the Event drop-down list (see Figure 2-4).

5. Type or paste the code in the newly created module, modifying the sheet name (if necessary) and the password. Note that you can protect additional sheets by adding additional statements before the `ActiveWorkbook.Save` statement.

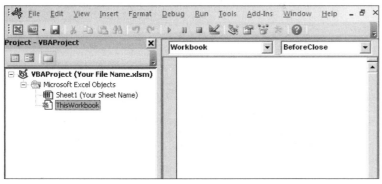

Figure 2-4: Type or paste your code in the Workbook_BeforeClose event code window.

Macro 5: Unprotect a Worksheet on Workbook Open

If you've distributed workbooks with protected sheets, you likely get the workbooks back with the sheets still protected. Often, you need to unprotect the worksheets in a workbook before continuing your work. If you find that you are continuously unprotecting worksheets, this macro may be just the ticket.

How it works

This code is triggered by the workbook's `Open` event. When you open a workbook, this event triggers, running the code within. This macro automatically unprotects the specified sheet with the given password when the workbook is opened.

```
Private Sub Workbook_Open()

'Step 1: Protect the sheet with a password
    Sheets("Sheet1").Unprotect Password:="RED"

End Sub
```

The macro explicitly names the sheet we want to unprotect — Sheet1, in this case. Then it passes the password required to unprotect the sheet. Be aware that Excel passwords are case-sensitive, so pay attention to the exact password and capitalization that you are using.

How to use it

To implement this macro, you need to copy and paste it into the `Workbook_Open` event code window. Placing the macro here allows it to run each time the workbook opens.

1. Activate the Visual Basic Editor by pressing ALT+F11.

2. In the Project window, find your project/workbook name and click the plus sign next to it in order to see all the sheets.

3. Click ThisWorkbook.

4. Select the `Open` event in the Event drop-down list (see Figure 2-5).

5. Type or paste the code in the newly created module, modifying the sheet name (if necessary) and the password. Note that you can unprotect additional sheets by adding additional statements.

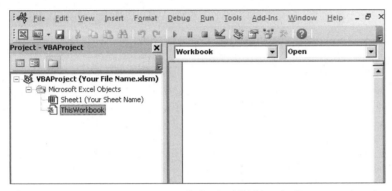

Figure 2-5: Type or paste your code in the Workbook_Open event code window.

Macro 6: Open a Workbook to a Specific Tab

In some situations, it's imperative that your workbook be started on a specific worksheet. With this macro, if a user is working with your workbook, they can't go astray because the workbook starts on the exact worksheet it needs to.

How it works

This macro uses the workbook's Open event to start the workbook on the specified sheet when the workbook is opened.

```
Private Sub Workbook_Open()

'Step 1: Select the specified sheet
    Sheets("Sheet1").Select

End Sub
```

The macro explicitly names the sheet the workbook should jump to when it's opened.

How to use it

To implement this macro, you need to copy and paste it into the Workbook_Open event code window. Placing the macro here allows it to run each time the workbook opens.

1. Activate the Visual Basic Editor by pressing ALT+F11 on your keyboard.

2. In the Project window, find your project/workbook name and click the plus sign next to it in order to see all the sheets.

3. Click ThisWorkbook.

4. Select the `Open` event in the Event drop-down list (see Figure 2-6).

5. Type or paste the code in the newly created module, changing the sheet name, if necessary.

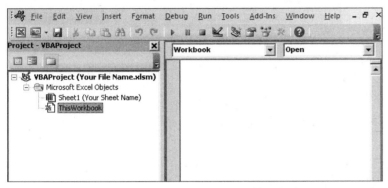

Figure 2-6: Type or paste your code in the Workbook_Open event code window.

Macro 7: Opening a Specific Workbook Defined by the User

Want to give yourself or your users a quick way to search for and open a file? This macro uses a simple technique that opens a friendly dialog box, allowing you to browse for and open the Excel file of your choosing.

How it works

This macro opens the dialog box you see in Figure 2-7, allowing the user to browse for and open an Excel file.

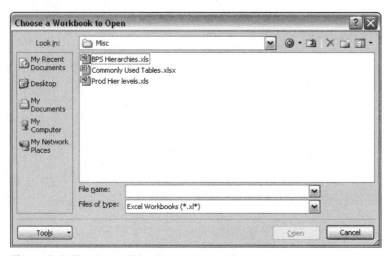

Figure 2-7: The Open dialog box activated by our macro.

Here's how this macro works:

```
Sub Macro7()

'Step 1: Define a string variable.
    Dim FName As Variant

'Step 2: GetOpenFilename Method activates dialog box.
    FName = Application.GetOpenFilename( _
                    FileFilter:="Excel Workbooks,*.xl*", _
                    Title:="Choose a Workbook to Open", _
                    MultiSelect:=False)
```

```
'Step 3: If a file was chosen, open it!
    If FName <> False Then
    Workbooks.Open Filename:=FName
    End If

End Sub
```

1. The first thing this macro does is to declare a variant variable that holds the filename that the user chooses. FName is the name of our variable.

2. In Step 2, we use the GetOpenFilename method to call up a dialog box that allows us to browse and select the file we need.

   The GetOpenFilename method supports a few customizable parameters. The FileFilter parameter allows us to specify the type of file we are looking for. The Title parameter allows us to change the title that appears at the top of the dialog box. The MultiSelect parameter allows us to limit the selection to one file.

3. If the user selects a file from the dialog box, the FName variable is filled with the name of the file they have chosen. In Step 3, we check for an empty FName variable. If the variable is not empty, we use the Open method of the Workbooks object to open the file.

How to use it

To implement this macro, you can copy and paste it into a standard module:

1. Activate the Visual Basic Editor by pressing ALT+F11.

2. Right-click the project/workbook name in the Project window.

3. Choose Insert➜Module.

4. Type or paste the code in the newly created module.

5. Optionally, you can assign the macro to a button (see the section "Assigning a macro to a button and other form controls" in Part I).

Macro 8: Determine Whether a Workbook Is Already Open

The previous macro automatically opened a workbook based on the user's selection. As we think about automatically opening workbooks, you must consider what may happen if you attempt to open a book that is already open. In the non-VBA world, Excel attempts to open the file again, with a warning that any unsaved changes will be lost. In VBA, it's a good idea to protect against such an occurrence by checking if a given file is already open before trying to open it again.

How it works

The first thing to notice about this macro is that it is a function, not a sub procedure. As you will see, making this macro a function enables us to pass any filename to it to test whether that file is already open.

The gist of this code is simple. We are testing a given filename to see if it can be assigned to an object variable. Only opened workbooks can be assigned to an object variable. When we try to assign a closed workbook to the variable, an error occurs.

So if the given workbook can be assigned, the workbook is open; if an error occurs, the workbook is closed.

```
Function FileIsOpenTest(TargetWorkbook As String) As Boolean

'Step 1:  Declare variables
    Dim TestBook As Workbook

'Step 2: Tell Excel to Resume on Error
    On Error Resume Next

'Step 3: Try to assign the target workbook to TestBook
    Set TestBook = Workbooks(TargetWorkbook)

'Step 4: If no error occurred then Workbook is already open
    If Err.Number = 0 Then
    FileIsOpenTest = True
    Else
    FileIsOpenTest = False
    End If

End Function
```

1. The first thing the macro does is to declare a string variable that will hold the filename that the user chooses. `TestBook` is the name of our string variable.

2. In Step 2, we are telling Excel that there may be an error running this code. In the event of an error, resume the code. Without this line, the code would simply stop when an error occurs. Again, we are testing a given filename to see if it can be assigned to an object variable. So if the given workbook can be assigned, it's open; if an error occurs, it's closed. We need to have the code continue if an error occurs.

3. In Step 3, we are attempting to assign the given workbook to the `TestBook` object variable. The workbook we are trying to assign is itself a string variable called `TargetWorkbook`. `TargetWorkbook` is passed to the function in the function declarations (see the first line of the code). This structure eliminates the need to hard-code a workbook name, allowing us to pass it as a variable instead.

4. In Step 4, we simply check to see if an error occurred. If an error did not occur, the workbook is open, so we set the `FileIsOpenTest` to `True`. If an error occurred, that means the workbook is not open. In that case, we set the `FileIsOpenTest` to `False`.

Tip

Again, this is a function that can be used to evaluate any file you pass to it, via its `TargetWorkbook` **argument. That is the beauty of putting this macro into a function.**

The following macro demonstrates how to implement this function. Here, we are using the same macro you saw in the previous section, "Macro 7: Opening a Specific Workbook Defined by the User," but this time, we are calling the new `FileIsOpenTest` function to make sure the user cannot open an already open file.

```
Sub Macro8()

'Step 1: Define a string variable.
    Dim FName As Variant
    Dim FNFileOnly As String


'Step 2: GetOpenFilename Method activates dialog box.
    FName = Application.GetOpenFilename( _
                    FileFilter:="Excel Workbooks,*.xl*", _
                    Title:="Choose a Workbook to Open", _
                    MultiSelect:=False)

'Step 3: Open the chosen file if not already opened.
    If FName <> False Then
    FNFileOnly = StrReverse(Left(StrReverse(FName), _
            InStr(StrReverse(FName), "\") - 1))
```

continued

continued

```
    If FileIsOpenTest(FNFileOnly) = True Then
        MsgBox "The given file is already open"
    Else
        Workbooks.Open Filename:=FName

    End If
    End If

End Sub
```

How to use it

To implement this macro, you can copy and paste both pieces of code into a standard module:

1. Activate the Visual Basic Editor by pressing ALT+F11 on your keyboard.

2. Right-click the project/workbook name in the Project window.

3. Choose Insert➜Module.

4. Type or paste the code in the newly created module.

5. Optionally, you can assign the macro to a button (see the section on "Assigning a macro to a button and other form controls" in Part I).

Macro 9: Determine Whether a Workbook Exists in a Directory

You may have a process that manipulates a file somewhere on your PC. For example, you may need to open an existing workbook to add new data to it on a daily basis. In these cases, you may need to test to see whether the file you need to manipulate actually exists. This macro allows you to pass a file path to evaluate whether the file is there.

How it works

The first thing to notice about this macro is that it is a function, not a sub procedure. Making this macro a function enables us to pass any file path to it.

In this macro, we use the Dir function. The Dir function returns a string that represents the name of the file that matches what you pass to it. This function can be used in lots of ways, but here, we are using it to check if the file path we pass to it exists.

```
Function FileExists(FPath As String) As Boolean

'Step 1: Declare your variables.
    Dim FName As String

'Step 2: Use the Dir function to get the file name
    FName = Dir(FPath)

'Step 3:  If file exists, return True else False
    If FName <> "" Then FileExists = True _
    Else: FileExists = False

End Function
```

1. Step 1 declares a string variable that holds the filename that returns from the Dir function. FName is the name of the string variable.

2. In Step 2, we attempt to set the FName variable. We do this by passing the FPath variable to the Dir function. This FPath variable is passed via the function declarations (see the first line of the code). This structure prevents us from having to hard-code a file path, passing it as a variable instead.

3. If the FName variable can't be set, this means the path we passed does not exist. Thus the FName variable is empty. Step 3 merely translates that result to a True or False expression.

Tip

Again, this is a function that can be used to evaluate any file path you pass to it. That's the beauty of writing this macro as a function.

The following macro demonstrates how to use this function:

```
Sub Macro9)

    If FileExists("C:\Temp\MyNewBook.xlsx") = True Then
        MsgBox "File exists."
    Else
        MsgBox "File does not exist."
    End If

End Sub
```

How to use it

To implement this macro, you can copy and paste both pieces of code into a standard module:

1. Activate the Visual Basic Editor by pressing ALT+F11 on your keyboard.
2. Right-click the project/workbook name in the Project window.
3. Choose Insert➜Module.
4. Type or paste the code in the newly created module.

Macro 10: Refresh All Data Connections in Workbook on Open

Your workbook may have connections to external data sources such as web queries, MSQuery connections, PivotTable connections, and so on. In these cases, it may be helpful to refresh these data connections automatically when the workbook is opened. This macro does the trick.

How it works

This macro is an easy one-liner that uses the `RefreshAll` method. This method refreshes all the connections in a given workbook or worksheet. In this case, we are pointing it to the entire workbook.

```vba
Private Sub Workbook_Open()

'Step 1:  Use the RefreshAll method
    Workbooks(ThisWorkbook.Name).RefreshAll

End Sub
```

The thing to note in this macro is that we are using the `ThisWorkbook` object. This object is an easy and safe way for you to point to the current workbook. The difference between `ThisWorkbook` and `ActiveWorkbook` is subtle but important. The `ThisWorkbook` object refers to the workbook that the code is contained in. The `ActiveWorkbook` object refers to the workbook that is currently active. They often return the same object, but if the workbook running the code is not the active workbook, they return different objects. In this case, you don't want to risk refreshing connections in other workbooks, so you use `ThisWorkbook`.

How to use it

To implement this macro, you need to copy and paste it into the `Workbook_Open` event code window. Placing the macro there allows it to run each time the workbook opens.

1. Activate the Visual Basic Editor by pressing ALT+F11.

2. In the Project window, find your project/workbook name and click the plus sign next to it in order to see all the sheets.

3. Click ThisWorkbook.

4. Select the Open event in the Event drop-down list (see Figure 2-8).

5. Type or paste the code in the newly created module.

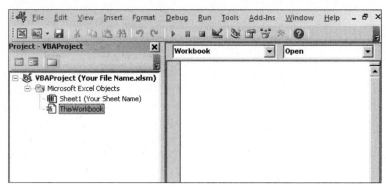

Figure 2-8: Enter or Paste your code in the Workbook_Open event code window.

Macro 11: Close All Workbooks at Once

One of the more annoying things in Excel is closing many workbooks at once. For each workbook you have opened, you need to activate the work, close it, and confirm save changes. There is no easy way to close them all down at one time. This little macro takes care of that annoyance.

How it works

In this macro, the `Workbooks` collection loops through all the open workbooks. As the macro loops through each workbook, it saves and closes them down.

```
Sub Macro11()

'Step 1: Declare your variables
    Dim wb As Workbook

'Step 2: Loop through workbooks, save and close
    For Each wb In Workbooks
        wb.Close SaveChanges:=True
    Next wb

End Sub
```

1. Step 1 declares an object variable that represents a Workbook object. This allows us to enumerate through all the open workbooks, capturing their names as we go.

2. Step 2 simply loops through the open workbooks, saving and closing them. If you don't want to save them, change the `SaveChanges` argument from `True` to `False`.

How to use it

The best place to store this macro is in your Personal Macro Workbook. This way, the macro is always available to you. The Personal Macro Workbook is loaded whenever you start Excel. In the VBE Project window, it is named personal.xlsb.

1. Activate the Visual Basic Editor by pressing ALT+F11 on your keyboard.

2. Right-click personal.xlb in the Project window.

3. Choose Insert➜Module.

4. Type or paste the code in the newly created module.

If you don't see personal.xlb in your project window, it doesn't exist yet. You'll have to record a macro, using Personal Macro Workbook as the destination.

Tip

To record the macro in your Personal Macro Workbook, select the Personal Macro Workbook option in the Record Macro dialog box before you start recording. This option is in the Store Macro In **drop-down box. Simply record a couple of cell clicks and then stop recording. You can discard the recorded macro and replace it with this one.**

Macro 12: Open All Workbooks in a Directory

Here's a scenario: You've written a cool macro that applies some automated processing to each workbook you open. Now the problem is that you need to go into your directory, open each workbook, run the macro, save it, close the workbook, and then open the next one. Opening each workbook in a directory is typically a time-consuming manual process. This macro solves that problem.

How it works

In this macro, we use the `Dir` function. The `Dir` function returns a string that represents the name of the file that matches what you pass to it.

In this code, we use the `Dir` function to enumerate through all the .xlsx files in a given directory, capturing each file's name. Then we open each file, run some code, and finally close the file after saving.

```
Sub Macro12()

'Step 1:Declare your variables
    Dim MyFiles As String

'Step 2: Specify a target directory
    MyFiles = Dir("C:\Temp\*.xlsx")
    Do While MyFiles <> ""


'Step 3: Open Workbooks one by one
    Workbooks.Open "C:\Temp\" & MyFiles

    'run some code here
    MsgBox ActiveWorkbook.Name

    ActiveWorkbook.Close SaveChanges:=True

'Step 4: Next File in the Directory
    MyFiles = Dir
    Loop

End Sub
```

1. Step 1 declares the `MyFiles` string variable that will capture each filename that is in the enumeration.

2. In Step 2, the macro uses the `Dir` function to specify the directory and file type we are looking for. Note that the code here is looking for *.xlsx. This means that only .xlsx files will be looped through. If you are looking for .xls files, you need to change that (along with the directory you need to search). This macro passes any filename it finds to the `MyFiles` string variable.

3. Step 3 opens the file, does some stuff (this is where you would put in any macro code to perform the desired actions), and then we save and close the file. In this simple example, we are calling a message box to show each filename as it opens.

4. The last step of the macro loops back to find more files. If there are no more files, the `MyFiles` variable will be blank. If that is the case, the loop and macro end.

How to use it

To implement this macro, you can copy and paste it into a standard module:

1. Activate the Visual Basic Editor by pressing ALT+F11.

2. Right-click the project/workbook name in the Project window.

3. Choose Insert➜Module.

4. Type or paste the code in the newly created module.

Macro 13: Print All Workbooks in a Directory

If you need to print from multiple workbooks in a directory, you can use this macro.

How it works

In this macro, we use the `Dir` function to return a string that represents the name of the file that matches what you pass to it.

In this code, we use the `Dir` function to enumerate through all the .xlsx files in a given directory, capturing each file's name. Then we open each file, print, and close the file.

```
Sub Macro13()

'Step 1:Declare your variables
    Dim MyFiles As String

'Step 2: Specify a target directory
    MyFiles = Dir("C:\Temp\*.xlsx")
    Do While MyFiles <> ""

'Step 3: Open Workbooks one by one
    Workbooks.Open "C:\Temp\" & MyFiles
    ActiveWorkbook.Sheets("Sheet1").PrintOut Copies:=1
    ActiveWorkbook.Close SaveChanges:=False

'Step 4: Next File in the Directory
    MyFiles = Dir
    Loop

End Sub
```

1. Step 1 declares the `MyFiles` string variable that will capture each filename that is in the enumeration.

2. Step 2 uses the `Dir` function to specify the directory and file type we are looking for. Note that the code here is looking for `*.xlsx`. This means that only .xlsx files will be looped through. If you are looking for .xls files, you will need to specify that (along with the directory you need to search). The macro passes any filename it finds to the `MyFiles` string variable.

3. Step 3 opens the file and then prints out one copy of Sheet1. Needless to say, you will probably want to change which sheets to print. You can also change the number of copies to print.

4. Step 4 loops back to find more files. If there are no more files, the `MyFiles` variable is blank. If that is the case, the loop and macro end.

How to use it

To implement this macro, you can copy and paste it into a standard module:

1. Activate the Visual Basic Editor by pressing ALT+F11.

2. Right-click the project/workbook name in the Project window.

3. Choose Insert➔Module.

4. Type or paste the code in the newly created module, modifying the print statement as needed.

Macro 14: Preventing the Workbook from Closing Until a Cell Is Populated

There are times when you don't want a user closing out a workbook without entering a specific piece of data. In these situations, you want Excel to deny the user the ability to close the workbook until the target cell is filled in. This is where this macro comes in.

How it works

This code is triggered by the workbook's `BeforeClose` event. When you try to close the workbook, this event fires, running the code within. This macro checks to see if the target cell (cell C7, in this case) is empty. If it is empty, the close process is cancelled. If C7 is not empty, the workbook saves and closes.

```
Private Sub Workbook_BeforeClose(Cancel As Boolean)

'Step 1: Check to see if Cell C7 is blank
If Sheets("Sheet1").Range("C7").Value = "" Then

'Step 2: Blank: cancel the Close and tell the user
    Cancel = True
    MsgBox "Cell C7 cannot be blank"

'Step 3: Not Blank; Save and Close
Else
    ActiveWorkbook.Close SaveChanges:=True
End If

End Sub
```

1. Step 1 checks to see whether C7 is blank.

2. If it is blank, Step 2 takes effect, cancelling the close process. This is done by passing `True` to the Cancel Boolean. Step 2 also activates a message box notifying the user of their stupidity (well, it's not quite that harsh, really).

3. If cell C7 is not blank, the workbook saves and closes.

How to use it

To implement this macro, you need to copy and paste it into the `Workbook_BeforeClose` event code window. Placing the macro here allows it to run each time you try to close the workbook.

1. Activate the Visual Basic Editor by pressing ALT+F11.

2. In the Project window, find your project/workbook name and click the plus sign next to it in order to see all the sheets.

3. Click ThisWorkbook.

4. Select the `BeforeClose` event in the Event drop-down list (see Figure 2-9).

5. Type or paste the code in the newly created module.

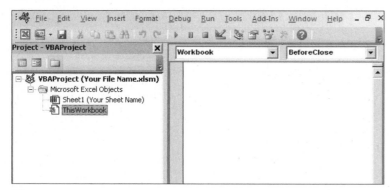

Figure 2-9: Type or paste your code in the Workbook_BeforeClose event code window.

Macro 15: Create a Backup of a Current Workbook with Today's Date

We all know that making backups of your work is important. Now you can have a macro do it for you. This simple macro saves your workbook to a new file with today's date as part of the name.

How it works

The trick to this macro is piecing together the new filename. The new filename has three pieces: the path, today's date, and the original filename.

The path is captured by using the `Path` property of the `ThisWorkbook` object. Today's date is grabbed with the `Date` function.

You'll notice that we are formatting the date (`Format(Date, "mm-dd-yy")`). This is because by default, the `Date` function returns mm/dd/yyyy. We use hyphens instead of forward slashes because the forward slashes would cause the file save to fail. (Windows does not allow forward slashes in filenames.)

The last piece of the new filename is the original filename. We use the `Name` property of the `ThisWorkbook` object to capture that:

```
Sub Macro15()

'Step 1: Save workbook with new filename
        ThisWorkbook.SaveCopyAs _
     Filename:=ThisWorkbook.Path & "\" & _
     Format(Date, "mm-dd-yy") & " " & _
     ThisWorkbook.Name

End Sub
```

In the one and only step, the macro builds a new filename and uses the `SaveCopyAs` method to save the file.

How to use it

To implement this macro, you can copy and paste it into a standard module:

1. Activate the Visual Basic Editor by pressing ALT+F11.

2. Right-click the project/workbook name in the Project window.

3. Choose Insert→Module.

4. Type or paste the code in the newly created module.

PART III

Automating Worksheet Tasks with Macros

This Part addresses macros that work at the worksheet level. In this Part, you'll find macros for adding, deleting, and renaming worksheets, and much more.

In This Part

Excel analysts often need to automate tasks related to worksheets. Whether it is un-hiding all sheets in a workbook, or printing all sheets at the same time, many tasks can be automated to save time and gain efficiencies. In this Part, we cover some of the more useful macros related to worksheets.

Tip

If you're brand-new to Excel VBA, we highly recommend you take a quick look at Part 1. There we provide the basic foundation you'll need to understand many of the concepts found in the macros in this part.

Tip

You can find the code for this Part on this book's companion website. See this book's Introduction for more on the companion website.

Macro 16: Add and Name a New Worksheet

We start off this chapter with one of the simplest worksheet-related automations you can apply with a macro — adding and naming a new worksheet.

How it works

If you read through the lines of the code, you'll see this macro is relatively intuitive.

```
Sub Macro16()

'Step 1: Tell Excel what to do if Error
    On Error GoTo MyError


'Step 2:  Add a sheet and name it
    Sheets.Add
    ActiveSheet.Name = _
    WorksheetFunction.Text(Now(), "m-d-yyyy h_mm_ss am/pm")
    Exit Sub


'Step 3: If here, an error happened; tell the user
    MyError:
    MsgBox "There is already a sheet called that."

End Sub
```

Here's how this macro works:

1. You must anticipate that if you give the new sheet a name that already exists, an error occurs. So in Step 1, the macro tells Excel to immediately skip to the line that says `MyError` (in Step 3) if there is an error.

2. Step 2 uses the `Add` method to add a new sheet. By default, the sheet is called Sheet*xx*, where *xx* represents the number of the sheet. We give the sheet a new name by changing the `Name` property of the `ActiveSheet` object. In this case, we are naming the worksheet with the current date and time.

   As with workbooks, each time you add a new sheet via VBA, it automatically becomes the active sheet. Finally, in Step 2, notice that the macro exits the procedure. It has to do this so that it doesn't accidentally go into Step 3 (which should come into play only if an error occurs).

3. Step 3 notifies the user that the sheet name already exists. Again, this step should only be activated if an error occurs.

How to use it

To implement this macro, you can copy and paste it into a standard module:

1. Activate the Visual Basic Editor by pressing ALT+F11.

2. Right-click the project/workbook name in the Project window.

3. Choose Insert➔Module.

4. Type or paste the code in the newly created module.

Macro 17: Delete All but the Active Worksheet

At times, you may want to delete all but the active worksheet. In these situations, you can use this macro.

How it works

This macro loops the worksheets and matches each worksheet name to the active sheet's name. Each time the macro loops, it deletes any unmatched worksheet. Note the use of the `DisplayAlerts` method in Step 4. This effectively turns off Excel's warnings so you don't have to confirm each delete.

```
Sub Macro17()

'Step 1:  Declare your variables
    Dim ws As Worksheet

'Step 2: Start looping through all worksheets
    For Each ws In ThisWorkbook.Worksheets

'Step 3: Check each worksheet name
    If ws.Name <> ThisWorkbook.ActiveSheet.Name Then

'Step 4: Turn off warnings and delete
    Application.DisplayAlerts = False
    ws.Delete
    Application.DisplayAlerts = True
    End If

'Step 5:  Loop to next worksheet
    Next ws

End Sub
```

1. The macro first declares an object called `ws`. This creates a memory container for each worksheet it loops through.

2. In Step 2, the macro begins to loop, telling Excel it will evaluate all worksheets in this workbook. There is a difference between `ThisWorkbook` and `ActiveWorkbook`. The `ThisWorkbook` object refers to the workbook that the code is contained in. The `ActiveWorkbook` object refers to the workbook that is currently active. They often return the same object, but if the workbook running the code is not the active workbook, they return different objects. In this case, we don't want to risk deleting sheets in other workbooks, so we use `ThisWorkbook`.

3. In this step, the macro simply compares the active sheet name to the sheet that is currently being looped.

4. If the sheet names are different, the macro deletes the sheet. As mentioned before, we use `DisplayAlerts` to suppress any confirmation checks from Excel.

5. In Step 5, the macro loops back to get the next sheet. After all sheets are evaluated, the macro ends.

How to use it

To implement this macro, you can copy and paste it into a standard module:

1. Activate the Visual Basic Editor by pressing ALT+F11.

2. Right-click the project/workbook name in the Project window.

3. Choose Insert→Module.

4. Type or paste the code in the newly created module.

Note

Note that when you use `ThisWorkbook` **in a macro instead of** `ActiveWorkbook`**, you can't run the macro from the Personal Macro Workbook. This is because** `ThisWorkbook` **refers to the Personal Macro Workbook, not the workbook to which the macro should apply.**

Macro 18: Hide All but the Active Worksheet

You may not want to delete all but the active sheet as we did in the last macro. Instead, a more gentle option is to simply hide the sheets. Excel doesn't let you hide all sheets in a workbook — at least one has to be showing. However, you can hide all but the active sheet.

How it works

This macro loops the worksheets and matches each worksheet name to the active sheet's name. Each time the macro loops, it hides any unmatched worksheet.

```
Sub Macro18()

'Step 1:  Declare your variables
    Dim ws As Worksheet

'Step 2: Start looping through all worksheets
    For Each ws In ThisWorkbook.Worksheets

'Step 3: Check each worksheet name
    If ws.Name <> ThisWorkbook.ActiveSheet.Name Then

'Step 4: Hide the sheet
        ws.Visible = xlSheetHidden
    End If

'Step 5:  Loop to next worksheet
    Next ws

End Sub
```

1. Step 1 declares an object called `ws`. This creates a memory container for each worksheet the macro loops through.

2. Step 2 begins the looping, telling Excel to evaluate all worksheets in this workbook. There is a difference between `ThisWorkbook` and `ActiveWorkbook`. The `ThisWorkbook` object refers to the workbook that the code is contained in. The `ActiveWorkbook` object refers to the workbook that is currently active. They often return the same object, but if the workbook running the code is not the active workbook, they return different objects. In this case, we don't want to risk hiding sheets in other workbooks, so we use `ThisWorkbook`.

3. In this step, the macro simply compares the active sheet name to the sheet that is currently being looped.

4. If the sheet names are different, the macro hides the sheet.

5. In Step 5, we loop back to get the next sheet. After all of the sheets are evaluated, the macro ends.

Tip

You'll notice that we used `xlSheetHidden` in our macro. This applies the default hide state you would normally get when you right-click a sheet and select Hide. In this default hide state, a user can right-click on any tab and choose Unhide. This shows all the sheets that are hidden. But there is another hide state that is more clandestine than the default. If you use `xlSheetVeryHidden` to hide your sheets, users will not be able to see them at all — not even if they right-click on any tab and choose Unhide. The only way to unhide a sheet hidden in this manner is by using VBA.

How to use it

To implement this macro, you can copy and paste it into a standard module:

1. Activate the Visual Basic Editor by pressing ALT+F11.

2. Right-click the project/workbook name in the Project window.

3. Choose Insert➜Module.

4. Type or paste the code in the newly created module.

Macro 19: Unhide All Worksheets in a Workbook

If you've ever had to unhide multiple sheets in Excel, you know what a pain it is. You need to click four times for each sheet you want to unhide. Although that may not sound like a lot, try to unhide ten or more sheets — it gets to be a pain fast. This macro makes easy work of that task.

How it works

This macro loops the worksheets and changes the visible state.

```
Sub Macro19()

'Step 1:  Declare your variables
    Dim ws As Worksheet

'Step 2: Start looping through all worksheets
    For Each ws In ActiveWorkbook.Worksheets

'Step 3:  Loop to next worksheet
    ws.Visible = xlSheetVisible
    Next ws

End Sub
```

1. Step 1 declares an object called `ws`. This creates a memory container for each worksheet the macro loops through.

2. In Step 2, the macro starts the looping, telling Excel to enumerate through all worksheets in this workbook.

3. Step 3 changes the visible state to `xlSheetVisible`. Then it loops back to get the next worksheet.

How to use it

The best place to store this macro is in your Personal Macro Workbook. That way, the macro is always available to you. The Personal Macro Workbook is loaded whenever you start Excel. In the VBE Project window, it is named personal.xlsb.

1. Activate the Visual Basic Editor by pressing ALT+F11.

2. Right-click personal.xlb in the Project window.

3. Choose Insert→Module.

4. Type or paste the code in the newly created module.

If you don't see personal.xlb in your project window, it means it doesn't exist yet. You'll have to record a macro using Personal Macro Workbook as the destination.

To record the macro in your Personal Macro Workbook, select the Personal Macro Workbook option in the Record Macro dialog box before you start recording. This option is in the Store Macro In drop-down box. Simply record a couple of cell clicks and then stop recording. You can discard the recorded macro and replace it with this one.

Macro 20: Moving Worksheets Around

We've all had to rearrange our spreadsheet so that some sheet came before or after other sheet. If you find that you often have to do this, here is a macro that can help.

How it works

When you want to rearrange sheets, you use the `Move` method of either the `Sheets` object or the `ActiveSheet` object. When using the `Move` method, you need to specify where to move the sheet to. You can do this using the `After` argument, the `Before` argument, or both.

```
Sub Macro20()

'Move the active sheet to the end
    ActiveSheet.Move After:=Worksheets(Worksheets.Count)

'Move the active sheet to the beginning
    ActiveSheet.Move Before:=Worksheets(1)

'Move Sheet 1 before Sheet 12
    Sheets("Sheet1").Move Before:=Sheets("Sheet12")

End Sub
```

This macro does three things. First, it moves the active sheet to the end. Nothing in VBA lets you point to "the last sheet." But you can find the maximum count of worksheets, and then use that number as an index for the `Worksheets` object. This means that we can enter something like `Worksheets(3)` to point to the third sheet in a workbook. Thus, you can use `Worksheet(Worksheets.Count)` to point to the last sheet.

Next, this macro moves the active sheet to the beginning of the workbook. This one is simple; we use `Worksheets(1)` to point to the first sheet in the workbook, and then move the active sheet before that one.

Finally, the macro demonstrates that you can move sheets simply by calling them out by name. In this example, we are moving Sheet1 before Sheet12.

How to use it

The best place to store this kind of a macro is in your Personal Macro Workbook. This way, the macro is always available to you. The Personal Macro Workbook is loaded whenever you start Excel. In the VBE Project window, it is named personal.xlsb.

1. Activate the Visual Basic Editor by pressing ALT+F11.
2. Right-click personal.xlb in the Project window.

3. Choose Insert➜Module.

4. Type or paste the code in the newly created module.

If you don't see personal.xlb in your project window, it means it doesn't exist yet. You'll have to record a macro, using Personal Macro Workbook as the destination.

To record the macro in your Personal Macro Workbook, select the Personal Macro Workbook option in the Record Macro dialog box before you start recording. This option is in the Store Macro In drop-down list. Simply record a couple of cell clicks and then stop recording. You can discard the recorded macro and replace it with this one.

Macro 21: Sort Worksheets by Name

You may often need to sort worksheets alphabetically by name. You would think Excel would have a native function to do this, but alas, it does not. If you don't want to manually sort your spreadsheets anymore, you can use this macro to do it for you.

How it works

This macro looks more complicated than it is. The activity in this macro is actually fairly simple. It simply iterates through the sheets in the workbook, comparing the current sheet to the previous one. If the name of the previous sheet is greater than the current sheet (alphabetically), the macro moves the current sheet before it. By the time all the iterations are done, you've got a sorted workbook!

```
Sub Macro21()

'Step 1: Declare your Variables
    Dim CurrentSheetIndex As Integer
    Dim PrevSheetIndex As Integer

'Step 2: Set the starting counts and start looping
    For CurrentSheetIndex = 1 To Sheets.Count
    For PrevSheetIndex = 1 To CurrentSheetIndex - 1

'Step 3: Check Current Sheet against Previous Sheet
    If UCase(Sheets(PrevSheetIndex).Name) > _
       UCase(Sheets(CurrentSheetIndex).Name) Then

'Step 4: If Move Current sheet Before Previous
    Sheets(CurrentSheetIndex).Move _
    Before:=Sheets(PrevSheetIndex)
    End If

'Step 5 Loop back around to iterate again
    Next PrevSheetIndex
    Next CurrentSheetIndex

End Sub
```

Note

Note that this technique is doing a text-based sort, so you may not get the results you were expecting when working with number-based sheet names. For instance, Sheet10 comes before Sheet2 because textually, 1 comes before 2. Excel doesn't do the numbers-based sorting that says 2 comes before 10.

1. Step 1 declares two integer variables. The `CurrentSheetIndex` holds the index number for the current sheet iteration, and the `PrevSheetIndex` variable holds the index number for the previous sheet iteration.

2. In Step 2, the macro starts iteration counts for both variables. Note that the count for the `PrevSheetIndex` is one number behind the `CurrentSheetIndex`. After the counts are set, we start looping.

3. In Step 3, we check to see whether the name of the previous sheet is greater than that of the current sheet.

   In this step, note the use of the `UCase` function. We use this to get both names in the same uppercase state. This prevents sorting errors due to differing case states.

4. Step 4 is reached only if the previous sheet name is greater than the current sheet name. In this step, we use the `Move` method to move the current sheet before the previous sheet.

5. In Step 5, we go back around to the start of the loop. Every iteration of the loop increments both variables up one number until the last worksheet is touched. After all iterations have been spent, the macro ends.

How to use it

The best place to store this macro is in your Personal Macro Workbook. This way, the macro is always available to you. The Personal Macro Workbook is loaded whenever you start Excel. In the VBE Project window, it is named personal.xlsb.

1. Activate the Visual Basic Editor by pressing ALT+F11.

2. Right-click personal.xlb in the Project window.

3. Choose Insert→Module.

4. Type or paste the code in the newly created module.

If you don't see personal.xlb in your project window, it means it doesn't exist yet. You'll have to record a macro, using Personal Macro Workbook as the destination.

To record the macro in your Personal Macro Workbook, select the Personal Macro Workbook option in the Record Macro dialog box before you start recording. This option is in the Store Macro In drop-down list. Simply record a couple of cell clicks and then stop recording. You can discard the recorded macro and replace it with this one.

Macro 22: Group Worksheets by Color

Many of us assign colors to our worksheet tabs. This allows for the visual confirmation that the data in a certain tab is somehow related to another tab because both have the same color. This macro groups worksheets based on their tab colors.

How it works

You may think it's impossible to sort or group by color, but Excel offers a way. Excel assigns an index number to every color. A light yellow color may have an index number of 36, whereas a maroon color has the index number 42.

This macro iterates through the sheets in the workbook, comparing the tab color index of the current sheet to that of the previous one. If the previous sheet has the same color index number as the current sheet, the macro moves the current sheet before it. By the time all the iterations are done, all of the sheets are grouped together based on their tab colors.

```
Sub Macro22()

'Step 1: Declare your Variables
    Dim CurrentSheetIndex As Integer
    Dim PrevSheetIndex As Integer

'Step 2: Set the starting counts and start looping
    For CurrentSheetIndex = 1 To Sheets.Count
    For PrevSheetIndex = 1 To CurrentSheetIndex - 1

'Step 3: Check Current Sheet against Previous Sheet
    If Sheets(PrevSheetIndex).Tab.ColorIndex = _
    Sheets(CurrentSheetIndex).Tab.ColorIndex Then

'Step 4: If Move Current sheet Before Previous
    Sheets(PrevSheetIndex).Move _
    Before:=Sheets(CurrentSheetIndex)
    End If

'Step 5 Loop back around to iterate again
    Next PrevSheetIndex
    Next CurrentSheetIndex

End Sub
```

1. Step 1 declares two integer variables. The `CurrentSheetIndex` holds the index number for the current sheet iteration, and the `PrevSheetIndex` variable holds the index number for the previous sheet iteration.

2. Step 2 starts iteration counts for both variables. Note that the count for the `PrevSheetIndex` is one number behind the `CurrentSheetIndex`. After the counts are set, the macro starts looping.

3. In Step 3, the macro checks to see whether the color index of the previous sheet is the same as that of the current sheet. Note the use of the `Tab.ColorIndex` property.

4. Step 4 is reached only if the color index of the previous sheet is equal to the color index of the current sheet. In this step, the macro uses the `Move` method to move the current sheet before the previous sheet.

5. In Step 5, the macro goes back around to the start of the loop. Every iteration of the loop increments both variables up one number until the last worksheet is touched. After all of the iterations have run, the macro ends.

How to use it

The best place to store this macro is in your Personal Macro Workbook. This way, the macro is always available to you. The Personal Macro Workbook is loaded whenever you start Excel. In the VBE Project window, it is named personal.xlsb.

1. Activate the Visual Basic Editor by pressing ALT+F11.

2. Right-click personal.xlb in the Project window.

3. Choose Insert➜Module.

4. Type or paste the code in the newly created module.

If you don't see personal.xlb in your project window, it doesn't exist yet. You'll have to record a macro, using Personal Macro Workbook as the destination.

To record the macro in your Personal Macro Workbook, select the Personal Macro Workbook option in the Record Macro dialog box before you start recording. This option is in the Store Macro In drop-down list. Simply record a couple of cell clicks and then stop recording. You can discard the recorded macro and replace it with this one.

Macro 23: Copy a Worksheet to a New Workbook

In Excel, you can manually copy an entire sheet to a new workbook by right-clicking the target sheet and selecting the Move or Copy option. Unfortunately, if you try to record a macro while you do this, the macro recorder fails to accurately write the code to reflect the task. So if you need to programmatically copy an entire sheet to a brand new workbook, this macro delivers.

How it works

In this macro, the active sheet is first being copied. Then we use the `Before` parameter to send the copy to a new workbook that is created on the fly. The copied sheet is positioned as the first sheet in the new workbook.

The use of the `ThisWorkbook` object is important here. This ensures that the active sheet that is being copied is from the workbook that the code is in, not the new workbook that is created.

```
Sub Macro23()

'Copy sheet, and send to new workbook
    ThisWorkbook.ActiveSheet.Copy _
    Before:=Workbooks.Add.Worksheets(1)

End Sub
```

How to use it

To implement this macro, you can copy and paste it into a standard module:

1. Activate the Visual Basic Editor by pressing ALT+F11.
2. Right-click the project/workbook name in the Project window.
3. Choose Insert➜Module.
4. Type or paste the code in the newly created module.

Macro 24: Create a New Workbook for Each Worksheet

Many Excel analysts need to parse their workbooks into separate books per worksheet tab. In other words, they need to create a new workbook for each of the worksheets in their existing workbook. You can imagine what an ordeal this would be if you were to do it manually. The following macro helps automate that task.

How it works

In this macro, you are looping the worksheets, copying each sheet, and then sending the copy to a new workbook that is created on the fly. The thing to note here is that the newly created workbooks are being saved in the same directory as your original workbook, with the same filename as the copied sheet (wb.SaveAs ThisWorkbook.Path & "\" & ws.Name).

```
Sub Macro24()

'Step 1:  Declare all the variables.
    Dim ws As Worksheet
    Dim wb As Workbook

'Step 2:  Start the looping through sheets
    For Each ws In ThisWorkbook.Worksheets

'Step 3:  Create new workbook and save it.
    Set wb = Workbooks.Add
    wb.SaveAs ThisWorkbook.Path & "\" & ws.Name

'Step 4:  Copy the target sheet to the new workbook
    ws.Copy Before:=wb.Worksheets(1)
    wb.Close SaveChanges:=True

'Step 5:  Loop back around to the next worksheet
    Next ws

End Sub
```

Note

Not all valid worksheet names translate to valid filenames. Windows has specific rules that prevent you from naming files with certain characters. You cannot use these characters when naming a file: backslash (\), forward slash (/), colon (:), asterisk (*), question mark (?), pipe (|), double quote ("), greater than (>), and less than (<). The twist is that you can use a few of these restricted characters in your sheet names; specifically, double quote, pipe (|), greater than (>), and less than (<).

As you're running this macro, naming the newly created files to match the sheet name may cause an error. For instance, the macro throws an error when creating a new file from a sheet called May| Revenue (because of the pipe character). To make a long story short, avoid naming your worksheets with these restricted characters.

1. Step 1 declares two object variables. The `ws` variable creates a memory container for each worksheet the macro loops through. The `wb` variable creates the container for the new workbooks we create.

2. In Step 2, the macro starts looping through the sheets. The use of the `ThisWorkbook` object ensures that the active sheet that is being copied is from the workbook the code is in, not the new workbook that is created.

3. In Step 3, we create the new workbook and save it. We save this new book in the same path as the original workbook (`ThisWorkbook`). The filename is set to be the same name as the currently active sheet.

4. Step 4 copies the currently active sheet and uses the `Before` parameter to send it to the new book as the first tab.

5. Step 5 loops back to get the next sheet. After all of the sheets are evaluated, the macro ends.

How to use it

To implement this macro, you can copy and paste it into a standard module:

1. Activate the Visual Basic Editor by pressing ALT+F11.

2. Right-click the project/workbook name in the Project window.

3. Choose Insert➜Module.

4. Type or paste the code in the newly created module.

Macro 25: Print Specified Worksheets

If you want to print specific sheets manually in Excel, you need to hold down the CTRL key on the keyboard, select the sheets you want to print, and then click Print. If you do this often enough, you may consider using this very simple macro.

How it works

This one is easy. All we have to do is pass the sheets we want printed in an array as seen here in this macro. Then we use the `PrintOut` method to trigger the print job. All the sheets you have entered are printed in one go.

```
Sub Macro25()

'Print Certain Sheets
    ActiveWorkbook.Sheets( _
    Array("Sheet1", "Sheet3", "Sheet5")).PrintOut Copies:=1

End Sub
```

Want to print all worksheets in a workbook? This one is even easier.

```
Sub Macro25()

'Print All Sheets
    ActiveWorkbook.Worksheets.PrintOut Copies:=1

End Sub
```

How to use it

The best place to store this macro is in your Personal Macro Workbook. This way, the macro is always available to you. The Personal Macro Workbook is loaded whenever you start Excel. In the VBE Project window, it is named personal.xlsb.

1. Activate the Visual Basic Editor by pressing ALT+F11.
2. Right-click personal.xlb in the Project window.

3. Choose Insert➜Module.

4. Type or paste the code in the newly created module.

If you don't see personal.xlb in your project window, it means it doesn't exist yet. You'll have to record a macro using Personal Macro Workbook as the destination.

To record the macro in your Personal Macro Workbook, select the Personal Macro Workbook option in the Record Macro dialog box before you start recording. This option is in the Store Macro In drop-down list. Simply record a couple of cell clicks and then stop recording. You can discard the recorded macro and replace it with this one.

Macro 26: Protect All Worksheets

Before you distribute your workbook, you may want to apply sheet protection to all of the sheets. Instead of protecting each sheet manually, you can use this macro.

How it works

In this macro, you are looping the worksheets and simply applying protection with a password. The `Password` argument defines the password needed to remove the protection. The `Password` argument is completely optional. If you omit it altogether, the sheet will still be protected; you just won't need to enter a password to unprotect it. Also, be aware that Excel passwords are case-sensitive, so you'll want to pay attention to the exact capitalization you are using.

```
Sub Macro26()

'Step 1:  Declare your variables
    Dim ws As Worksheet

'Step 2: Start looping through all worksheets
    For Each ws In ActiveWorkbook.Worksheets

'Step 3:  Protect and loop to next worksheet
    ws.Protect Password:="RED"
    Next ws

End Sub
```

1. Step 1 declares an object called `ws`. This creates a memory container for each worksheet we loop through.

2. Step 2 starts the looping, telling Excel we want to enumerate through all worksheets in this workbook.

3. In Step 3, the macro applies protection with the given password, and then loops back to get the worksheet.

How to use it

The best place to store this macro is in your Personal Macro Workbook. This way, the macro is always available to you. The Personal Macro Workbook is loaded whenever you start Excel. In the VBE Project window, it is named personal.xlsb.

1. Activate the Visual Basic Editor by pressing ALT+F11.

2. Right-click personal.xlb in the Project window.

3. Choose Insert➜Module.

4. Type or paste the code in the newly created module.

If you don't see personal.xlb in your project window, it doesn't exist yet. You'll have to record a macro using Personal Macro Workbook as the destination.

To record the macro in your Personal Macro Workbook, select the Personal Macro Workbook option in the Record Macro dialog box before you start recording. This option is in the Store Macro In drop-down list. Simply record a couple of cell clicks and then stop recording. You can discard the recorded macro and replace it with this one.

Macro 27: Unprotect All Worksheets

You may find yourself constantly having to unprotect multiple worksheets manually. The following macro does the same thing programmatically.

How it works

This macro loops the worksheets and uses the `Password` argument to unprotect each sheet.

```
Sub Macro27()

'Step 1:  Declare your variables
    Dim ws As Worksheet

'Step 2: Start looping through all worksheets
    For Each ws In ActiveWorkbook.Worksheets

'Step 3:  Loop to next worksheet
    ws.UnProtect Password:="RED"
    Next ws

End Sub
```

1. Step 1 declares an object called `ws`. This creates a memory container for each worksheet we loop through.

2. Step 2 starts the looping, telling Excel to enumerate through all worksheets in this workbook.

3. Step 3 unprotects the active sheet, providing the password as needed, and then loops back to get the worksheet.

Obviously, the assumption is that all the worksheets that need to be unprotected have the same password. If this is not the case, you need to explicitly unprotect each sheet with its corresponding password.

```
Sub Macro27b()

Sheets("Sheet1").UnProtect Password:="RED"
Sheets("Sheet2").UnProtect Password:="BLUE"
Sheets("Sheet3").UnProtect Password:="YELLOW"
Sheets("Sheet4").UnProtect Password:="GREEN"

End Sub
```

How to use it

The best place to store this kind of a macro is in your Personal Macro Workbook. This way, the macro is always available to you. The Personal Macro Workbook is loaded whenever you start Excel. In the VBE Project window, it will be named personal.xlsb.

1. Activate the Visual Basic Editor by pressing ALT+F11.

2. Right-click personal.xlb in the Project window.

3. Choose Insert➜Module.

4. Type or paste the code in the newly created module.

If you don't see personal.xlb in your project window, it means it doesn't exist yet. You'll have to record a macro, using Personal Macro Workbook as the destination.

To record the macro in your Personal Macro Workbook, select the Personal Macro Workbook option in the Record Macro dialog box before you start recording. This option is in the Store Macro In drop-down list. Simply record a couple of cell clicks and then stop recording. You can discard the recorded macro and replace it with this one.

Macro 28: Create a Table of Contents for Your Worksheets

Outside of sorting worksheets, creating a table of contents for the worksheets in a workbook is the most commonly requested Excel macro. The reason is probably not lost on you. We often have to work with files that have more worksheet tabs than can easily be seen or navigated. A table of contents definitely helps.

The following macro not only creates a list of worksheet names in the workbook, but it also ads hyperlinks so that you can easily jump to a sheet with a simple click.

How it works

It's easy to get intimidated when looking at this macro. There is a lot going on here. However, if you step back and consider the few simple actions it does, it becomes a little less scary:

- ➤ It removes any previous Table of Contents sheet
- ➤ It creates a new Table of Contents sheet
- ➤ It grabs the name of each worksheet and pastes it on the Table of Contents
- ➤ It adds a hyperlink to each entry in the Table of Contents

That doesn't sound so bad. Now look at the code:

```
Sub Macro28()

'Step 1: Declare Variables
    Dim i As Long

'Step 2:  Delete Previous TOC if Exists
    On Error Resume Next
    Application.DisplayAlerts = False
    Sheets("Table Of Contents").Delete
    Application.DisplayAlerts = True
    On Error GoTo 0

'Step 3:  Add a new TOC sheet as the first sheet
    ThisWorkbook.Sheets.Add _
    Before:=ThisWorkbook.Worksheets(1)
    ActiveSheet.Name = "Table Of Contents"
```

```
'Step 4: Start the i Counter
    For i = 1 To Sheets.Count

'Step 5: Select Next available row
    ActiveSheet.Cells(i, 1).Select

'Step 6:  Add Sheet Name and Hyperlink
    ActiveSheet.Hyperlinks.Add _
    Anchor:=ActiveSheet.Cells(i, 1), _
    Address:="", _
    SubAddress:="'" & Sheets(i).Name & "'!A1", _
    TextToDisplay:=Sheets(i).Name

'Step 7: Loop back increment i
    Next i

End Sub
```

1. Step 1 declares an integer variable called `i` to serve as the counter as the macro iterates through the sheets.

    Note that this macro is not looping through the sheets the way previous macros in this Part did. In previous macros, we looped through the worksheets collection and selected each worksheet there. In this procedure, we are using a counter (our `i` variable). The main reason is because we not only have to keep track of the sheets, but we also have to manage to enter each sheet name on a new row into a table of contents. The idea is that as the counter progresses through the sheets, it also serves to move the cursor down in the table of contents so each new entry goes on a new row.

2. Step 2 essentially attempts to delete any previous sheet called Table of Contents. Because there may not be any Table of Contents sheet to delete, we have to start Step 2 with the `On Error Resume Next` error handler. This tells Excel to continue the macro if an error is encountered here. We then delete the Table of Contents sheet using the `DisplayAlerts` method, which effectively turns off Excel's warnings so we don't have to confirm the deletion. Finally, we reset the error handler to trap all errors again by entering `On Error GoTo 0`.

3. In Step 3, we add a new sheet to the workbook using the `Before` argument to position the new sheet as the first sheet. We then name the sheet Table of Contents. As we mentioned previously in this Part, when you add a new worksheet, it automatically becomes the active sheet. Because this new sheet has the focus throughout the procedure, any references to `ActiveSheet` in this code refer to the Table of Contents sheet.

4. Step 4 starts the `i` counter at 1 and ends it at the maximum count of all sheets in the workbook. Again, instead of looping through the Worksheets collection like we've done in previous macros, we are simply using the `i` counter as an index number that we can pass to the `Sheets` object. When the maximum number is reached, the macro ends.

5. Step 5 selects the corresponding row in the Table of Contents sheet. That is to say, if the `i` counter is on 1, it selects the first row in the Table of Contents sheet. If the `i` counter is at 2, it selects the second row, and so on.

   We are able to do this using the `Cells` item. The `Cells` item provides an extremely handy way of selecting ranges through code. It requires only relative row and column positions as parameters. So `Cells(1,1)` translates to row 1, column 1 (or cell A1). `Cells(5, 3)` translates to row 5, column 3 (or cell C5). The numeric parameters in the `Cells` item are particularly handy when you want to loop through a series of rows or columns using an incrementing index number.

6. Step 6 uses the `Hyperlinks.Add` method to add the sheet name and hyperlinks to the selected cell. This step feeds the `Hyperlinks.Add` method the parameters it needs to build out the hyperlinks.

7. The last step in the macro loops back to increment the `i` counter to the next count. When the i counter reaches a number that equals the count of worksheets in the workbook, the macro ends.

How to use it

To implement this macro, you can copy and paste it into a standard module:

1. Activate the Visual Basic Editor by pressing ALT+F11.

2. Right-click the project/workbook name in the Project window.

3. Choose Insert→Module.

4. Type or paste the code in the newly created module.

Macro 29: Zooming In and Out of a Worksheet with Double-Click

Some spreadsheets are huge. Sometimes, we are forced to shrink the font size down so that we can see a decent portion of the spreadsheet on the screen. If you find that you are constantly zooming in and out of a spreadsheet, alternating between scanning large sections of data and reading specific cells, here is a handy macro that will auto-zoom on double-click.

How it works

With this macro in place, you can double-click on a cell in the spreadsheet to zoom in 200 percent. Double-click again and Excel zooms back to 100 percent. Obviously, you can change the values and complexity in the code to fit your needs.

```
Private Sub Worksheet_BeforeDoubleClick(ByVal Target As Range, Cancel As
   Boolean)

'Check current Zoom state
'Zoom to 100% if to at 100
'Zoom 200% if currently at 100
    If ActiveWindow.Zoom <> 100 Then
    ActiveWindow.Zoom = 100
    Else
    ActiveWindow.Zoom = 200
    End If

End Sub
```

Note

Note that the side effect of double-clicking a cell is that it goes into edit mode. You can exit edit mode by pressing Esc on your keyboard. If you find it annoying to repeatedly press Esc when triggering this macro, you can add this statement to the end of the procedure:

```
Application.SendKeys ("{ESC}")
```

This statement mimics you pressing Esc on your keyboard.

How to use it

To implement this macro, you need to copy and paste it into the `Worksheet_BeforeDouble Click` event code window. Placing the macro there allows it to run each time you double-click on the sheet.

1. Activate the Visual Basic Editor by pressing ALT+F11.

2. In the Project window, find your project/workbook name and click the plus sign next to it in order to see all the sheets.

3. Click on the sheet from which you want to trigger the code.

4. Select the `BeforeDoubleClick` event from the Event drop-down list (see Figure 3-1).

5. Type or paste the code in the newly created module.

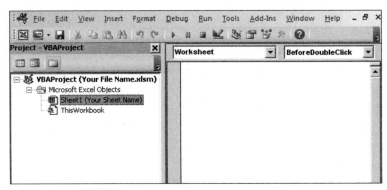

Figure 3-1: Type or paste your code into the Worksheet_BeforeDoubleClick event code window.

Macro 30: Highlight the Active Row and Column

When looking at a table of numbers, it would be nice if Excel automatically highlighted the row and column you're on (as demonstrated in Figure 3-2). This effect gives your eyes a lead line up and down the column as well as left and right across the row.

⊿	A	B	C	D	E	F	G
1							
2		Jan	Feb	Mar	Apr	May	Jun
3	Product 1	$74,084	$41,353	$37,032	$77,941	$35,221	$55
4	Product 2	$70,049	$42,425	$51,966	$25,159	$35,929	$16
5	Product 3	$13,513	$98,468	$18,818	$27,001	$11,373	$2
6	Product 4	$72,705	$25,553	$68,709	$86,278	$58,278	$47
7	Product 5	$35,637	$81,467	$83,445	$51,797	$58,971	$52
8	Product 6	$61,118	$71,932	$42,153	$20,370	$44,917	$25
9	Product 7	$42,303	$19,757	$78,250	$32,396	$1,863	$30
10	Product 8	$74,735	$53,599	$52,357	$55,778	$89,745	$43
11	Product 9	$29,764	$31,476	$92,661	$76,510	$93,957	$90
12	Product 10	$37,577	$68,726	$42,900	$60,592	$7,627	$17
13	Product 11	$98,304	$19,809	$56,834	$62,311	$54,039	$55
14	Product 12	$64,827	$85,195	$16,953	$47,824	$26,565	$52
15							

Figure 3-2: A highlighted row and column makes it easy to track data horizontally and vertically.

The following macro enables the effect you see in Figure 3-2 with just a simple double-click. When the macro is in place, Excel highlights the row and column for the cell that is active, greatly improving your ability to view and edit a large grid.

How it works

Take a look at how this macro works:

```
Private Sub Worksheet_BeforeDoubleClick(ByVal Target As Range, Cancel As
   Boolean)

'Step 1:  Declare Variables
    Dim strRange As String

'Step2:  Build the range string
    strRange = Target.Cells.Address & "," & _
               Target.Cells.EntireColumn.Address & "," & _
               Target.Cells.EntireRow.Address

'Step 3: Pass the range string to a Range
    Range(strRange).Select

End Sub
```

1. We first declare an object called `strRange`. This creates a memory container we can use to build a range string.

2. A range string is nothing more than the address for a range. `"A1"` is a range string that points to cell A1. `"A1:G5"` is also a range string; this points to a range of cells encompassing cells A1 to G5. In Step 2, we are building a range string that encompasses the double-clicked cell (called `Target` in this macro), the entire active row, and the entire active column. The `Address` properties for these three ranges are captured and pieced together into the `strRange` variable.

3. In Step 3, we feed the `strRange` variable as the address for a `Range.Select` statement. This is the line of the code that finally highlights the double-clicked selection.

How to use it

To implement this macro, you need to copy and paste it into the `Worksheet_BeforeDouble Click` event code window. Placing the macro there allows it to run each time you double-click on the sheet.

1. Activate the Visual Basic Editor by pressing ALT+F11.

2. In the Project window, find your project/workbook name and click the plus sign next to it in order to see all the sheets.

3. Click on the sheet from which you want to trigger the code.

4. Select the `BeforeDoubleClick` event from the Event drop-down list (see Figure 3-3).

5. Type or paste the code in the newly created module.

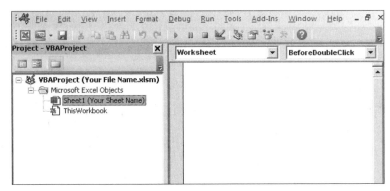

Figure 3-3: Type or paste your code into the Worksheet_BeforeDoubleClick event code window.

Selecting and Modifying Ranges

This Part is all about ranges: selecting them, modifying them, hiding them, and more.

In This Part

One of the most important things you do in Excel is navigating the worksheet. When you work with Excel manually, you are constantly navigating to appropriate ranges, finding the last row, moving to the last column, hiding and unhiding ranges, and so on. This all comes instinctively as part of doing work in Excel.

When you attempt to automate your work through VBA, you'll find that navigating your spreadsheet remains an important part of the automation process. In many cases, you need to dynamically navigate and manipulate Excel ranges, just as you would manually — only through VBA code. This chapter provides some of the most commonly used macros in terms of navigating and working with ranges.

Tip

The code for this Part can be found on this book's companion website. See this book's Introduction for more on the companion website.

Macro 31: Selecting and Formatting a Range

One of the basic things you need to do in VBA is to select a specific range to do something with it. This simple macro selects the range D5:D16.

How it works

In this macro, you explicitly define the range to select by using the `Range` object.

```
Sub Macro31a()

Range("D5:D16").Select

End Sub
```

After the range of cells is selected, you can use any of the `Range` properties to manipulate the cells. We've altered this macro so that the range is colored yellow, converted to number formatting, and bold.

```
Sub Macro31a()

    Range("D5:D16").Select
    Selection.NumberFormat = "#,##0"
    Selection.Font.Bold = True
    Selection.Interior.ColorIndex = 36

End Sub
```

You don't have to memorize all the properties of the cell object in order to manipulate them. You can simply record a macro, do your formatting, and then look at the code that Excel has written. After you've seen what the correct syntax is, you can apply it as needed. Many Excel programmers start learning VBA this way.

You notice that we refer to `Selection` many times in the previous sample code. To write more efficient code, you can simply refer to the range, using the `With...End With` statement. This statement tells Excel that any action you perform applies to the object to which you've pointed. Note that this macro doesn't actually select the range at all. This is a key point. In a macro, we can work with a range without selecting it first.

```
Sub Macro31a()

    With Range("D5:D16")
        .NumberFormat = "#,##0"
        .Font.Bold = True
        .Interior.ColorIndex = 36
    End With

End Sub
```

Another way you can select a range is by using the `Cells` item of the `Range` object.

The `Cells` item gives us an extremely handy way of selecting ranges through code. It requires only relative row and column positions as parameters. `Cells(5, 4)` translates to row 5, column 4 (or Cell D5). `Cells(16, 4)` translates to row 16, column 4 (or cell D16).

If you want to select a range of cells, simply pass two items into the `Range` object. This macro performs the same selection of range D5:D16:

```
Sub Macro31a()

Range(Cells(5, 4), Cells(16, 4)).Select

End Sub
```

Here is the full formatting code using the `Cells` item. Again, note that this macro doesn't actually select the range we are altering. We can work with a range without selecting it first.

```
Sub Macro31a()

    With Range(Cells(5, 4), Cells(16, 4))
        .NumberFormat = "#,##0"
        .Font.Bold = True
        .Interior.ColorIndex = 36
    End With

End Sub
```

How to use it

To implement this kind of a macro, you can copy and paste it into a standard module:

1. Activate the Visual Basic Editor by pressing ALT+F11 on your keyboard.

2. Right-click the project/workbook name in the Project window.

3. Choose Insert➜Module.

4. Type or paste the code into the code window.

Macro 32: Creating and Selecting Named Ranges

One of the more useful features in Excel is the ability to name your range (that is, to give your range a user-friendly name, so that you can more easily identify and refer to it via VBA).

Here are the steps you would perform to create a named range manually.

1. Select the range you wish to name.

2. Go to the Formulas tab in the Ribbon and choose the Define Name command (see Figure 4-1).

3. Give the chosen range a user-friendly name in the New Name dialog box, as shown in Figure 4-2.

When you click OK, your range is named. To confirm this, you can go to the Formula tab and select the Name Manager command. This activates the Name Manager dialog box (see Figure 4-3), where you can see all the applied named ranges.

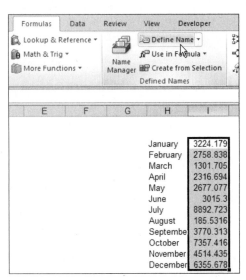

Figure 4-1: Click the Define Name command to name a chosen range.

Figure 4-2: Give your range a name.

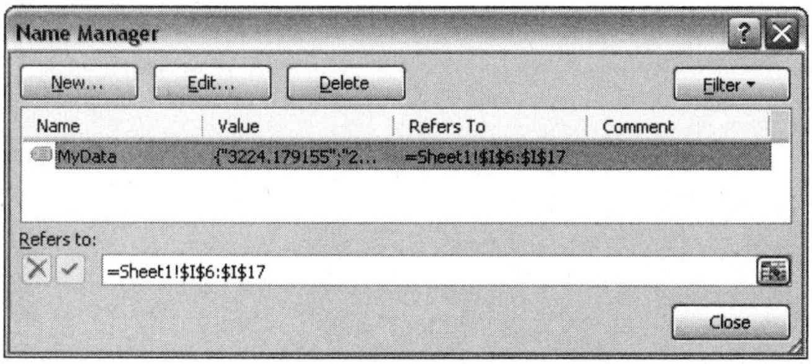

Figure 4-3: The Name Manager dialog box lists all the applied named ranges.

Creating a named range via VBA is much less involved. You can directly define the `Name` property of the `Range` object:

```
Sub Macro32a()

Range("D6:D17").Name = "MyData"

End Sub
```

Admittedly, you'd be hard pressed to find a situation where you would need to automate the creation of named ranges. The real efficiency comes in manipulating them via VBA.

How it works

You simply pass the name of the range through the `Range` object. This allows you to select the range:

```
Sub Macro32b()

Range("MyData").Select

End Sub
```

As with normal ranges, you can refer to the range using the With...End With statement. This statement tells Excel that any action you perform applies to the object to which you've pointed. This not only prevents you from having to repeat syntax, but it also allows for the easy addition of actions by simply adding them between the With and End With statements.

```
Sub Macro32a()

    With Range("MyData")
        .NumberFormat = "#,##0"
        .Font.Bold = True
        .Interior.ColorIndex = 36
    End With

End Sub
```

How to use it

To implement this kind of a macro, you can copy and paste it into a standard module:

1. Activate the Visual Basic Editor by pressing ALT+F11.
2. Right-click the project/workbook name in the Project window.
3. Choose Insert➜Module.
4. Type or paste the code.

Macro 33: Enumerating Through a Range of Cells

One must-have VBA skill is the ability to enumerate (or loop) through a range. If you do any serious macro work in Excel, you will soon encounter the need to go through a range of cells one by one and perform some action.

This basic macro shows you a simple way to enumerate through a range.

How it works

In this macro, we are essentially using two `Range` object variables. One of the variables captures the scope of data we are working with, whereas the other is used to hold each individual cell as we go through the range. Then we use the `For Each` statement to activate or bring each cell in the target range into focus:

```vba
Sub Macro33()

'Step1:  Declare your variables.
    Dim MyRange As Range
    Dim MyCell As Range

'Step 2:  Define the target Range.
    Set MyRange = Range("D6:D17")

'Step 3:  Start looping through the range.
    For Each MyCell In MyRange

'Step 4:  Do something with each cell.

    If MyCell.Value > 3000 Then
        MyCell.Font.Bold = True
    End If

'Step 5: Get the next cell in the range
    Next MyCell

End Sub
```

1. The macro first declares two `Range` object variables. One, called `MyRange`, holds the entire target range. The other, called `MyCell`, holds each cell in the range as the macro enumerates through them one by one.

2. In Step 2, we fill the `MyRange` variable with the target range. In this example, we are using `Range("D6:D17")`. If your target range is a named range, you could simply enter its name — `Range("MyNamedRange")`.

3. In this step, the macro starts looping through each cell in the target range, activating each cell as it goes through.

4. After a cell is activated, you would do something with it. That "something" really depends on the task at hand. You may want to delete rows when the active cell has a certain value, or you may want to insert a row between each active cell. In this example, the macro is changing the font to Bold for any cell that has a value greater than 3,000.

5. In Step 5, the macro loops back to get the next cell. After all cells in the target range are activated, the macro ends.

How to use it

To implement this macro, you can copy and paste it into a standard module:

1. Activate the Visual Basic Editor by pressing ALT+F11 on your keyboard.

2. Right-click the project/workbook name in the Project window.

3. Choose Insert→Module.

4. Type or paste the code.

Macro 34: Select and Format All Named Ranges

If you spend your time auditing other people's worksheets, you'll know that Excel users love their named ranges. It's not uncommon to encounter spreadsheets where dozens of cells and ranges are given individual names. This makes auditing a spreadsheet an extremely muddy experience. It sometimes helps to know where the named ranges are. Here is a macro you can use to color all of the named ranges in a workbook yellow.

How it works

In this macro, we are looping through the `Names` collection of the active workbook to capture each named range. When a named range is captured, we color the range.

```
Sub Macro34()

'Step 1:  Declare your variables.
    Dim RangeName As Name
    Dim HighlightRange As Range

'Step 2: Tell Excel to Continue if Error.
    On Error Resume Next

'Step 3: Loop through each Named Range.
    For Each RangeName In ActiveWorkbook.Names

'Step 4: Capture the RefersToRange
    Set HighlightRange = RangeName.RefersToRange

'Step 5:  Color the Range
    HighlightRange.Interior.ColorIndex = 36

'Step 6:  Loop back around to get the next range
    Next RangeName

End Sub
```

1. We first declare two object variables. The first variable called `RangeName` holds each named range as the macro enumerates through the `Names` collection. The second variable called `HighlightRange` captures the range to which `RangeName` is referring.

2. Technically, an Excel user can assign a "name" to things that are not actually a range (such as constants or formulas). So with that in mind, we have to anticipate that Excel will throw an error if the `RefersToRange` property of the named range does not represent a range address. In this step, we tell Excel to ignore any error that is thrown and continue to the next line of code. This ensures that the code doesn't abruptly stop due to a bad range address.

3. In this step, the macro starts looping through each name in the active workbooks `Names` collection.

4. After a named range is activated, the macro captures the address in our `HighlightRange` object variable. This exposes all the properties we can use to format the range.

5. In Step 5, we assign a color to the cells in the captured range.

6. Finally, we loop back to get the next named range. The macro ends after we have enumerated through all of the names.

How to use it

The best place to store this macro is in your Personal Macro Workbook. This way, the macro is always available to you. The Personal Macro Workbook is loaded whenever you start Excel. In the VBE Project window, it will be named personal.xlb.

1. Activate the Visual Basic Editor by pressing ALT+F11.

2. Right-click personal.xlb in the Project window.

3. Choose Insert➜Module.

4. Type or paste the code.

If you don't see personal.xlb in your project window, it doesn't exist yet. You'll have to record a macro, using Personal Macro Workbook as the destination.

To record the macro in your Personal Macro Workbook, select the Personal Macro Workbook option in the Record Macro dialog box before you start recording. This option is in the `Store Macro In` drop-down list. Simply record a couple of cell clicks and then stop recording. You can discard the recorded macro and replace it with this one.

Macro 35: Inserting Blank Rows in a Range

Occasionally, you may need to dynamically insert rows into your dataset. Although blank rows are generally bothersome, in some situations, the final formatted version of your report requires them to separate data. The macro in this section adds blank rows into a range.

How it works

This macro performs a reverse loop through the chosen range using a counter. It starts at the last row of the range inserting two blank rows, and then moves to the previous row in the range. It keeps doing that same insert for every loop, each time incrementing the counter to the previous row.

```
Sub Macro35()

'Step1:  Declare your variables.
    Dim MyRange As Range
    Dim iCounter As Long

'Step 2:  Define the target Range.
    Set MyRange = Range("C6:D17")

'Step 3:  Start reverse looping through the range.
    For iCounter = MyRange.Rows.Count To 2 Step -1

'Step 4: Insert two blank rows.
    MyRange.Rows(iCounter).EntireRow.Insert
    MyRange.Rows(iCounter).EntireRow.Insert

'Step 5: Increment the counter down
    Next iCounter

End Sub
```

1. We first declare two variables. The first variable is an object variable called `MyRange`. This is an object variable that defines the target range. The other variable is a `Long Integer` variable called `iCounter`. This variable serves as an incremental counter.

2. In Step 2, the macro fills the `MyRange` variable with the target range. In this example, we are using `Range("C6:D17")`. If your target range is a named range, you could simply enter its name — `Range("MyNamedRange")`.

3. In this step, the macro sets the parameters for the incremental counter to start at the max count for the range (`MyRange.Rows.Count`) and end at 2 (the second row of the chosen range). Note that we are using the `Step-1` qualifier. Because we specify `Step -1`, Excel knows we are going to increment the counter backwards, moving back one increment on each iteration. In all, Step 3 tells Excel to start at the last row of the chosen range, moving backward until it gets to the second row of the range.

4. When working with a range, you can explicitly call out a specific row in the range by passing a row index number to the `Rows` collection of the range. For instance, `Range("D6:D17").Rows(5)` points to the fifth row in the range D6:D17.

    In Step 4, the macro uses the `iCounter` variable as an index number for the `Rows` collection of `MyRange`. This helps pinpoint which exact row the macro is working with in the current loop. The macro then uses the `EntireRow.Insert` method to insert a new blank row. Because we want two blank rows, we do this twice.

5. In Step 5, the macro loops back to increment the counter down.

How to use it

To implement this macro, you can copy and paste it into a standard module:

1. Activate the Visual Basic Editor by pressing ALT+F11.

2. Right-click the project/workbook name in the Project window.

3. Choose Insert➜Module.

4. Type or paste the code.

Macro 36: Unhide All Rows and Columns

When you are auditing a spreadsheet that you did not create, you often want to ensure you're getting a full view of what is exactly in the spreadsheet. To do so, you need to ensure that no columns and rows are hidden. This simple macro automatically unhides all rows and columns for you.

How it works

In this macro, we call on the `Columns` collection and the `Rows` collection of the worksheet. Each collection has properties that dictate where their objects are hidden or visible. Running this macro unhides every column in the `Columns` collection and every row in the `Rows` collection.

```
Sub Macro36()

Columns.EntireColumn.Hidden = False
Rows.EntireRow.Hidden = False

End Sub
```

How to use it

The best place to store this macro is in your Personal Macro Workbook. This way, the macro is always available to you. The Personal Macro Workbook is loaded whenever you start Excel. In the VBE Project window, it is named personal.xlb.

1. Activate the Visual Basic Editor by pressing ALT+F11.
2. Right-click personal.xlb in the Project window.
3. Choose Insert➜Module.
4. Type or paste the code.

If you don't see personal.xlb in your project window, it means it doesn't exist yet. You'll have to record a macro, using Personal Macro Workbook as the destination.

To record the macro in your Personal Macro Workbook, select the Personal Macro Workbook option in the Record Macro dialog box before you start recording. This option is in the `Store Macro In` drop-down list. Simply record a couple of cell clicks and then stop recording. You can discard the recorded macro and replace it with this one.

Macro 37: Deleting Blank Rows

Work with Excel long enough, and you'll find out that blank rows can often cause havoc on many levels. They can cause problems with formulas, introduce risk when copying and pasting, and sometimes cause strange behaviors in PivotTables. If you find that you are manually searching out and deleting blank rows in your data sets, this macro can help automate that task.

How it works

In this macro, we are using the UsedRange property of the Activesheet object to define the range we are working with. The UsedRange property gives us a range that encompasses the cells that have been used to enter data. We then establish a counter that starts at the last row of the used range to check if the entire row is empty. If the entire row is indeed empty, we remove the row. We keep doing that same delete for every loop, each time incrementing the counter to the previous row.

```
Sub Macro37()

'Step1:  Declare your variables.
    Dim MyRange As Range
    Dim iCounter As Long

'Step 2:  Define the target Range.
    Set MyRange = ActiveSheet.UsedRange

'Step 3:  Start reverse looping through the range.
    For iCounter = MyRange.Rows.Count To 1 Step -1

'Step 4: If entire row is empty then delete it.
        If Application.CountA(Rows(iCounter).EntireRow) = 0 Then
        Rows(iCounter).Delete
        End If

'Step 5: Increment the counter down
    Next iCounter

End Sub
```

1. The macro first declares two variables. The first variable is an Object variable called MyRange. This is an object variable that defines our target range. The other variable is a Long Integer variable called iCounter. This variable serves as an incremental counter.

2. In Step 2, the macro fills the `MyRange` variable with the `UsedRange` property of the `ActiveSheet` object. The `UsedRange` property gives us a range that encompasses the cells that have been used to enter data. Note that if we wanted to specify an actual range or a named range, we could simply enter its name — `Range("MyNamedRange")`.

3. In this step, the macro sets the parameters for the incremental counter to start at the max count for the range (`MyRange.Rows.Count`) and end at 1 (the first row of the chosen range). Note that we are using the `Step-1` qualifier. Because we specify `Step -1`, Excel knows we are going to increment the counter backwards, moving back one increment on each iteration. In all, Step 3 tells Excel to start at the last row of the chosen range, moving backward until it gets to the first row of the range.

4. When working with a range, you can explicitly call out a specific row in the range by passing a row index number to the `Rows` collection of the range. For instance, `Range("D6:D17").Rows(5)` points to the fifth row in the range D6:D17.

   In Step 4, the macro uses the `iCounter` variable as an index number for the `Rows` collection of `MyRange`. This helps pinpoint which exact row we are working with in the current loop. The macro checks to see whether the cells in that row are empty. If they are, the macro deletes the entire row.

5. In Step 5, the macro loops back to increment the counter down.

How to use it

The best place to store this macro is in your Personal Macro Workbook. This way, the macro is always available to you. The Personal Macro Workbook is loaded whenever you start Excel. In the VBE Project window, it is named personal.xlb.

1. Activate the Visual Basic Editor by pressing ALT+F11.

2. Right-click personal.xlb in the Project window.

3. Choose Insert➜Module.

4. Type or paste the code.

If you don't see personal.xlb in your project window, it means it doesn't exist yet. You'll have to record a macro, using Personal Macro Workbook as the destination.

To record the macro in your Personal Macro Workbook, select the Personal Macro Workbook option in the Record Macro dialog box before you start recording. This option is in the `Store Macro In` drop-down list. Simply record a couple of cell clicks and then stop recording. You can discard the recorded macro and replace it with this one.

Macro 38: Deleting Blank Columns

Just as with blank rows, blank columns also have the potential of causing unforeseen errors. If you find that you are manually searching out and deleting blank columns in your data sets, this macro can automate that task.

How it works

In this macro, we are using the UsedRange property of the ActiveSheet object to define the range we are working with. The UsedRange property gives us a range that encompasses the cells that have been used to enter data. We then establish a counter that starts at the last column of the used range, checking if the entire column is empty. If the entire column is indeed empty, we remove the column. We keep doing that same delete for every loop, each time incrementing the counter to the previous column.

```
Sub Macro38()

'Step1:  Declare your variables.
    Dim MyRange As Range
    Dim iCounter As Long

'Step 2:  Define the target Range.
    Set MyRange = ActiveSheet.UsedRange

'Step 3:  Start reverse looping through the range.
    For iCounter = MyRange.Columns.Count To 1 Step -1


'Step 4: If entire column is empty then delete it.
        If Application.CountA(Columns(iCounter).EntireColumn) = 0 Then
        Columns(iCounter).Delete
        End If

'Step 5: Increment the counter down
    Next iCounter

End Sub
```

1. Step 1 first declares two variables. The first variable is an object variable called MyRange. This is an Object variable that defines the target range. The other variable is a Long Integer variable called iCounter. This variable serves as an incremental counter.

2. Step 2 fills the `MyRange` variable with the `UsedRange` property of the `ActiveSheet` object. The `UsedRange` property gives us a range that encompasses the cells that have been used to enter data. Note that if we wanted to specify an actual range or a named range, we could simply enter its name — `Range("MyNamedRange")`.

3. In this step, the macro sets the parameters for our incremental counter to start at the max count for the range (`MyRange.Columns.Count`) and end at 1 (the first row of the chosen range). Note that we are using the `Step-1` qualifier. Because we specify `Step -1`, Excel knows we are going to increment the counter backwards; moving back one increment on each iteration. In all, Step 3 tells Excel that we want to start at the last column of the chosen range, moving backward until we get to the first column of the range.

4. When working with a range, you can explicitly call out a specific column in the range by passing a column index number to the `Columns` collection of the range. For instance, `Range("A1:D17").Columns(2)` points to the second column in the range (column B).

   In Step 4, the macro uses the `iCounter` variable as an index number for the `Columns` collection of `MyRange`. This helps pinpoint exactly which column we are working with in the current loop. The macro checks to see whether all the cells in that column are empty. If they are, the macro deletes the entire column.

5. In Step 5, the macro loops back to increment the counter down.

How to use it

The best place to store this macro is in your Personal Macro Workbook. This way, the macro is always available to you. The Personal Macro Workbook is loaded whenever you start Excel. In the VBE Project window, it is named personal.xlb.

1. Activate the Visual Basic Editor by pressing ALT+F11.

2. Right-click personal.xlb in the Project window.

3. Choose Insert➜Module.

4. Type or paste the code.

If you don't see personal.xlb in your project window, it doesn't exist yet. You'll have to record a macro, using Personal Macro Workbook as the destination.

To record the macro in your Personal Macro Workbook, select the Personal Macro Workbook option in the Record Macro dialog box before you start recording. This option is in the `Store Macro In` drop-down box. Simply record a couple of cell clicks and then stop recording. You can discard the recorded macro and replace it with this one.

Macro 39: Select and Format All Formulas in a Workbook

When auditing an Excel workbook, it's paramount to have a firm grasp of all the formulas in each sheet. This means finding all the formulas, which can be an arduous task if done manually. However, Excel provides us with a slick way of finding and tagging all the formulas on a worksheet. The macro in this section exploits this functionality to dynamically find all cells that contain formulas.

How it works

Excel has a set of predefined "special cells" that you can select by using the Go To Special dialog box. To select special cells manually, go to the Home tab on the Ribbon and select Go To Special. This brings up the Go To Special dialog box shown in Figure 4-4. Here, you can select a set of cells based on a few defining attributes. One of those defining attributes is formulas. Selecting the Formulas option effectively selects all cells that contain formulas.

Figure 4-4: The Go To Special dialog box.

This macro programmatically does the same thing for the entire workbook at the same time. Here, we are using the `SpecialCells` method of the `Cells` collection. The `SpecialCells` method requires type parameter that represents the type of special cell. In this case, we are using `xlCellTypeFormulas`.

In short, we are referring to a special range that consists only of cells that contain formulas. We refer to this special range using the `With...End With` statement. This statement tells Excel that any action you perform applies only to the range to which you've pointed. Here, we are coloring the interior of the cells in the chosen range.

```
Sub Macro39()

'Step 1:  Declare your Variables
    Dim ws As Worksheet

'Step 2: Avoid Error if no formulas are found
    On Error Resume Next

'Step 3:  Start looping through worksheets
    For Each ws In ActiveWorkbook.Worksheets

'Step 4:  Select cells and highlight them
    With ws.Cells.SpecialCells(xlCellTypeFormulas)
    .Interior.ColorIndex = 36
    End With

'Step 5: Get next worksheet
    Next ws

End Sub
```

1. Step 1 declares an object called ws. This creates a memory container for each worksheet the macro loops through.

2. If the spreadsheet contains no formulas, Excel throws an error. To avoid the error, we tell Excel to continue with the macro if an error is triggered.

3. Step 3 begins the looping, telling Excel to evaluate all worksheets in the active workbook.

4. In this Step, the macro selects all cells containing formulas, and then formats them.

5. In Step 5, we loop back to get the next sheet. After all of the sheets are evaluated, the macro ends.

How to use it

The best place to store this macro is in your Personal Macro Workbook. This way, the macro is always available. The Personal Macro Workbook is loaded whenever you start Excel. In the VBE Project window, it's named personal.xlb.

1. Activate the Visual Basic Editor by pressing ALT+F11.

2. Right-click personal.xlb in the Project window.

3. Choose Insert➜Module.

4. Type or paste the code.

If you don't see personal.xlb in your project window, it doesn't exist yet. You'll have to record a macro, using Personal Macro Workbook as the destination.

To record the macro in your Personal Macro Workbook, select the Personal Macro Workbook option in the Record Macro dialog box before you start recording. This option is in the `Store Macro In` drop-down list. Simply record a couple of cell clicks and then stop recording. You can discard the recorded macro and replace it with this one.

Macro 40: Find and Select the First Blank Row or Column

You may often run across scenarios where you have to append rows or columns to an existing data set. When you need to append rows, you will need to be able to find the last used row and then move down to the next empty cell. Likewise, in situations where you need to append columns, you need to be able to find the last used column and then move over the next empty cell. The macros in this section allow you to dynamically find and select the first blank row or column. They are meant to be used in conjunction with other macros. After all, these macros simply find and select the first blank row or column.

How it works

These macros both use the `Cells` item and the `Offset` property as key navigation tools.

The `Cells` item belongs to the `Range` object. It gives us an extremely handy way of selecting ranges through code. It requires only relative row and column positions as parameters. `Cells(5,4)` translates to row 5, column 4 (or Cell D5). `Cells(16, 4)` translates to row 16, column 4 (or cell D16).

In addition to passing hard numbers to the Cells item, you can also pass expressions.

`Cells(Rows.Count, 1)` is the same as selecting the last row in the spreadsheet and the first column in the spreadsheet. In Excel 2010, that essentially translates to cell A1048576.

`Cells(1, Columns.Count)` is the same as selecting the first row in the spreadsheet and the last column in the spreadsheet. In Excel 2010, that translates to cell XFD1.

Combining the `Cells` statement with the `End` property allows you to jump to the last used row or column. This statement is equivalent to going to cell A1048576 and pressing Ctrl+Shift+Up Arrow on the keyboard. When you run this, Excel automatically jumps to the last used row in column A.

```
Cells(Rows.Count, 1).End(xlUp).Select
```

Running this statement is equivalent to going to cell XFD1 and pressing Ctrl+Shift+Left Arrow on the keyboard. This gets you to the last used column in row 1.

```
Cells(1, Columns.Count).End(xlToLeft).Select
```

When you get to the last used row or column, you can use the `Offset` property to move down or over to the next blank row or column.

The `Offset` property uses a row and column index to specify a changing base point.

For example, this statement selects cell A2 because the row index in the offset is moving the row base point by one:

```
Range("A1").Offset(1, 0).Select
```

This statement selects cell C4 because the row and column indexes move the base point by three rows and two columns:

```
Range("A1").Offset(3, 2).Select
```

Pulling all these concepts together, we can create a macro that selects the first blank row or column.

This macro selects the first blank row.

```
Sub Macro40a()

'Step 1:   Declare Your Variables.
    Dim LastRow As Long

'Step 2:   Capture the last used row number.
    LastRow = Cells(Rows.Count, 1).End(xlUp).Row

'Step 3:   Select the next row down
    Cells(LastRow, 1).Offset(1, 0).Select

End Sub
```

1. Step 1 first declares a `Long Integer` variable called `LastRow` to hold the row number of the last used row.

2. In Step 2, we capture the last used row by starting at the very last row in the worksheet and using the `End` property to jump up to the first non-empty cell (the equivalent of going to cell A1048576 and pressing Ctrl+Shift+Up Arrow on the keyboard).

3. In this step, we use the `Offset` property to move down one row and select the first blank cell in column A.

This macro selects the first blank column:

```
Sub Macro40b()

'Step 1:  Declare Your Variables.
    Dim LastColumn As Long

'Step 2:  Capture the last used column number.
    LastColumn = Cells(5, Columns.Count).End(xlToLeft).Column

'Step 3:  Select the next column over
    Cells(5, LastColumn).Offset(0, 1).Select

End Sub
```

1. We first declare a `Long Integer` variable called `LastColumn` to hold the column number of the last used column.

2. In Step 2, we capture the last used column by starting at the very last column in the worksheet and using the `End` property to jump up to the first non-empty column (the equivalent of going to cell XFD5 and pressing Ctrl+Shift+Left Arrow on the keyboard).

3. In this step, we use the `Offset` property to move over one column and select the first blank column in row 5.

How to use it

You can implement these macros by pasting them into a standard module:

1. Activate the Visual Basic Editor by pressing ALT+F11.

2. Right-click the project/workbook name in the Project window.

3. Choose Insert➔Module.

4. Type or paste the code.

Macro 41: Apply Alternate Color Banding

Color banding is an effect where each row of a data set is colored in alternating shades (see Figure 4-5). You would typically apply alternating row colors to reports you distribute to people who need to review each row of data. Color banding makes the data a little easier to read. This macro allows you to automatically apply alternating colors to each row in the selected range.

5		January	February	March	April	May	Ju
6	Product 1	72,542	70,916	49,289	3,538	87,442	
7	Product 10	64,906	54,698	93,271	29,388	29,712	
8	Product 11	68,672	29,475	58,379	16,282	2,953	
9	Product 12	38,676	1,457	3,833	98,225	99,695	
10	Product 2	28,187	18,175	71,645	99,211	10,516	
11	Product 3	75,043	8,280	24,234	40,255	77,472	
12	Product 4	4,984	31,805	47,905	45,292	89,648	
13	Product 5	42,680	47,574	35,982	18,860	56,353	
14	Product 6	16,140	3,676	76,712	27,619	68,199	
15	Product 7	97,001	56,895	40,052	79,893	78,703	
16	Product 8	21,227	28,168	97,923	16,585	1,843	
17	Product 9	56,692	17,489	82,649	28,960	68,233	

Figure 4-5: Color banding helps make your data sets easier to read.

How it works

In this macro, we are essentially using two `Range` object variables. One of the variables captures the scope of data we are working with, whereas the other is used to hold each individual cell as we go through the range. Then we use the `For Each` statement to activate or bring each cell in the target range into focus. When each row is in focus, we use the `Offset` property to evaluate the color index of the previous row. If the color index is white, we apply the alternate green color index.

```
Sub Macro41()

'Step1:  Declare your variables.
    Dim MyRange As Range
    Dim MyRow As Range

'Step 2:  Define the target Range.
    Set MyRange = Selection

'Step 3:  Start looping through the range.
    For Each MyRow In MyRange.Rows

'Step 4:  Check if the row is an even number.
    If MyRow.Row Mod 2 = 0 Then

'Step 5:  Apply appropriate alternate color.
    MyRow.Interior.ColorIndex = 35
    Else
```

```
    MyRow.Interior.ColorIndex = 2
    End If

'Step 6:  Loop back to get next row.
    Next MyRow

End Sub
```

1. We first declare two `Range` object variables. One, called `MyRange`, holds the entire target range. The other, called `MyCell`, holds each cell in the range as the macro enumerates through them one by one.

2. Step 2 fills the `MyRange` variable with the target range. In this example, we are using the selected range — the range that was selected on the spreadsheet. You can easily set the `MyRange` variable to a specific range such as `Range("A1:Z100")`. Also, if your target range is a named range, you could simply enter its name: `Range("MyNamedRange")`.

3. In this step, the macro starts through each cell in the target range, activating each cell as it goes through.

4. When a cell is activated, we determine if the current row is an even row number.

5. If the row number is indeed even, the macro uses the alternate green color index 35. If not, it uses the color index 2.

6. In Step 6, the macro loops back to get the next cell. After all of the cells in the target range are activated, the macro ends.

How to use it

The best place to store this macro is in your Personal Macro Workbook. This way, the macro is always available to you. The Personal Macro Workbook is loaded whenever you start Excel. In the VBE Project window, it will be named personal.xlb.

1. Activate the Visual Basic Editor by pressing ALT+F11.

2. Right-click personal.xlb in the Project window.

3. Choose Insert➜Module.

4. Type or paste the code.

If you don't see personal.xlb in your project window, it doesn't exist yet. You'll have to record a macro, using Personal Macro Workbook as the destination.

To record the macro in your Personal Macro Workbook, select the Personal Macro Workbook option in the Record Macro dialog box before you start recording. This option is in the `Store Macro In` drop-down list. Simply record a couple of cell clicks and then stop recording. You can discard the recorded macro and replace it with this one.

Macro 42: Sort a Range on Double-Click

When you distribute your Excel reports to your customers, it's often nice to add a few bells and whistles. One of the easier enhancements to apply is the ability to sort when a column header is double-clicked. Although this may sound complicated, it's relatively easy with this macro.

How it works

In this macro, we first find the last non-empty row (using the concepts outlined in this chapter under "Macro 40: Find and Select the First Blank Row or Column"). We then use that row number to define the target range of rows we need to sort. Using the Sort method, we sort the target rows by the column we doubled-clicked.

 Note **Double-clicking will put Excel in Edit mode, which you can cancel by pressing Esc.**

```
Private Sub Worksheet_BeforeDoubleClick(ByVal Target As Range, Cancel As
    Boolean)

'Step 1: Declare your Variables
    Dim LastRow As Long

'Step 2:  Find last non-empty row
    LastRow = Cells(Rows.Count, 1).End(xlUp).Row

'Step 3:  Sort ascending on double-clicked column
    Rows("6:" & LastRow).Sort _
    Key1:=Cells(6, ActiveCell.Column), _
    Order1:=xlAscending

End Sub
```

1. We first declare a Long Integer variable called LastRow to hold the row number of the last non-empty row.

2. In Step 2, we capture the last non-empty row by starting at the very last row in the worksheet and using the End property to jump up to the first non-empty cell (equivalent of going to cell A1048576 and pressing Ctrl+Shift+Up Arrow on the keyboard).

Note that you need to change the column number in this cell to one that is appropriate for your data set. That is to say, if your table starts on Column J, you would need to change the statement in Step 2 to `Cells(Rows.Count, 10).End(xlUp).Row` because column J is the tenth column in the worksheet.

3. In this step, we define the total row range for our data. Keep in mind that the range of rows has to start with the first row of data (excluding headers) and end with the last non-empty row. In this case, our data set starts on row 6. So we use the Sort method on `Rows("6:" & LastRow)`. The `Key` argument here tells Excel which range to sort on.

    Again, you will want to ensure the range you use here starts with the first row of data (excluding the headers).

How to use it

To implement this macro, you need to copy and paste it into the `Worksheet_BeforeDouble Click` event code window. Placing the macro there allows it to run each time you double-click on the sheet.

1. Activate the Visual Basic Editor by pressing ALT+F11.

2. In the Project window, find your project/workbook name and click the plus sign next to it in order to see all the sheets.

3. Click on the sheet from which you want to trigger the code.

4. Select the `BeforeDoubleClick` event from the Event drop-down list (see Figure 4-6).

5. Type or paste the code.

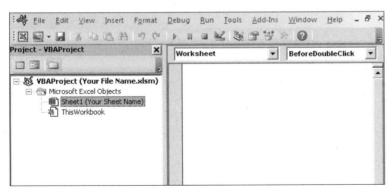

Figure 4-6: Type or paste your code in the Worksheet `BeforeDoubleClick` event code window.

Macro 43: Limit Range Movement to a Particular Area

Excel gives you the ability to limit the range of cells that a user can scroll through. The macro we demonstrate here is something you can easily implement today.

How it works

Excel's `ScrollArea` property allows you to set the scroll area for a particular worksheet. For instance, this statement sets the scroll area on Sheet1 so the user cannot activate any cells outside of A1:M17.

```
Sheets("Sheet1").ScrollArea = "A1:M17"
```

Because this setting is not saved with a workbook, you'll have to reset it each time the workbook is opened. You can accomplish this by implementing this statement in the Workbook_Open event:

```
Private Sub Worksheet_Open()
Sheets("Sheet1").ScrollArea = "A1:M17"End Sub
```

If for some reason you need to clear the scroll area limits, you can remove the restriction with this statement:

```
ActiveSheet.ScrollArea = ""
```

How to use it

To implement this macro, you need to copy and paste it into the `Workbook_Open` event code window. Placing the macro here allows it to run each time the workbook opens.

1. Activate the Visual Basic Editor by pressing ALT+F11.

2. In the Project window, find your project/workbook name and click the plus sign next to it in order to see all the sheets.

3. Click ThisWorkbook.

4. Select the `Open` event in the Event drop-down list (see Figure 4-7).

5. Type or paste the code.

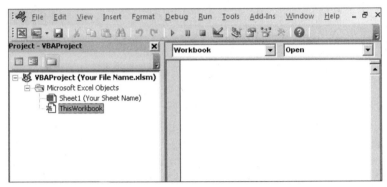

Figure 4-7: Type or paste your code in the Workbook Open event code window.

Macro 44: Dynamically Set the Print Area of a Worksheet

In certain situations, you may find yourself constantly adding data to your spreadsheets. When you do, you may have to constantly resize the print area of the worksheet to encapsulate any new data that you've added. Why keep doing this manually when you can implement a macro to dynamically adjust the print area to capture any new data you've added?

How it works

In this simple macro, we use the `PrintArea` property to define the range of cells that will be included when printing. As you can see, we are simply feeding the `PrintArea` property with the address of the `UsedRange` property. The `UsedRange` property gives us a range that encompasses the cells that have been used to enter data.

To keep this dynamic, we implement the code in the worksheet's `Change` event:

```
Private Sub Worksheet_Change(ByVal Target As Range)
ActiveSheet.PageSetup.PrintArea = ActiveSheet.UsedRange.Address
End Sub
```

How to use it

To implement this macro, you need to copy and paste it into the `Worksheet_Change` event code window. Placing the macro here allows it to run each time you double-click on the sheet.

1. Activate the Visual Basic Editor by pressing ALT+F11.

2. In the Project window, find your project/workbook name and click the plus sign next to it in order to see all the sheets.

3. Click on the sheet in which you want to trigger the code.

4. Select the `Change` event from the Event drop-down list (see Figure 4-8).

5. Type or paste the code.

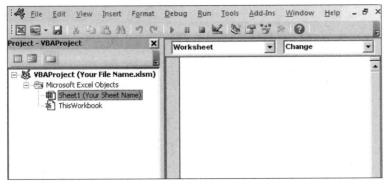

Figure 4-8: Type or paste your code in the Worksheet_Change event code window.

PART V

Working with Data

This Part is all about managing data: cleaning it up, formatting it, and more.

In This Part

When working with information in Excel, you often have to transform the data in some way. Transforming it generally means cleaning, standardizing, or shaping data in ways that are appropriate for your work. This can mean anything from cleaning out extra spaces, to padding numbers with zeros, to filtering data for certain criteria.

The macros in this Part shows you some of the more useful macros you can use to dynamically transform the data in your workbooks. If you like, you can combine these macros into one, running each piece of code in a sequence that essentially automates the scrubbing and shaping of your data.

Tip

The code for this Part can be found on this book's companion website. See this book's Introduction for more on the companion website.

Macro 45: Copy and Paste a Range

One of the basic data manipulation skills you'll need to learn is copying and pasting a range of data. It's fairly easy to do this manually. Luckily, it's just as easy to copy and paste via VBA.

How it works

In this macro, we use the `Copy` method of the `Range` object to copy data from D6:D17 and paste to L6:L17. Note the use of the `Destination` argument. This argument tells Excel where to paste the data.

```
Sub Macro45a()

Sheets("Sheet1").Range("D6:D17").Copy _
Destination:=Sheets("Sheet1").Range("L6:L17")

End Sub
```

When working with your spreadsheet, you likely often have to copy formulas and paste them as values. To do this in a macro, you can use the `PasteSpecial` method. In this example, we copy the formulas F6:F17 to M6:M17. Notice that we are not only pasting as values using `xlPasteValues`, but we are also using `xlPasteFormats` to apply the formatting from the copied range.

```
Sub Macro45b()

Sheets("Sheet1").Range("F6:F17").Copy
Sheets("Sheet1").Range("M6:M17").PasteSpecial xlPasteValues
Sheets("Sheet1").Range("M6:M17").PasteSpecial xlPasteFormats

End Sub
```

Note

Keep in mind that the ranges specified here are for demonstration purposes. Alter the ranges to suit the data in your worksheet.

How to use it

To implement this macro, you can copy and paste it into a standard module:

1. Activate the Visual Basic Editor by pressing ALT+F11 on your keyboard.

2. Right-click the project/workbook name in the Project window.

3. Choose Insert→Module.

4. Type or paste the code.

Macro 46: Convert All Formulas in a Range to Values

In some situations, you may want to apply formulas in a certain workbook, but you don't necessarily want to keep or distribute the formulas with your workbook. In these situations, you may want to convert all the formulas in a given range to values.

How it works

In this macro, we essentially use two `Range` object variables. One of the variables captures the scope of data we are working with, whereas the other is used to hold each individual cell as we go through the range. Then we use the `For Each` statement to activate or bring each cell in the target range into focus. Every time a cell is activated, we check to see whether the cell contains a formula. If it does, we replace the formula with the value that is shown in the cell.

```
Sub Macro46()

'Step 1: Declare your variables
    Dim MyRange As Range
    Dim MyCell As Range


'Step 2:  Save the Workbook before changing cells?
    Select Case MsgBox("Can't Undo this action.  " & _
                        "Save Workbook First?", vbYesNoCancel)
        Case Is = vbYes
        ThisWorkbook.Save

        Case Is = vbCancel
        Exit Sub
    End Select


'Step 3:  Define the target Range.
    Set MyRange = Selection


'Step 4:  Start looping through the range.
    For Each MyCell In MyRange


'Step 5:  If cell has formula, set to the value shown.
    If MyCell.HasFormula Then
    MyCell.Formula = MyCell.Value
    End If
```

```
'Step 6: Get the next cell in the range
    Next MyCell
End Sub
```

1. Step 1 declares two `Range` object variables, one called `MyRange` to hold the entire target range, and the other called `MyCell` to hold each cell in the range as we enumerate through them one by one.

2. When you run a macro, it destroys the undo stack. This means you can't undo the changes a macro makes. Because we are actually changing data, we need to give ourselves the option of saving the workbook before running the macro. This is what Step 2 does.

   Here, we call up a message box that asks if we want to save the workbook first. It then gives us three choices: Yes, No, and Cancel. Clicking Yes saves the workbook and continues with the macro. Clicking Cancel exits the procedure without running the macro. Clicking No runs the macro without saving the workbook.

3. Step 3 fills the `MyRange` variable with the target range. In this example, we use the selected range — the range that was selected on the spreadsheet. You can easily set the `MyRange` variable to a specific range such as `Range("A1:Z100")`. Also, if your target range is a named range, you can simply enter its name: `Range("MyNamedRange")`.

4. This step starts looping through each cell in the target range, activating each cell as it goes through.

5. After a cell is activated, the macro uses the `HasFormula` property to check whether the cell contains a formula. If it does, we set the cell to equal the value that is shown in the cell. This effectively replaces the formula with a hard-coded value.

6. Step 6 loops back to get the next cell. After all cells in the target range are activated, the macro ends.

How to use it

To implement this macro, you can copy and paste it into a standard module:

1. Activate the Visual Basic Editor by pressing ALT+F11 on your keyboard.

2. Right-click the project/workbook name in the Project window.

3. Choose Insert→Module.

4. Type or paste the code.

Macro 47: Perform the Text to Columns Command on All Columns

When you import data from other sources, you may sometimes wind up with cells where the number values are formatted as text. You typically recognize this problem because no matter what you do, you can't format the numbers in these cells to numeric, currency, or percentage formats. You may also see a smart tag on the cells (see Figure 5-1) that tells you the cell is formatted as text.

	A	B	C
1		Revenue	
2	◇ ▾	3224.1791553785	
3		2758.83834214959	
4		The number in this cell is formatted as text	
5		2316.69407974405	
6		2677.07735743106	
7		3015.29997101164	
8		8892.72320795156	
9		3185.53161972604	
10		3770.3130347558	
11		7357.41604042586	
12		4514.43505181198	
13		6355.67839756981	

Figure 5-1: Imported numbers are sometimes formatted as text.

It's easy enough to fix this manually by clicking on the Text to Columns command on the Data tab (Figure 5-2). This opens the Text to Columns dialog box shown in Figure 5-3. There is no need to go through all the steps in this Wizard; simply click the Finish button to apply the fix.

Figure 5-2: Click on the Text to Columns command.

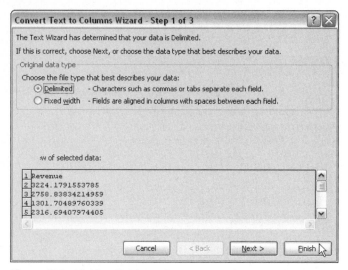

Figure 5-3: Clicking finish on the Text to Columns dialog box corrects incorrectly formatted numbers.

Again, this is a fairly simple action. The problem, however, is that Excel doesn't let you perform the Text to Columns fix on multiple columns. You have to apply this fix one column at a time. This can be a real nuisance if you've got this issue in many columns.

Here is where a simple macro can help you save your sanity.

How it works

In this macro, we use two `Range` object variables to go through our target range, leveraging the `For Each` statement to activate each cell in the target range. Every time a cell is activated, we simply reset the value of the cell. This in effect does the same thing as the Text to Columns command.

```
Sub Macro47()

'Step 1: Declare your variables
  Dim MyRange As Range
    Dim MyCell As Range


'Step 2:  Save the Workbook before changing cells?
    Select Case MsgBox("Can't Undo this action.  " & _
                    "Save Workbook First?", vbYesNoCancel)
        Case Is = vbYes
```

```
        ThisWorkbook.Save

        Case Is = vbCancel
        Exit Sub
    End Select


'Step 3:  Define the target Range.
    Set MyRange = Selection


'Step 4:  Start looping through the range.
    For Each MyCell In MyRange


'Step 5:  Reset the cell value.
    If Not IsEmpty(MyCell) Then
    MyCell.Value = MyCell.Value
    End If


'Step 6: Get the next cell in the range
    Next MyCell

End Sub
```

1. Step 1 declares two `Range` object variables, one called `MyRange` to hold the entire target range, and the other called `MyCell` to hold each cell in the range as the macro enumerates through them one by one.

2. When you run a macro, it destroys the undo stack. This means you can't undo the changes a macro makes. Because the macro is actually changing data, we need to give ourselves the option of saving the workbook before running the macro. This is what Step 2 does. Here, we call up a message box that asks if we want to save the workbook first. It gives us three choices: Yes, No, and Cancel. Clicking Yes saves the workbook and continues with the macro. Clicking Cancel exits the procedure without running the macro. Clicking No runs the macro without saving the workbook.

3. Step 3 fills the `MyRange` variable with the target range. In this example, we are using the selected range — the range that was selected on the spreadsheet. You can easily set the `MyRange` variable to a specific range such as `Range("A1:Z100")`. Also, if your target range is a named range, you can simply enter its name: `Range("MyNamedRange")`.

4. Step 4 starts looping through each cell in the target range, activating each cell as we go through.

5. After a cell is activated, the macro uses the `IsEmpty` function to make sure the cell is not empty. We do this to save a little on performance by skipping the cell if there is nothing in it. We then simply reset the cell to its own value. This removes any formatting mismatch.

6. Step 6 loops back to get the next cell. After all cells in the target range are activated, the macro ends.

How to use it

To implement this macro, you can copy and paste it into a standard module:

1. Activate the Visual Basic Editor by pressing ALT+F11 on your keyboard.

2. Right-click the project/workbook name in the Project window.

3. Choose Insert➔Module.

4. Type or paste the code.

Macro 48: Convert Trailing Minus Signs

Legacy and mainframe systems are notorious for outputting trailing minus signs. In other words, instead of a number like -142, some systems output 142-. This obviously wreaks havoc on your spreadsheet — especially if you need to perform mathematic operations on the data. This nifty macro goes through a target range and fixes all the negative minus signs so that they show up in front of the number instead of at the end.

How it works

In this macro, we use two `Range` object variables to go through our target range, leveraging the `For Each` statement to activate each cell in the target range. Every time a cell is activated, we convert the value of the cell into a `Double` numeric data type by using the `Cdbl` function. The `Double` data type forces any negative signs to show at the front of the number.

```
Sub Macro48()

'Step 1:  Declare your variables
    Dim MyRange As Range
    Dim MyCell As Range


'Step 2:  Save the Workbook before changing cells?
    Select Case MsgBox("Can't Undo this action.  " & _
                       "Save Workbook First?", vbYesNoCancel)

        Case Is = vbYes
        ThisWorkbook.Save

        Case Is = vbCancel
        Exit Sub
    End Select


'Step 3:  Define the target Range.
    Set MyRange = Selection


'Step 4:  Start looping through the range.
    For Each MyCell In MyRange


'Step 5:  Convert the value to a Double.
    If IsNumeric(MyCell) Then
        MyCell = CDbl(MyCell)
    End If
```

```
'Step 6: Get the next cell in the range
    Next MyCell

End Sub
```

1. Step 1 declares two `Range` object variables, one called `MyRange` to hold the entire target range, and the other called `MyCell` to hold each cell in the range as we enumerate through them one by one.

2. When you run a macro, it destroys the undo stack. This means you can't undo the changes a macro makes. Because we are actually changing data, we need to give ourselves the option of saving the workbook before running the macro. This is what Step 2 does. Here, we call up a message box that asks if we want to save the workbook first. It then gives us three choices: Yes, No, and Cancel. Clicking Yes saves the workbook and continues with the macro. Clicking Cancel exits the procedure without running the macro. Clicking No runs the macro without saving the workbook.

3. Step 3 fills the `MyRange` variable with the target range. In this example, we are using the selected range — the range that was selected on the spreadsheet. You can easily set the `MyRange` variable to a specific range such as `Range("A1:Z100")`. Also, if your target range is a named range, you can simply enter its name — `Range("MyNamedRange")`.

4. Step 4 starts looping through each cell in the target range, activating each cell as it goes through.

5. After a cell is activated, Step 5 uses the `IsNumeric` function to check to see if the value can be evaluated as a number. This is to ensure we don't affect textual fields. We then pass the cell's value through the `Cdbl` function. This effectively converts the value to the `Double` numeric data type, forcing the minus sign to the front.

6. Step 6 loops back to get the next cell. After all cells in the target range are activated, the macro ends.

Note   **Because we define the target range as the current selection, you want to be sure to select the area where your data exists before running this code. In other words, you wouldn't want to select the entire worksheet. Otherwise, every empty cell in the spreadsheet would be filled with a zero. Of course, you can ensure this is never a problem by explicitly defining the target range, such as** `Set MyRange = Range("A1:Z100")`**.**

How to use it

To implement this macro, you can copy and paste it into a standard module:

1. Activate the Visual Basic Editor by pressing ALT+F11.

2. Right-click the project/workbook name in the Project window.

3. Choose Insert➜Module.

4. Type or paste the code.

Macro 49: Trim Spaces from All Cells in a Range

A frequent problem when you import dates from other sources is leading or trailing spaces. That is, the values that are imported have spaces at the beginning or end of the cell. This obviously makes it difficult to do things like VLOOKUP or sorting. Here is a macro that makes it easy to search for and remove extra spaces in your cells.

How it works

In this macro, we enumerate through a target range, passing each cell in that range through the Trim function.

```
Sub Macro49()

'Step 1:Declare your variables
    Dim MyRange As Range
    Dim MyCell As Range


'Step 2:  Save the Workbook before changing cells?
    Select Case MsgBox("Can't Undo this action.  " & _
                       "Save Workbook First?", vbYesNoCancel)
        Case Is = vbYes
        ThisWorkbook.Save

        Case Is = vbCancel
        Exit Sub
    End Select


'Step 3:  Define the target Range.
    Set MyRange = Selection


'Step 4:  Start looping through the range.
    For Each MyCell In MyRange


'Step 5:  Trim the Spaces.
    If Not IsEmpty(MyCell) Then
    MyCell = Trim(MyCell)
    End If


'Step 6: Get the next cell in the range
    Next MyCell

End Sub
```

1. Step 1 declares two `Range` object variables, one called `MyRange` to hold the entire target range, and the other called `MyCell` to hold each cell in the range as the macro enumerates through them one by one.

2. When you run a macro, it destroys the undo stack. You can't undo the changes a macro makes. Because we are actually changing data, we need to give ourselves the option of saving the workbook before running the macro. Step 2 does this. Here, we call up a message box that asks if we want to save the workbook first. It then gives us three choices: Yes, No, and Cancel. Clicking Yes saves the workbook and continues with the macro. Clicking Cancel exits the procedure without running the macro. Clicking No runs the macro without saving the workbook.

3. Step 3 fills the `MyRange` variable with the target range. In this example, we are using the selected range — the range that was selected on the spreadsheet. You can easily set the `MyRange` variable to a specific range such as `Range("A1:Z100")`. Also, if your target range is a named range, you can simply enter its name — `Range("MyNamedRange")`.

4. Step 4 starts looping through each cell in the target range, activating each cell as we go through.

5. After a cell is activated, the macro uses the `IsEmpty` function to make sure the cell is not empty. We do this to save a little on performance by skipping the cell if there is nothing in it. We then pass the value of that cell to the `Trim` function. The `Trim` function is a native Excel function that removes leading and trailing spaces.

6. Step 6 loops back to get the next cell. After all cells in the target range are activated, the macro ends.

How to use it

To implement this macro, you can copy and paste it into a standard module:

1. Activate the Visual Basic Editor by pressing ALT+F11.

2. Right-click the project/workbook name in the Project window.

3. Choose Insert➡Module.

4. Type or paste the code.

Macro 50: Truncate ZIP Codes to the Left Five

U.S. ZIP codes come in either 5 or 10 digits. Some systems output a 10-digit ZIP code, which, for the purposes of a lot of Excel analysis, is too many. A common data standardization task is to truncate ZIP codes to the left five digits. Many of us use formulas to do this, but if you are constantly cleaning up your ZIP codes, the macro outlined in this section can help automate that task.

It's important to note that although this macro solves a specific problem, the concept of truncating data remains useful for many other types of data cleanup activities.

How it works

This macro uses the `Left` function to extract the left five characters of each ZIP code in the given range.

```
Sub Macro50()

'Step 1:  Declare your variables
    Dim MyRange As Range
    Dim MyCell As Range


'Step 2:  Save the Workbook before changing cells?
    Select Case MsgBox("Can't Undo this action.  " & _
                       "Save Workbook First?", vbYesNoCancel)
        Case Is = vbYes
        ThisWorkbook.Save

        Case Is = vbCancel
        Exit Sub
    End Select


'Step 3:  Define the target Range.
    Set MyRange = Selection


'Step 4:  Start looping through the range.
    For Each MyCell In MyRange


'Step 5:  Extract out the left 5 characters.
    If Not IsEmpty(MyCell) Then
    MyCell = Left(MyCell, 5)
    End If


'Step 6: Get the next cell in the range
```

```
    Next MyCell

End Sub
```

1. Step 1 declares two `Range` object variables, one called `MyRange` to hold the entire target range, and the other called `MyCell` to hold each cell in the range as the macro enumerates through them one by one.

2. When you run a macro, it destroys the undo stack. This means you can't undo the changes a macro makes. Because we are actually changing data, we need to give ourselves the option of saving the workbook before running the macro. This is what Step 2 does. Here, we call up a message box that asks if we want to save the workbook first. It gives us three choices: Yes, No, and Cancel. Clicking Yes saves the workbook and continues with the macro. Clicking Cancel exits the procedure without running the macro. Clicking No runs the macro without saving the workbook.

3. Step 3 fills the `MyRange` variable with the target range. In this example, we are using the selected range — the range that was selected on the spreadsheet. You can easily set the `MyRange` variable to a specific range such as `Range("A1:Z100")`. Also, if your target range is a named range, you can simply enter its name: `Range("MyNamedRange")`.

4. Step 4 starts looping through each cell in the target range, activating each cell.

5. After a cell is activated, Step 5 uses the `IsEmpty` function to make sure the cell is not empty. We do this to save a little on performance by skipping the cell if there is nothing in it. We then pass the cell's value through `Left` function. The `Left` function allows you to extract out the *n*th left-most characters in a string. In this scenario, we need the left five characters in order to truncate the ZIP code to five digits.

6. Step 6 loops back to get the next cell. After all of the cells in the target range are activated, the macro ends.

Tip   As you may have guessed, you can also use the `Right` function to extract out the *n*th right-most characters in a string. As an example, it's not uncommon to work with product numbers where the first few characters hold a particular attribute or meaning, whereas the last few characters point to the actual product (as in 100-4567). You can extract out the actual product by using `Right(Product_Number, 4)`.

Note   Because we define the target range as the current selection, be sure to select the area where your data exists before running this code. In other words, you wouldn't want to select cells that don't conform to the logic you placed in this macro. Otherwise, every cell you select is truncated, whether you mean it to be or not. Of course, you can ensure this is never a problem by explicitly defining the target range, such as `Set MyRange = Range("A1:Z100")`.

How to use it

To implement this macro, you can copy and paste it into a standard module:

1. Activate the Visual Basic Editor by pressing ALT+F11.

2. Right-click project/workbook name in the Project window.

3. Choose Insert➜Module.

4. Type or paste the code into the newly created module.

Macro 51: Padding Cells with Zeros

Many systems require unique identifiers (such as customer number, order number, or product number) to have a fixed character length. For instance, you frequently see customer numbers that look like this: 00000045478. This concept of taking a unique identifier and forcing it to have a fixed length is typically referred to as *padding*. The number is padded with zeros to achieve the prerequisite character length.

It's a pain to do this manually in Excel. However, with a macro, padding numbers with zeros is a breeze.

Note

Some Excel gurus are quick to point out that you can apply a custom number format to pad numbers with zeros by going to the Format Cells dialog box, selecting Custom on the Number tab, and entering 0000000000 as the custom format.

The problem with this solution is that the padding is cosmetic only. A quick glance at the formula bar reveals that the data actually remains numeric without the padding (it does not become textual). So if you copy and paste the data into another platform or non-Excel table, you lose the cosmetic padding.

How it works

Say that all your customer numbers need to be 10 characters long. So for each customer number, you need to pad the number with enough zeros to get it to 10 characters. This macro does just that.

As you review this macro, keep in mind that you need to change the padding logic in Step 5 to match your situation.

```
Sub Macro51()

'Step 1:  Declare your variables
    Dim MyRange As Range
    Dim MyCell As Range


'Step 2:  Save the Workbook before changing cells?
    Select Case MsgBox("Can't Undo this action.  " & _
                        "Save Workbook First?", vbYesNoCancel)

        Case Is = vbYes
        ThisWorkbook.Save

        Case Is = vbCancel
        Exit Sub
    End Select
```

```
'Step 3:  Define the target Range.
    Set MyRange = Selection


'Step 4:  Start looping through the range.
    For Each MyCell In MyRange


'Step 5: Pad with ten zeros then take the right 10
    If Not IsEmpty(MyCell) Then

        MyCell.NumberFormat = "@"
        MyCell = "0000000000" & MyCell
        MyCell = Right(MyCell, 10)

    End If


'Step 6: Get the next cell in the range
    Next MyCell

End Sub
```

1. Step 1 declares two `Range` object variables, one called `MyRange` to hold the entire target range, and the other called `MyCell` to hold each cell in the range as the macro enumerates through them one by one.

2. When you run a macro, it destroys the undo stack, meaning that you can't undo the changes a macro makes. Because we are actually changing data, we need to give ourselves the option of saving the workbook before running the macro. This is what Step 2 does. Here, we call up a message box that asks if we want to save the workbook first. It then gives us three choices: Yes, No, and Cancel. Clicking Yes saves the workbook and continues with the macro. Clicking Cancel exits the procedure without running the macro. Clicking No runs the macro without saving the workbook.

3. Step 3 fills the `MyRange` variable with the target range. In this example, we use the selected range — the range that was selected on the spreadsheet. You can easily set the `MyRange` variable to a specific range such as `Range("A1:Z100")`. Also, if your target range is a named range, you can simply enter its name: `Range("MyNamedRange")`.

4. Step 4 starts looping through each cell in the target range, activating each cell.

5. After a cell is activated, Step 5 uses the `IsEmpty` function to make sure the cell is not empty. We do this to save a little on performance by skipping the cell if there is nothing in it.

   The macro then ensures that the cell is formatted as text. This is because a cell formatted as a number cannot have leading zeros — Excel would automatically remove them. On the next line, we use the `NumberFormat` property to specify that the format is `@`. This symbol indicates text formatting.

   Next, the macro concatenates the cell value with 10 zeros. We do this simply by explicitly entering 10 zeros in the code, and then using the ampersand (&) to combine them with the cell value.

   Finally, Step 5 uses the `Right` function to extract out the 10 right-most characters. This effectively gives us the cell value, padded with enough zeros to make 10 characters.

6. Step 6 loops back to get the next cell. After all cells in the target range are activated, the macro ends.

How to use it

To implement this macro, you can copy and paste it into a standard module:

1. Activate the Visual Basic Editor by pressing ALT+F11 on your keyboard.

2. Right-click the project/workbook name in the Project window.

3. Choose Insert➡Module.

4. Type or paste the code.

Macro 52: Replace Blanks Cells with a Value

In some analyses, blank cells can cause of all kinds of trouble. They can cause sorting issues, they can prevent proper auto filling, they can cause your pivot tables to apply the Count function instead of the Sum function, and so on.

Blanks aren't always bad, but if they are causing you trouble, this is a macro you can use to quickly replace the blanks in a given range with a value that indicates a blank cell.

How it works

This macro enumerates through the cells in the given range, and then uses the Len function to check the length of the value in the active cell. Blank cells have a character length of 0. If the length is indeed 0, the macro enters a 0 in the cell, effectively replacing the blanks.

```
Sub Macro52()

'Step 1:  Declare your variables
    Dim MyRange As Range
    Dim MyCell As Range


'Step 2:  Save the Workbook before changing cells?
    Select Case MsgBox("Can't Undo this action.  " & _
                        "Save Workbook First?", vbYesNoCancel)

        Case Is = vbYes
        ThisWorkbook.Save

        Case Is = vbCancel
        Exit Sub
    End Select


'Step 3:  Define the target Range.
    Set MyRange = Selection


'Step 4:  Start looping through the range.
    For Each MyCell In MyRange


'Step 5:  Ensure the cell has Text formatting.
    If Len(MyCell.Value) = 0 Then
  MyCell = 0
```

```
   End If


'Step 6: Get the next cell in the range
   Next MyCell

End Sub
```

1. We first declare two `Range` object variables, one called `MyRange` to hold the entire target range, and the other called `MyCell` to hold each cell in the range as the macro enumerates through them one by one.

2. When you run a macro, it destroys the undo stack. This means you can't undo the changes a macro makes. Because we are actually changing data, we need to give ourselves the option of saving the workbook before running the macro. This is what Step 2 does. Here, we call up a message box that asks if we want to save the workbook first. It then gives us three choices: Yes, No, and Cancel. Clicking Yes saves the workbook and continues with the macro. Clicking Cancel exits the procedure without running the macro. Clicking No runs the macro without saving the workbook.

3. Step 3 fills the `MyRange` variable with the target range. In this example, we are using the selected range — the range that was selected on the spreadsheet. You can easily set the `MyRange` variable to a specific range such as `Range("A1:Z100")`. Also, if your target range is a named range, you can simply enter its name: `Range("MyNamedRange")`.

4. Step 4 starts looping through each cell in the target range, activating each cell.

5. After a cell is activated, we use the `IsEmpty` function to make sure the cell is not empty. We do this to save a little on performance by skipping the cell if there is nothing in it. We then use the `Len` function, which is a standard Excel function that returns a number corresponding to the length of the string being evaluated. If the cell is blank, the length will be 0, at which point, the macro replaces the blank with a 0. You could obviously replace the blank with any value you'd like (`N/A`, `TBD`, `No Data`, and so on).

6. Step 6 loops back to get the next cell. After all cells in the target range are activated, the macro ends.

Note

Because we define the target range as the current selection, you want to be sure to select the area where your data exists before running this code. That is to say, you wouldn't want to select the entire worksheet. Otherwise, every empty cell in the spreadsheet would be filled with a zero. Of course, you can ensure this is never a problem by explicitly defining a range, such as `Set MyRange = Range("A1:Z100")`.

How to use it

To implement this macro, you can copy and paste it into a standard module:

1. Activate the Visual Basic Editor by pressing ALT+F11.

2. Right-click the project/workbook name in the Project window.

3. Choose Insert➜Module.

4. Type or paste the code.

Macro 53: Append Text to the Left or Right of Your Cells

Every so often, you may come upon a situation where you need to attach data to the beginning or end of the cells in a range. For instance, you may need to add an area code to a set of phone numbers. This macro demonstrates how you can automate the data standardization tasks that require appending data to values.

How it works

This macro uses two `Range` object variables to go through the target range, leveraging the `For Each` statement to activate each cell in the target range. Every time a cell is activated, the macro attaches an area code to the beginning of the cell value.

```
Sub Macro53()

'Step 1:  Declare your variables
    Dim MyRange As Range
    Dim MyCell As Range


'Step 2:  Save the Workbook before changing cells?
    Select Case MsgBox("Can't Undo this action.  " & _
                       "Save Workbook First?", vbYesNoCancel)

        Case Is = vbYes
        ThisWorkbook.Save

        Case Is = vbCancel
        Exit Sub
    End Select


'Step 3:  Define the target Range.
    Set MyRange = Selection


'Step 4:  Start looping through the range.
    For Each MyCell In MyRange


'Step 5:  Ensure the cell has Text formatting.
    If Not IsEmpty(MyCell) Then
```

```
    MyCell = "(972) " & MyCell
    End If



'Step 6: Get the next cell in the range
    Next MyCell

End Sub
```

1. Step 1 declares two `Range` object variables, one called `MyRange` to hold the entire target range, and the other called `MyCell` to hold each cell in the range as we enumerate through them one by one.

2. When you run a macro, it destroys the undo stack. This means you can't undo the changes a macro makes. Because we are actually changing data, we need to give ourselves the option of saving the workbook before running the macro. This is what Step 2 does. Here, we call up a message box that asks if we want to save the workbook first. It then gives us three choices: Yes, No, and Cancel. Clicking Yes saves the workbook and continues with the macro. Clicking Cancel exits the procedure without running the macro. Clicking No runs the macro without saving the workbook.

3. Step 3 fills the `MyRange` variable with the target range. In this example, we are using the selected range — the range that was selected on the spreadsheet. You can easily set the `MyRange` variable to a specific range such as `Range("A1:Z100")`. Also, if your target range is a named range, you can simply enter its name: `Range("MyNamedRange")`.

4. Step 4 starts looping through each cell in the target range, activating each cell as we go through.

5. After a cell is activated, we use the ampersand (&) to combine an area code with the cell value. If you need to append text to the end of the cell value, you would simply place the ampersand and the text at the end. For instance, `MyCell = MyCell & "Added Text"`.

6. Step 6 loops back to get the next cell. After all cells in the target range are activated, the macro ends.

How to use it

To implement this macro, you can copy and paste it into a standard module:

1. Activate the Visual Basic Editor by pressing ALT+F11.

2. Right-click the project/workbook name in the Project window.

3. Choose Insert➜Module.

4. Type or paste the code.

Macro 54: Create a Super Data Cleanup Macro

As we mentioned at the beginning of this Part, you can combine the macros we have covered thus far into a super data cleanup macro. This allows you to clean and standardize your data in one fell swoop, saving loads of time and headaches.

How it works

In this macro, we combine several of the data transformation macros we have covered into one. Note that we only need to declare the two `Range` object variables one time. With each action, we point these variables to different ranges. Although you have to alter the ranges and the tasks in this macro, it gives you a good idea of how to start an all-purpose data cleanup procedure that suits your needs.

```
Sub Macro54()

'Step 1:  Declare your variables
    Dim MyRange As Range
    Dim MyCell As Range


'Step 2:  Save the Workbook before changing cells?
    Select Case MsgBox("Can't Undo this action.  " & _
                        "Save Workbook First?", vbYesNoCancel)

        Case Is = vbYes
        ThisWorkbook.Save

        Case Is = vbCancel
        Exit Sub
    End Select


'Step 3:  Perform Text to Columns
    Set MyRange = Range("F6:I17")
    For Each MyCell In MyRange
        If Not IsEmpty(MyCell) Then
            MyCell.Value = MyCell.Value
        End If
    Next MyCell


'Step 4:  Pad Customer Numbers with zeros
    Set MyRange = Range("B6:B17")
    For Each MyCell In MyRange
```

```vba
        If Not IsEmpty(MyCell) Then
            MyCell.NumberFormat = "@"
            MyCell = "0000000000" & MyCell
            MyCell = Right(MyCell, 10)
        End If
    Next MyCell


'Step 5:  Truncate Postal Codes to 5 digits
    Set MyRange = Range("C6:C17")
    For Each MyCell In MyRange
        If Not IsEmpty(MyCell) Then
            MyCell = Left(MyCell, 5)
        End If
    Next MyCell


'Step 6:  Add Area code to Phone Numbers
    Set MyRange = Range("D6:D17")
    For Each MyCell In MyRange
        If Not IsEmpty(MyCell) Then
            MyCell = "(972) " & MyCell
        End If
    Next MyCell


'Step 7:  Trim Spaces from Product Numbers
    Set MyRange = Range("E6:E17")
    For Each MyCell In MyRange
        If Not IsEmpty(MyCell) Then
            MyCell = Trim(MyCell)
        End If
    Next MyCell


'Step 8: Replace Blanks with zeros
    Set MyRange = Range("F6:I17")
    For Each MyCell In MyRange
        If Len(MyCell.Value) = 0 Then
            MyCell = 0
        End If
    Next MyCell

End Sub
```

How to use it

To implement this kind of a macro, you can copy and paste it into a standard module:

1. Activate the Visual Basic Editor by pressing ALT+F11 on your keyboard.

2. Right-click the project/workbook name in the Project window.

3. Choose Insert➜Module.

4. Type or paste the code.

Macro 55: Clean Up Non-Printing Characters

Sometimes you have non-printing characters in your data such as line feeds, carriage returns, and non-breaking spaces. These characters often need to be removed before you can use the data for serious analysis.

Now, anyone who has worked with Excel for more than a month knows about the Find and Replace functionality. You may have even recorded a macro while performing a Find and Replace (a recorded macro is an excellent way to automate your find and replace procedures). So your initial reaction may be to simply find and replace these characters. The problem is that these non-printing characters are for the most part invisible and thus difficult to clean up with the normal Find and Replace routines. The easiest way to clean them up is through VBA.

If you find yourself struggling with those pesky invisible characters, use this general purpose macro to find and remove all the non-printing characters.

How it works

This macro is a relatively simple Find and Replace routine. We are using the `Replace` method, telling Excel what to find and what to replace it with. This is similar to the syntax you would see when recording a macro while manually performing a Find and Replace.

The difference is that instead of hard-coding the text to find, this macro uses character codes to specify our search text. Every character has an underlying `ASCII` code, similar to a serial number. For instance, the lowercase letter `a` has an `ASCII` code of 97. The lower case letter `c` has an `ASCII` code of 99. Likewise, invisible characters also have a code:

> The line feed character code is 10.
>
> The carriage return character code is 13.
>
> The non-breaking space character code is 160.

This macro utilizes the `Replace` method, passing each character's ASCII code as the search item. Each character code is then replaced with an empty string:

```
Sub Macro55()

'Step 1: Remove Line Feeds
    ActiveSheet.UsedRange.Replace What:=Chr(10), Replacement:=""

'Step 2: Remove Carriage Returns
    ActiveSheet.UsedRange.Replace What:=Chr(13), Replacement:=""

'Step 3: Remove Non-Breaking Spaces
    ActiveSheet.UsedRange.Replace What:=Chr(160), Replacement:=""

End Sub
```

1. Step 1 looks for and removes the Line Feed character. The code for this character is 10. We can identify the code 10 character by passing `id` through the `Chr` function. After `Chr(10)` is identified as the search item, this step then passes an empty string to the `Replacement` argument.

   Note the use of `ActiveSheet.UsedRange`. This essentially tells Excel to look in all the cells that have had data entered into them. You can replace the `UsedRange` object with an actual range if needed.

2. Step 2 finds and removes the carriage return character.

3. Step 3 finds and removes the non-breaking spaces character.

Note

The characters covered in this macro are only a few of many non-printing characters. However, these are the ones you most commonly run into. If you work with others, you can simply add a new line of code, specifying the appropriate character code. Type ASCII code listing into any search engine to see a list of the codes for various characters.

How to use it

To implement this macro, you can copy and paste it into a standard module:

1. Activate the Visual Basic Editor by pressing ALT+F11 on your keyboard.

2. Right-click the project/workbook name in the Project window.

3. Choose Insert→Module.

4. Type or paste the code.

Macro 56: Highlight Duplicates in a Range of Data

Ever wanted to expose the duplicate values in a range? The macro in this section does just that. There are many manual ways to find and highlight duplicates — ways involving formulas, conditional formatting, sorting, and so on. However, all these manual methods take setup and some level of maintenance as the data changes. This macro simplifies the task, allowing you to find and highlight duplicates in your data with a click of the mouse.

How it works

This macro enumerates through the cells in the target range, leveraging the For Each statement to activate each cell one at a time. We then use the CountIf function to count the number of times the value in the active cell occurs in the range selected. If that number is greater than one, we format the cell yellow.

```
Sub Macro56()

'Step 1:  Declare your variables
    Dim MyRange As Range
    Dim MyCell As Range


'Step 2:  Define the target Range.
    Set MyRange = Selection

'Step 3:  Start looping through the range.
    For Each MyCell In MyRange


'Step 4:  Ensure the cell has Text formatting.
    If WorksheetFunction.CountIf(MyRange, MyCell.Value) > 1 Then
    MyCell.Interior.ColorIndex = 36
    End If


'Step 5: Get the next cell in the range
    Next MyCell

End Sub
```

1. Step 1 declares two `Range` object variables, one called `MyRange` to hold the entire target range, and the other called `MyCell` to hold each cell in the range as the macro enumerates through them one by one.

2. Step 2 fills the `MyRange` variable with the target range. In this example, we are using the selected range — the range that was selected on the spreadsheet. You can easily set the `MyRange` variable to a specific range such as `Range("A1:Z100")`. Also, if your target range is a named range, you can simply enter its name: `Range("MyNamedRange")`.

3. Step 3 starts looping through each cell in the target range, activating each cell.

4. The `WorksheetFunction` object provides a way for us to be able to run many of Excel's spreadsheet functions in VBA. Step 4 uses the `WorksheetFunction` object to run a `CountIf` function in VBA.

   In this case, we are counting the number of times the active cell value (`MyCell.Value`) is found in the given range (`MyRange`). If the `CountIf` expression evaluates to greater than 1, the macro changes the interior color of the cell.

5. Step 5 loops back to get the next cell. After all cells in the target range are activated, the macro ends.

How to use it

To implement this macro, you can copy and paste it into a standard module:

1. Activate the Visual Basic Editor by pressing ALT+F11 on your keyboard.

2. Right-click the project/workbook name in the Project window.

3. Choose Insert➔Module.

4. Type or paste the code.

Macro 57: Hide All Rows but Those Containing Duplicate Data

With the previous macro, you can quickly find and highlight duplicates in your data. This in itself can be quite useful. But if you have many records in your range, you may want to take the extra step of hiding all the non-duplicate rows. Doing so exposes the duplicate values further because they will be the only rows showing.

How it works

This macro enumerates through the cells in the target range, leveraging the For Each statement to activate each cell one at a time. We then use the CountIf function to count the number of times the value in the active cell occurs in the range selected. If that number is one, we hide the row in which the active cell resides. If that number is *greater* than one, we format the cell yellow and leave the row visible.

```vba
Sub Macro57()

'Step 1: Declare your variables
    Dim MyRange As Range
    Dim MyCell As Range


'Step 2:  Define the target Range.
    Set MyRange = Selection


'Step 3:  Start looping through the range.
    For Each MyCell In MyRange


'Step 4:  Ensure the cell has Text formatting.
    If Not IsEmpty(MyCell) Then

        If WorksheetFunction.CountIf(MyRange, MyCell) > 1 Then
            MyCell.Interior.ColorIndex = 36
            MyCell.EntireRow.Hidden = False
        Else
            MyCell.EntireRow.Hidden = True
        End If

    End If

'Step 5: Get the next cell in the range
    Next MyCell

End Sub
```

1. Step 1 declares two `Range` object variables, one called `MyRange` to hold the entire target range, and the other called `MyCell` to hold each cell in the range as we enumerate through them one by one.

2. Step 2 fills the `MyRange` variable with the target range. In this example, we are using the selected range — the range that was selected on the spreadsheet. You can easily set the `MyRange` variable to a specific range such as `Range("A1:Z100")`. Also, if your target range is a named range, you can simply enter its name: `Range("MyNamedRange")`.

3. Step 3 loops through each cell in the target range, activating each cell as we go through.

4. We first use the `IsEmpty` function to make sure the cell is not empty. We do this so the macro won't automatically hide rows with no data in the target range.

   We then use the `WorksheetFunction` object to run a `CountIf` function in VBA. In this particular scenario, we are counting the number of times the active cell value (`MyCell.Value`) is found in the given range (`MyRange`).

   If the `CountIf` expression evaluates to greater than 1, we change the interior color of the cell and set the `EntireRow` property to `Hidden=False`. This ensures the row is visible.

   If the `CountIf` expression *does not* evaluate to greater than 1, the macro jumps to the `Else` argument. Here we set the `EntireRow` property to `Hidden=True`. This ensures the row is not visible.

5. Step 5 loops back to get the next cell. After all cells in the target range are activated, the macro ends.

Note

Because we define the target range as the current selection, you want to be sure to select the area where your data exists before running this code. You wouldn't want to select an entire column or the entire worksheet. Otherwise, any cell that contains data that is unique (not duplicated) triggers the hiding of the row. Alternatively, you can explicitly define the target range to ensure this is never a problem — such as `Set MyRange = Range("A1:Z100")`.

How to use it

To implement this macro, you can copy and paste it into a standard module:

1. Activate the Visual Basic Editor by pressing ALT+F11 on your keyboard.

2. Right-click the project/workbook name in the Project window.

3. Choose Insert➜Module.

4. Type or paste the code.

Macro 58: Selectively Hide AutoFilter Drop-down Arrows

It goes without saying that the AutoFilter function in Excel is one of the most useful. Nothing else allows for faster on-the-spot filtering and analysis. The only problem is that the standard AutoFilter functionality applies drop-down arrows to every column in the chosen dataset (see Figure 5-4). This is all right in most situations, but what if you want to prevent your users from using the AutoFilter drop-down arrows on some of the columns in your data?

The good news is that with a little VBA, you can selectively hide AutoFilter drop-down arrows, as shown in Figure 5-5.

Region ▼	Q1 ▼	Q2 ▼	Q3 ▼	Q4 ▼	Product Number ▼
East	771	930	0	376	M2244
East	392	9	657	39	M3345
East	0	190	557	0	M7765
East	240	499	827	135	P8895
North	908	553	924	421	P8867
North	90	201	0	645	P8844
North	565	0	596	13	C3322
South	982	885	660	437	C5521
South	87	0	478	502	C5567
South	236	800	687	0	C8874
West	0	0	172	96	R7786
West	104	886	421	56	R7609

Figure 5-4: The standard AutoFilter functionality adds drop-down arrows to all of the columns in your data.

Region ▼	Q1	Q2	Q3	Q4	Product Number ▼
East	771	930	0	376	M2244
East	392	9	657	39	M3345
East	0	190	557	0	M7765
East	240	499	827	135	P8895
North	908	553	924	421	P8867
North	90	201	0	645	P8844
North	565	0	596	13	C3322
South	982	885	660	437	C5521
South	87	0	478	502	C5567
South	236	800	687	0	C8874
West	0	0	172	96	R7786
West	104	886	421	56	R7609

Figure 5-5: With a little VBA, you can choose to hide certain AutoFilter drop-down arrows.

How it works

In VBA, we can use the `AutoFilter` object to turn on AutoFilters for a specific range. For instance:

```
Range("B5:G5").AutoFilter
```

After an AutoFilter is applied, we can manipulate each of the columns in the AutoFilter by pointing to it. For example, you can perform some action on the third column in the AutoFilter, like this:

```
Range("B5:G5").AutoFilter Field:3
```

You can perform many actions on an AutoFilter field. In this scenario, we are interested in making the drop-down arrow on field three invisible. For this, we can use the `VisibleDropDown` parameter. Setting this parameter to `False` makes the drop-down arrow invisible.

```
Range("B5:G5").AutoFilter Field:3, VisibleDropDown:=False
```

Here is an example of a macro where we turn on AutoFilters, and then make only the first and last drop-down arrows visible.

```
Sub Macro58()

With Range("B5:G5")
.AutoFilter
.AutoFilter Field:=1, VisibleDropDown:=True
.AutoFilter Field:=2, VisibleDropDown:=False
.AutoFilter Field:=3, VisibleDropDown:=False
.AutoFilter Field:=4, VisibleDropDown:=False
.AutoFilter Field:=5, VisibleDropDown:=False
.AutoFilter Field:=6, VisibleDropDown:=True
End With

End Sub
```

Note

Not only are we pointing to a specific range, but we are also explicitly pointing to each field. When implementing this type of a macro in your environment, alter the code to suit your particular data set.

How to use it

To implement this macro, you can copy and paste it into a standard module:

1. Activate the Visual Basic Editor by pressing ALT+F11 on your keyboard.

2. Right-click the project/workbook name in the Project window.

3. Choose Insert→Module.

4. Type or paste the code.

Macro 59: Copy Filtered Rows to a New Workbook

Often, when you're working with a set of data that is AutoFiltered, you want to extract the filtered rows to a new workbook. Of course, you can manually copy the filtered rows, open a new workbook, paste the rows, and then format the newly pasted data so that all the columns fit. But if you are doing this frequently enough, you may want to have a macro to speed up the process.

How it works

This macro captures the AutoFilter range, opens a new workbook, then pastes the data.

```
Sub Macro59()

'Step 1: Check for AutoFilter - Exit if none exists
    If ActiveSheet.AutoFilterMode = False Then
    Exit Sub
    End If


'Step 2:  Copy the Autofiltered Range to new workbook
    ActiveSheet.AutoFilter.Range.Copy
    Workbooks.Add.Worksheets(1).Paste


'Step 3: Size the columns to fit
    Cells.EntireColumn.AutoFit

End Sub
```

1. Step 1 uses the `AutoFilterMode` property to check whether the sheet even has AutoFilters applied. If not, we exit the procedure.

2. Each `AutoFilter` object has a `Range` property. This `Range` property obligingly returns the rows to which the AutoFilter applies, meaning it returns only the rows that are shown in the filtered data set. In Step 2, we use the `Copy` method to capture those rows, and then we paste the rows to a new workbook. Note that we use `Workbooks.Add.Worksheets(1)`. This tells Excel to paste the data into the first sheet of the newly created workbook.

3. Step 3 simply tells Excel to size the column widths to autofit the data we just pasted.

How to use it

To implement this macro, you can copy and paste it into a standard module:

1. Activate the Visual Basic Editor by pressing ALT+F11 on your keyboard.

2. Right-click the project/workbook name in the Project window.

3. Choose Insert➡Module.

4. Type or paste the code.

Macro 60: Create a New Sheet for Each Item in an AutoFilter

One of the most common tasks an Excel user is confronted with is separating a data set into separate sheets. For instance, if you have a set of data that has rows for the east, west, south, and north regions of the U.S., you may be asked to create a new sheet for the east data, a new sheet for the west data, a new sheet for the south, and one for the north. In these situations, you would normally have to manually filter each region, and then copy and paste the data into new sheets. This can be quite a painful exercise if you have to do it one time. If you have to perform this same exercise on an ongoing basis? Well, let's just say it can be difficult to come to work.

The good news is that you can use a macro to do the heavy lifting for you.

How it works

The basic premise of this macro is in itself simple. We start with a data set that contains an AutoFilter (similar to the one shown in Figure 5-6).

Region ▼	Product Number ▼	Q1 Units ▼	Q2 Units ▼	Q3 Units ▼	Q4 Units ▼
East	M2244	771	930	0	376
East	M3345	392	9	657	39
East	M7765	0	190	557	0
East	P8895	240	499	827	135
North	P8867	908	553	924	421
North	P8844	90	201	0	645
North	C3322	565	0	596	13
South	C5521	982	885	660	437
South	C5567	87	0	478	502
South	C8874	236	800	687	0
West	R7786	0	0	172	96
West	R7609	104	886	421	56

Figure 5-6: Start with a data set that has an AutoFilter applied.

We point the macro to the field that is used to separate the data into separate sheets. In this case, we need to create a separate sheet for each region. As you can see in Figure 5-6, the Region field is the first field in the AutoFiltered data set.

The macro goes through this field, capturing the unique data items in this field (North, South, East, West). Then one at a time, it uses each unique data item as the filter criteria on the AutoFilter, effectively filtering the data for that item.

Each time a region is filtered, the macro copies the filtered range and pastes the data into a new sheet. After the data is pasted, it names the sheet the same name as the filter criteria.

This macro is a little tough to look at first glance, so take the time to walk through each step in detail.

```
Sub Macro60()

'Step 1: Declare your Variables
    Dim MySheet As Worksheet
    Dim MyRange As Range
    Dim UList As Collection
    Dim UListValue As Variant
    Dim i As Long


'Step 2:  Set the Sheet that contains the AutoFilter
    Set MySheet = ActiveSheet


'Step 3: If the sheet is not auto-filtered, then exit
    If MySheet.AutoFilterMode = False Then
        Exit Sub
    End If


'Step 4: Specify the Column # that holds the data you want filtered
    Set MyRange = Range(MySheet.AutoFilter.Range.Columns(1).Address)


'Step 5: Create a new Collection Object
    Set UList = New Collection


'Step 6:  Fill the Collection Object with Unique Values
    On Error Resume Next
    For i = 2 To MyRange.Rows.Count
    UList.Add MyRange.Cells(i, 1), CStr(MyRange.Cells(i, 1))
    Next i
    On Error GoTo 0


'Step 7: Start looping in through the collection Values
    For Each UListValue In UList


'Step 8: Delete any Sheets that may have been previously created
        On Error Resume Next
        Application.DisplayAlerts = False
        Sheets(CStr(UListValue)).Delete
        Application.DisplayAlerts = True
        On Error GoTo 0
```

```
'Step 9:  Filter the AutoFilter to match the current Value
     MyRange.AutoFilter Field:=1, Criteria1:=UListValue


'Step 10: Copy the AutoFiltered Range to new Sheet
     MySheet.AutoFilter.Range.Copy
     Worksheets.Add.Paste
     ActiveSheet.Name = Left(UListValue, 30)
     Cells.EntireColumn.AutoFit


'Step 11: Loop back to get the next collection Value
    Next UListValue


'Step 12: Go back to main Sheet and removed filters
    MySheet.AutoFilter.ShowAllData
    MySheet.Select

End Sub
```

1. Step 1 starts the macro by declaring five variables. `MySheet` is a worksheet variable that is used to identify the sheet in which the AutoFiltered data resides. `MyRange` is a range variable that holds the range of our main filter field (the Region field in this scenario). `UList` is a Collection object that helps us extract the unique items from our main filter field. `UListValue` holds the individual unique items as we enumerate through them. Finally, the `i` variable serves as a simple counter for our `MyRange` variable.

2. Step 2 sets the `MySheet` variable to hold the sheet in which the AutoFilter resides. It's important to do this because we need to refer back to this sheet throughout the macro. Here, we are assuming the macro will be fired from the sheet that holds the AutoFilter, so we use `ActiveSheet`.

   You can also alter the macro to explicitly use a sheet name instead of `ActiveSheet`, like `Set MySheet = Sheets("YourSheetName")`. This is safer because you have no risk of unintentionally firing the macro from the wrong sheet. But it essentially ensures that the macro only works for the sheet you explicitly specified.

3. Step 3 checks the `AutoFilterMode` property to see if the sheet even has AutoFilters applied. If not, it exits the procedure.

4. If the macro reaches Step 4, we have determined that there is indeed an AutoFilter applied in `MySheet`.

Now we need to capture the column number that holds the items that will be used to parse our data set into separate sheets. As you can see, in Figure 5-6, the region column is the first column in our AutoFilter range. So we set the `MyRange` field to `Columns(1)` of the AutoFilter range. This is important! We eventually use the specified column to create a unique list of items with which we parse our data. When you implement this macro in your environment, you need to change the column number used to match the field you need to parse.

5. Step 5 initializes the `UList Collection` object. A `Collection` object is a container that can hold an array of unique data items.

   In fact, a `Collection` object can *only* hold unique data. If you try to fill it with non-unique data, it throws an error. Because of this, it makes for an excellent way to quickly find and store a list of unique data items.

   We use the collection object to hold a unique list of items from our `MyRange` variable. In this scenario, because our `MyRange` variable points to the Region column, the `Collection` object eventually holds a unique list of regions (East, North, South, West).

6. Step 6 fills the `UList` Collection object with the unique data items in MyRange.

   To do so, it uses the `i` variable to loop through the rows of the MyRange column. You'll notice that we start `i` at 2; this is because row 1 contains the header label (Region). We don't want to include the header label as one of the unique items in our collection object.

   On each loop, the macro tries to add the current cell to the `UList` collection. The syntax to add an item to a collection is

   ```
   CollectionName.Add ItemName, UniqueKeyIdentifier
   ```

   In this case, we are adding each cell in `MyRange` as both the item name and unique key identifier. Because the `UList` collection throws an error if the data items are not unique, we wrap the entire section in `On Error Resume Next` and `On Error Goto 0`. This ensures that if duplicate items are added, the `UList` collection ignores them. At the end of the loop, we have a unique list of all the data items in `MyRange`. Again, in this scenario, this means we have a unique list of regions (East, North, South, West).

7. Step 7 works exclusively with the `UList` collection. This collection holds the unique list of items we use as both the filter criteria for our AutoFilter and the Sheet names for our newly created sheets. The macro starts looping through the list with the `UListValue` variable.

8. Each time we run this macro, a new sheet is added for each unique item in our target filter field, with sheet names to match. If we run this macro more than one time, an error may be thrown because we will be creating a sheet that already exists. To ensure this doesn't happen, Step 8 deletes any sheet whose name matches the `UListValue` data item.

9. Step 9 uses the `UListValue` to filter the AutoFilter. We are dynamically passing the UListValue as the `Criteria` for `Field1`:

```
MyRange.AutoFilter Field:=1, Criteria1:=UListValue
```

The field number here is very important! Because the Region field is the first field (see Figure 5-6), we are specifying Field 1. When you implement this macro in your environment, you need to change the field number to match the field you need to parse.

10. Each `AutoFilter` object has a `Range` property. This `Range` property returns the rows to which the AutoFilter applies, meaning it returns only the rows that are shown in the filtered data set. Step 10 uses the `Copy` method to capture the newly filtered rows and paste the rows to a new sheet. The macro then names the sheet to match `UListValue`.

Note that we are wrapping `UListValue` in the `Left` function. Specifically, we are telling Excel to limit the name of the sheet to the left 31 characters in the `UListValue`. We do this because the limit for sheet names is 31 characters. Anything longer than 31 characters throws an error.

11. Step 11 loops back to get the next value from the `UList` collection.

12. The macro ends by jumping to the original AutoFiltered data and clearing all filters.

You may be wondering how to create a new workbook for each item in an AutoFilter.

This is a relatively easy change. Simply replace the code in Step 10 with this code.

```
'Step 10: Copy the AutoFiltered Range to new Workbook
  ActiveSheet.AutoFilter.Range.Copy
    Workbooks.Add.Worksheets(1).Paste

    Cells.EntireColumn.AutoFit

    ActiveWorkbook.SaveAs _
    Filename:="C:\Temp\" & CStr(UListValue) & ".xlsx"

    ActiveWorkbook.Close
```

Tip

Pay special attention to the fact that the path in this code is hard-coded to save in the `C:Temp` **folder. If you like, you can change this to suit your needs.**

How to use it

To implement this macro, you can copy and paste it into a standard module:

1. Activate the Visual Basic Editor by pressing ALT+F11 on your keyboard.

2. Right-click the project/workbook name in the Project window.

3. Choose Insert→Module.

4. Type or paste the code.

Macro 61: Show Filtered Columns in the Status Bar

When you have a large table with many columns that are AutoFiltered, it is sometimes hard to tell which columns are filtered and which aren't. Of course, you could scroll through the columns, peering at each AutoFilter drop-down list for the telltale icon indicating the column is filtered, but that can get old quickly.

This macro helps by specifically listing all the columns that are filtered in the status bar. The status bar is the bar (seen here in Figure 5-7) that runs across the bottom of the Excel window.

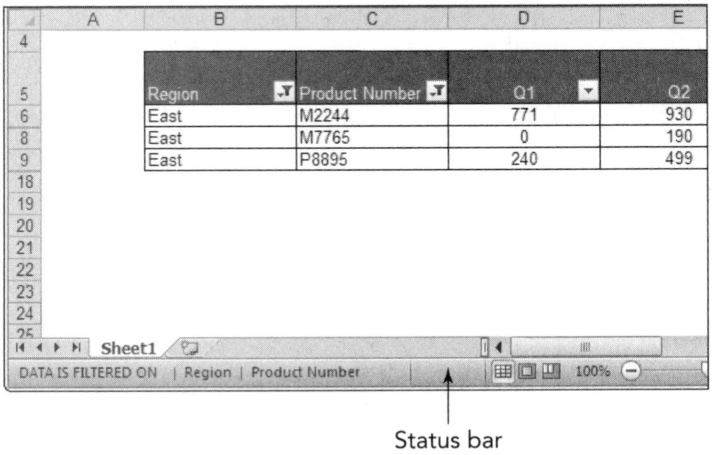

Status bar

Figure 5-7: This macro lists all filtered columns in the status bar.

How it works

This macro loops through the fields in our AutoFiltered data set. As we loop, we check to see if each field is actually filtered. If so, we capture the field name in a text string. After looping through all the fields, we pass the final string to the StatusBar property.

```
Sub Macro61()


'Step 1: Declare your Variables
    Dim AF As AutoFilter
    Dim TargetField As String
    Dim strOutput As String
    Dim i As Integer


'Step 2: Check if AutoFilter exists - If not Exit
    If ActiveSheet.AutoFilterMode = False Then
        Application.StatusBar = False
        Exit Sub
```

```
    End If


'Step 3: Set AutoFilter and start looping
    Set AF = ActiveSheet.AutoFilter
    For i = 1 To AF.Filters.Count


'Step 4: Capture filtered field names
  If AF.Filters(i).On Then
    TargetField = AF.Range.Cells(1, i).Value
  strOutput = strOutput & "  |  " & TargetField
  End If
  Next


'Step 5: Display the filters if there are any
   If strOutput = "" Then
   Application.StatusBar = False
   Else
   Application.StatusBar = "DATA IS FILTERED ON  " & strOutput
   End If

End Sub
```

1. Step 1 declares four variables. `AF` is an AutoFilter variable that is used to manipulate the AutoFilter object. `TargetField` is a string variable we use to hold the field names of any field that is actually filtered. `strOutput` is the string variable we use to build out the final text that goes into the status bar. Finally, the `i` variable serves as a simple counter, allowing us to iterate through the fields in our AutoFilter.

2. Step 2 checks the `AutoFilterMode` property to see if sheet even has AutoFilters applied. If not, we set the `StatusBar` property to `False`. This has the effect of clearing the status bar, releasing control back to Excel. We then exit the procedure.

3. Step 3 sets the `AF` variable to the AutoFilter on the active sheet. We then set our counter to count from 1 to the maximum number of columns in the AutoFiltered range. The AutoFilter object keeps track of its columns with index numbers. Column 1 is index 1; column 2 is index 2, and so on. The idea is that we can loop through each column in the AutoFilter by using the `i` variable as the index number.

4. Step 4 checks the status of `AF.Filters` object for each `(i)` – `i` being the index number of the column we are evaluating. If the AutoFilter for that column is filtered in any way, the status for that column is `On`.

If the filter for the column is indeed on, we capture the name of the field in the `TargetField` variable. We actually get the name of the field by referencing the `Range` of our `AF` AutoFilter object. With this range, we can use the `Cells` item to pinpoint the field name. `Cells(1,1)` captures the value in row one, column one. `Cells(1,2)` captures the value in row one, column two, and so on.

As you can see in Step 4, we have hard-coded the row to 1 and used the `i` variable to indicate the column index. This means that as the macro iterates through the columns, it always captures the value in row one as the `TargetField` name (row one is where the field name is likely to be).

After we have the `TargetField` name, we can pass that information a simple string container (`strOutput` in our case). `strOutput` simply keeps all the target field names we find and concatenates them into a readable text string.

5. Step 5 first checks to make sure that there is something in the `strOutput` string. If `strOutput` is empty, it means the macro found no columns in our AutoFilter that were filtered. In this case, Step 5 simply sets the `StatusBar` property to `False`, releasing control back to Excel.

   If `strOutput` is not empty, Step 5 sets the `StatusBar` property to equal some helper text along with our `strOutput` string.

How to use it

You ideally want this macro to run each time a field is filtered. However, Excel does not have an `OnAutoFilter` event. The closest thing to that is the `Worksheet_Calculate` event. That being said, AutoFilters in themselves don't actually calculate anything, so you need to enter a "volatile" function on the sheet that contains your AutoFiltered data. A volatile function is one that forces a recalculation when any change is made on the worksheet.

In the sample files that come with this book, notice that we use the `=Now()` function. The `Now` function is a volatile function that returns a date and time. With this on the sheet, the worksheet is sure to recalculate each time the AutoFilter is changed.

Place the `Now` function anywhere on your sheet (by typing `=Now()` in any cell). Then copy and paste the macro into the `Worksheet_Calculate` event code window:

1. Activate the Visual Basic Editor by pressing ALT+F11 on your keyboard.

2. In the Project window, find your project/workbook name and click the plus sign next to it in order to see all the sheets.

3. Click on the sheet from which you want to trigger the code.

4. Select the `Calculate` event from the Event drop-down list (see Figure 5-8).

5. Type or paste the code.

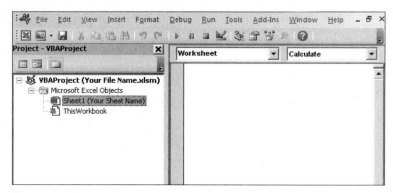

Figure 5-8: Type or paste your code in the Worksheet_Calculate event code window.

In order to make the code run as smoothly as possible, consider adding these two pieces of code under the worksheet calculate event:

```
Private Sub Worksheet_Deactivate()
Application.StatusBar = False
End Sub

Private Sub Worksheet_Activate()
Call Worksheet_Calculate
End Sub
```

Also, add this piece of code in the workbook `BeforeClose` event:

```
Private Sub Workbook_BeforeClose(Cancel As Boolean)
Application.StatusBar = False
End Sub
```

The `Worksheet_Deactivate` event clears the status bar when you move to another sheet or workbook. This avoids confusion as you move between sheets.

The `Worksheet_Activate` event fires the macro in `Worksheet_Calculate`. This brings back the Status Bar indicators when you navigate back to the filtered sheet.

The `Workbook_BeforeClose` event clears the status bar when you close the workbook. This avoids confusion as you move between workbooks.

PART VI

Working with PivotTables

This Part gives you the lowdown on PivotTables: sorting them, formatting them, hiding data, and more.

In This Part

Excel offers a fairly robust object model for PivotTables. You can use the macro recorder to create a macro that does just about anything with a PivotTable, and the macro gets you 90 percent of the way to automation. For instance, you can record a macro that builds a PivotTable, and that macro records your steps and duplicates your tasks with relatively high fidelity. So if you find yourself needing to automate tasks like filtering out the top 10 items or grouping data items, you can reliably turn to the macro recorder to help write the VBA needed.

That being said, certain PivotTable-related tasks are not easily solved with the macro recorder. This is what this Part focuses on. Here, we cover the most common scenarios where macros help you gain efficiencies when working with PivotTables.

Tip

The code for this Part can be found on this book's companion website. See this book's Introduction for more on the companion website.

Macro 62: Create a Backwards-Compatible PivotTable

If you are still using Excel 2003, you may know about the compatibility headaches that come with PivotTables between Excel 2003 and later versions. As you can imagine, the extraordinary increases in PivotTable limitations lead to some serious compatibility questions. For instance, later versions of Excel PivotTables can have more than 16,384 column fields and more than 1,000,000 unique data items. Excel 2003 can have only 256 column fields and 32,500 unique data items.

To solve these compatibility issues, Microsoft has initiated the concept of Compatibility mode. Compatibility mode is a state that Excel automatically enters when opening an xls file. When Excel is in Compatibility mode, it artificially takes on the limitations of Excel 2003. This means while you are working with an xls file, you cannot exceed any of the Excel 2003 PivotTable limitations, allowing you (as a user of Excel 2007 or 2010) to create PivotTables that work with Excel 2003.

If you are not in Compatibility mode (meaning you are working with an xlsx or xlsm file) and you create a PivotTable, the PivotTable object turns into a hard table when opened in Excel 2003. That is to say, PivotTables that are created in xlsx or xlsm files are destroyed when opened in Excel 2003.

To avoid this fiasco manually, Excel 2007 and 2010 users must go through these steps:

1. Create a blank workbook.
2. Save the file as an xls file.
3. Close the file.
4. Open it up again.
5. Start creating the PivotTable.

This is enough to drive you up the wall if you've got to do this every day.

An alternative is to use a macro that automatically starts a PivotTable in Table in the Excel 2003 version — even if you are not in Compatibility mode!

How it works

If you record a macro while creating a PivotTable in Excel 2007 or Excel 2010, the macro recorder generates the code to create your PivotTable. This code has several arguments in it. One of the arguments is the Version property. As the name implies, the Version property specifies the version of Excel the PivotTable was created in. The nifty thing is that you can change the Version in the code to force Excel to create a PivotTable that will work with Excel 2003.

Here is a listing of the different versions you can specify:

- ➤ **xlPivotTableVersion2000** - Excel 2000

- ➤ **xlPivotTableVersion10** - Excel 2002

- ➤ **xlPivotTableVersion11** - Excel 2003

- ➤ **xlPivotTableVersion12** - Excel 2007

- ➤ **xlPivotTableVersion14** - Excel 2010

Here is an example of a macro that starts a PivotTable using Range("A3:N86") on Sheet1 as the source data.

Note that we changed the Version and DefaultVersion properties to xlPivotTable Version11. This ensures that the PivotTable starts off as one that will work in Excel 2003.

No need to save your workbook as an .xls file first or to be in Compatibility mode. You can use a simple macro like this (just change the source data range) to create a PivotTable that will automatically work with Excel 2003.

```
Sub Macro62()

Dim SourceRange As Range
Set SourceRange = Sheets("Sheet1").Range("A3:N86")

ActiveWorkbook.PivotCaches.Create( _
SourceType:=xlDatabase, _
SourceData:=SourceRange, _
Version:=xlPivotTableVersion11).CreatePivotTable _
TableDestination:="", _
TableName:="", _
DefaultVersion:=xlPivotTableVersion11

End Sub
```

Note

Keep in mind that creating a PivotTable in the Excel 2003 version will essentially force the PivotTable to take on the limits of Excel 2003. This means any new PivotTable limit increases or PivotTable features added in Excel 2007 or Excel 2010 will not be available in your 2003 version PivotTable.

How to use it

To implement this macro, you can copy and paste it into a standard module:

1. Activate the Visual Basic Editor by pressing ALT+F11.
2. Right-click the project/workbook name in the Project window.
3. Choose Insert➜Module.
4. Type or paste the code.

Macro 63: Refresh All PivotTables Workbook

It's not uncommon to have multiple PivotTables in the same workbook. Many times, these PivotTables link to data that changes, requiring a refresh of the PivotTables. If you find that you need to refresh your PivotTables en masse, you can use this macro to refresh all PivotTables on demand.

How it works

It's important to know that each `PivotTable` object is a child of the worksheet it sits in. The macro has to first loop through the worksheets in a workbook first, and *then* loop through the PivotTables in each worksheet. This macro does just that — loops through the worksheets, and then loops through the PivotTables. On each loop, the macro refreshes the PivotTable.

```
Sub Macro63()

'Step 1: Declare your Variables
    Dim ws As Worksheet
    Dim pt As PivotTable


'Step 2: Loop through each sheet in workbook
    For Each ws In ThisWorkbook.Worksheets

'Step 3: Loop through each PivotTable
        For Each pt In ws.PivotTables
            pt.RefreshTable
        Next pt
    Next ws

End Sub
```

1. Step 1 first declares an object called `ws`. This creates a memory container for each worksheet we loop through. It also declares an object called `pt`, which holds each PivotTable the macro loops through.

2. Step 2 starts the looping, telling Excel we want to evaluate all worksheets in this workbook. Notice we are using `ThisWorkbook` instead of `ActiveWorkbook`. The `ThisWorkbook` object refers to the workbook that the code is contained in. The `ActiveWorkbook` object refers to the workbook that is currently active. They often return the same object, but if the workbook running the code is not the active workbook, they return different objects. In this case, we don't want to risk refreshing PivotTables in other workbooks, so we use `ThisWorkbook`.

3. Step 3 loops through all the PivotTables in each worksheet, and then triggers the `RefreshTable` method. After all PivotTables have been refreshed, the macro moves to the next sheet. After all sheets have been evaluated, the macro ends.

Note

As an alternative method for refreshing all PivotTables in the workbook, you can use `ThisWorkbook.RefreshAll`**. This refreshes all the PivotTables in the workbook. However, it also refreshes all query tables. So if you have data tables that are connected to an external source or the web, these will be affected by the** `RefreshAll` **method. If this is not a concern, you can simply enter** `ThisWorkbook.RefreshAll` **into a standard module.**

How to use it

To implement this macro, you can copy and paste it into a standard module:

1. Activate the Visual Basic Editor by pressing ALT+F11.

2. Right-click the project/workbook name in the Project window.

3. Choose Insert➜Module.

4. Type or paste the code.

Macro 64: Create a PivotTable Inventory Summary

When your workbook contains multiple PivotTables, it's often helpful to have an inventory summary (similar to the one shown here in Figure 6-1) that outlines basic details about the PivotTables. With this type of summary, you can quickly see important information like the location of each PivotTable, the location of each PivotTable's source data, and the pivot cache index each PivotTable is using.

	A	B	C	D	E	F
1	Pivot Name	Worksheet	Location	Cache Index	Source Data Location	Row Count
2	PivotTable10	Product Categories	$A$3:$I$11	2	Raw Data'!$A$3:$N$59469	59466
3	PivotTable9	Internet Sales	$A$3:$D$11	3	Raw Data'!$A$3:$N$59468	59465
4	PivotTable11	Units Sold	$A$3:$I$11	1	Raw Data'!$A$3:$N$59470	59467
5	PivotTable12	Sales by Year	$A$3:$I$45	2	Raw Data'!$A$3:$N$59469	59466

Figure 6-1: A PivotTable inventory summary.

The following macro outputs such a summary.

How it works

When you create a `PivotTable` object variable, you expose all of a PivotTable's properties — properties like its name, location, cache index, and so on. In this macro, we loop through each PivotTable in the workbook and extract specific properties into a new worksheet.

Because each `PivotTable` object is a child of the worksheet it sits in, we have to first loop through the worksheets in a workbook first, and *then* loop through the PivotTables in each worksheet.

Take a moment to walk through the steps of this macro in detail.

```
Sub Macro64()

'Step 1:  Declare your Variables
    Dim ws As Worksheet
    Dim pt As PivotTable
    Dim MyCell As Range


'Step 2: Add a new sheet with column headers
    Worksheets.Add
    Range("A1:F1") = Array("Pivot Name", "Worksheet", _
                           "Location", "Cache Index", _
                           "Source Data Location", _
                           "Row Count")
```

```
'Step 3:  Start Cursor at Cell A2 setting the anchor here
    Set MyCell = ActiveSheet.Range("A2")


'Step 4: Loop through each sheet in workbook
    For Each ws In Worksheets


'Step 5: Loop through each PivotTable
        For Each pt In ws.PivotTables
        MyCell.Offset(0, 0) = pt.Name
        MyCell.Offset(0, 1) = pt.Parent.Name
        MyRange.Offset(0, 2) = pt.TableRange2.Address
        MyRange.Offset(0, 3) = pt.CacheIndex
        MyRange.Offset(0, 4) = Application.ConvertFormula _
                            (pt.PivotCache.SourceData, xlR1C1, xlA1)
        MyRange.Offset(0, 5) = pt.PivotCache.RecordCount

'Step 6:  Move Cursor down one row and set a new anchor
            Set MyRange = MyRange.Offset(1, 0)


'Step 7:  Work through all PivotTables and worksheets
        Next pt
    Next ws


'Step 8: Size columns to fit
    ActiveSheet.Cells.EntireColumn.AutoFit

End Sub
```

1. Step 1 declares an object called `ws`. This creates a memory container for each worksheet we loop through. We then declare an object called `pt`, which holds each PivotTable we loop through. Finally, we create a range variable called `MyCell`. This variable acts as our cursor as we fill in the inventory summary.

2. Step 2 creates a new worksheet and adds column headings that range from A1 to F1. Note that we can add column headings using a simple array that contains our header labels. This new worksheet remains our active sheet from here on out.

3. Just as you would manually place your cursor in a cell if you were to start typing data, Step 3 places the `MyCell` cursor in cell A2 of the active sheet. This is our anchor point, allowing us to navigate from here.

   Throughout the macro, you see the use of the `Offset` property. The `Offset` property allows us to move a cursor x number of rows and x number of columns from an anchor point. For instance, `Range(A2).Offset(0,1)` would move the cursor one column to the right. If we wanted to move the cursor one row down, we would enter `Range(A2).Offset(1, 0)`.

In the macro, we navigate by using `Offset` on `MyCell`. For example, `MyCell.Offset(0,4)` would move the cursor four columns to the right of the anchor cell. After the cursor is in place, we can enter data.

4. Step 4 starts the looping, telling Excel we want to evaluate all worksheets in this workbook.

5. Step 5 loops through all the PivotTables in each worksheet. For each PivotTable it finds, it extracts out the appropriate property and fills in the table based on the cursor position (see Step 3).

We are using six `PivotTable` properties: `Name`, `Parent.Range`, `TableRange2.Address`, `CacheIndex`, `PivotCache.SourceData`, and `PivotCache.Recordcount`.

The `Name` property returns the name of the PivotTable.

The `Parent.Range` property gives us the sheet where the PivotTable resides. The `TableRange2.Address` property returns the range that the PivotTable object sits in.

The `CacheIndex` property returns the index number of the pivot cache for the PivotTable. A *pivot cache* is a memory container that stores all the data for a PivotTable. When you create a new PivotTable, Excel takes a snapshot of the source data and creates a pivot cache. Each time you refresh a PivotTable, Excel goes back to the source data and takes another snapshot, thereby refreshing the pivot cache. Each pivot cache has a `SourceData` property that identifies the location of the data used to create the pivot cache. The `PivotCache.SourceData` property tells us which range will be called upon when we refresh the PivotTable. You can also pull out the record count of the source data by using the `PivotCache.Recordcount` property.

6. Each time the macro encounters a new PivotTable, it moves the `MyCell` cursor down a row, effectively starting a new row for each PivotTable.

7. Step 7 tells Excel to loop back around to iterate through all PivotTables and all worksheets. After all PivotTables have been evaluated, we move to the next sheet. After all sheets have been evaluated, the macro moves to the last step.

8. Step 8 finishes off with a little formatting, sizing the columns to fit the data.

How to use it

To implement this macro, you can copy and paste it into a standard module:

1. Activate the Visual Basic Editor by pressing ALT+F11.

2. Right-click the project/workbook name in the Project window.

3. Choose Insert➜Module.

4. Type or paste the code.

Macro 65: Make All PivotTables Use the Same Pivot Cache

If you work with PivotTables enough, you will undoubtedly find the need to analyze the same dataset in multiple ways. In most cases, this process requires you to create separate PivotTables from the same data source.

The problem is that each time you create a PivotTable, you are storing a snapshot of the data source in a pivot cache. Every pivot cache that is created increases your memory usage and file size. The side effect of this behavior is that your spreadsheet bloats with redundant data. Making your PivotTables share the same cache prevents this.

Note

Starting with Excel 2007, Microsoft built in an automatic pivot cache sharing algorithm that recognizes when you are creating a PivotTable from the same source as an existing PivotTable. This reduces the instances of creating superfluous pivot caches. However, you can still inadvertently create multiple pivot caches if the number of rows or columns captured from your source range is different for each of your PivotTables.

In addition to the reduction in file size, there are other benefits to sharing a pivot cache:

> ➤ You can refresh one PivotTable and all others that share the pivot cache are refreshed also.

> ➤ When you add a Calculated Field to one PivotTable, your newly created calculated field shows up in the other PivotTables' field list.

> ➤ When you add a Calculated Item to one PivotTable, it shows up in the others as well.

> ➤ Any grouping or ungrouping you perform affects all PivotTables sharing the same cache.

How it works

With the last macro, you are able to take an inventory of all your PivotTables. In that inventory summary, you can see the pivot cache index of each PivotTable (see Figure 6-1). Using this, you can determine which PivotTable contains the most appropriate pivot cache, and then force all others to share the same cache.

In this example, we are forcing all PivotTables to the pivot cache used by PivotTable1 on the Units Sold sheet.

```
Sub Macro65()

'Step 1:  Declare your Variables
   Dim ws As Worksheet
```

```
    Dim pt As PivotTable


'Step 2: Loop through each sheet in workbook
    For Each ws In ThisWorkbook.Worksheets


'Step 3: Loop through each PivotTable
        For Each pt In ws.PivotTables

        pt.CacheIndex = _
        Sheets("Units Sold").PivotTables("PivotTable1").CacheIndex

        Next pt
    Next ws

End Sub
```

1. Step 1 declares an object called `ws`. This creates a memory container for each worksheet we loop through. We also declare an object called `pt`, which holds each PivotTable we loop through.

2. Step 2 starts the looping, telling Excel we want to evaluate all worksheets in this workbook. Notice we are using `ThisWorkbook` instead of `ActiveWorkbook`. `ThisWorkbook` object refers to the workbook that the code is contained in. `ActiveWorkbook` object refers to the workbook that is currently active. They often return the same object, but if the workbook running the code is not the active workbook, they return different objects. In this case, we don't want to risk affecting PivotTables in other workbooks, so we use `ThisWorkbook`.

3. Step 3 loops through all the PivotTables in each worksheet, and then sets the `CachIndex` to the same one used by PivotTable1 on the "Units Sold" sheet. After all PivotTables have been refreshed, we move to the next sheet. After all sheets have been evaluated, the macro ends.

How to use it

To implement this macro, you can copy and paste it into a standard module:

1. Activate the Visual Basic Editor by pressing ALT+F11.

2. Right-click the project/workbook name in the Project window.

3. Choose Insert➡Module.

4. Type or paste the code.

Macro 66: Hide All Subtotals in a PivotTable

When you create a PivotTable, Excel includes subtotals by default. This inevitably leads to a PivotTable report that inundates the eyes with all kinds of numbers, making it difficult to analyze. Figure 6-2 demonstrates this.

Region	Market	Product Category	Internet Order	Sum of Sale Amount
⊟North	⊟Dakotas	⊟Bar Equipment	FALSE	496
			TRUE	2,891
		Bar Equipment Total		3,387
		⊟Commercial Appliances	FALSE	6,132
			TRUE	1,155
		Commercial Appliances Total		7,287
		⊟Concession Equipment	FALSE	24,985
			TRUE	5,634
		Concession Equipment Total		30,619
		⊟Fryers	FALSE	3,237
			TRUE	14,792
		Fryers Total		18,029
		⊟Ovens and Ranges	FALSE	46,806
			TRUE	148,296
		Ovens and Ranges Total		195,102
		⊟Refrigerators and Coolers	FALSE	19,708
			TRUE	266,555
		Refrigerators and Coolers Total		286,263
		⊟Warmers	FALSE	5,902
			TRUE	20,319
		Warmers Total		26,221
	Dakotas Total			566,909
	⊟Great Lakes	⊟Bar Equipment	FALSE	9,554

Figure 6-2: Subtotals can sometimes hinder analysis.

Manually removing Subtotals is easy enough; right-click the field headers and uncheck the Subtotal option. But if you're constantly hiding subtotals, you can save a little time by automating the process with a simple macro.

Tip

You can manually hide all subtotals at once by going to the Ribbon and selecting PivotTable Tools→Design→Layout→Subtotals→Do Not Show Subtotals. But again, if you are building an automated process that routinely manipulates pivot tables without manual intervention, you may prefer the macro option.

How it works

If you record a macro while hiding a Subtotal in a PivotTable, Excel produces code similar to this:

```
ActiveSheet.PivotTables("Pvt1 ).PivotFields("Region").Subtotals =
   Array(False, False, False, False, False, False, False, False, False,
   False, False, False)
```

That's right; Excel passes an array with exactly 12 `False` settings. There are 12 instances of `False` because there are twelve types of Subtotals — `Sum`, `Avg`, `Count`, `Min`, and `Max`, just to name a few. So when you turn off Subtotals while recording a macro, Excel sets each of the possible Subtotal types to `False`.

An alternative way of turning off Subtotals is to first set one of the 12 Subtotals to `True`. This automatically forces the other 11 Subtotal types to `False`. We then set the same Subtotal to `False`, effectively hiding all Subtotals. In this piece of code, we are setting the first Subtotal to `True`, and then setting it to `False`. This removes the subtotal for Region.

```
With ActiveSheet.PivotTables("Pvt1 ).PivotFields("Region")
.Subtotals(1) = True
.Subtotals(1) = False
End With
```

In our macro, we use this trick to turn off subtotals for every pivot field in the active PivotTable.

```
Sub Macro66()

'Step 1: Declare your Variables
    Dim pt As PivotTable
    Dim pf As PivotField


'Step 2: Point to the PivotTable in the active cell
    On Error Resume Next
    Set pt = ActiveSheet.PivotTables(ActiveCell.PivotTable.Name)


'Step 3:  Exit if active cell is not in a PivotTable
    If pt Is Nothing Then
    MsgBox "You must place your cursor inside of a PivotTable."
    Exit Sub
    End If


'Step 4:  Loop through all pivot fields and remove totals
    For Each pf In pt.PivotFields
        pf.Subtotals(1) = True
        pf.Subtotals(1) = False
    Next pf

End Sub
```

1. Step 1 declares two object variables. This macro uses `pt` as the memory container for the PivotTable and uses `pf` as a memory container for the pivot fields. This allows us to loop through all the pivot fields in the PivotTable.

2. This macro is designed so that we infer the active PivotTable based on the active cell. That is to say, the active cell must be inside a PivotTable for this macro to run. The assumption is that when the cursor is inside a particular PivotTable, we want to perform the macro action on that pivot.

   Step 2 sets the `pt` variable to the name of the PivotTable on which the active cell is found. We do this by using the `ActiveCell.PivotTable.Name` property to get the name of the target pivot.

   If the active cell is not inside of a PivotTable, an error is thrown. This is why the macro uses the `On Error Resume Next` statement. This tells Excel to continue with the macro if there is an error.

3. Step 3 checks to whether the `pt` variable is filled with a PivotTable object. If the `pt` variable is set to `Nothing`, the active cell was not on a PivotTable, thus no PivotTable could be assigned to the variable. If this is the case, we tell the user in a message box, and then we exit the procedure.

4. If the macro reaches Step 4, it has successfully pointed to a PivotTable. We are ready to loop to all the fields in the PivotTable. We use a `For Each` statement to iterate through each pivot field. Each time a new pivot field is selected, we apply our Subtotal logic. After all the fields have been evaluated, the macro ends.

How to use it

To implement this macro, you can copy and paste it into a standard module:

1. Activate the Visual Basic Editor by pressing ALT+F11.

2. Right-click the project/workbook name in the Project window.

3. Choose Insert➜Module.

4. Type or paste the code.

Macro 67: Adjust All Pivot Data Field Titles

When you create a PivotTable, Excel tries to help you out by prefacing each data field header with `Sum of`, `Count of`, or whichever operation you use. Often, this is not conducive to your reporting needs. You want clean titles that match your data source as closely as possible. Although it's true that you can manually adjust the titles for you data fields (one at a time), this macro fixes them all in one go.

How it works

Ideally, the name of the each data item matches the field name from your source data set (the original source data used to create the PivotTable). Unfortunately, PivotTables won't allow you to name a data field the exact name as the source data field. The workaround for this is to add a space to the end of the field name. Excel considers the field name (with a space) to be different from the source data field name, so it allows it. Cosmetically, the readers of your spreadsheet don't notice the space after the name.

This macro utilizes this workaround to rename your data fields. It loops through each data field in the PivotTable, and then resets each header to match its respective field in the source data plus a space character.

```
Sub Macro67()

'Step 1: Declare your Variables
    Dim pt As PivotTable
    Dim pf As PivotField


'Step 2: Point to the PivotTable in the active cell
    On Error Resume Next
    Set pt = ActiveSheet.PivotTables(ActiveCell.PivotTable.Name)


'Step 3:  Exit if active cell is not in a PivotTable
    If pt Is Nothing Then
    MsgBox "You must place your cursor inside of a PivotTable."
    Exit Sub
    End If


'Step 4:  Loop through all pivot fields adjust titles
    For Each pf In pt.DataFields
        pf.Caption = pf.SourceName & Chr(160)
    Next pf

End Sub
```

1. Step 1 declares two object variables. It uses `pt` as the memory container for our PivotTable and `pf` as a memory container for the data fields. This allows the macro to loop through all the data fields in the PivotTable.

2. This macro is designed so that we infer the active PivotTable based on the active cell. In other words, the active cell must be inside a PivotTable for this macro to run. We assume that when the cursor is inside a particular PivotTable, we want to perform the macro action on that pivot.

   Step 2 sets the `pt` variable to the name of the PivotTable on which the active cell is found. We do this by using the `ActiveCell.PivotTable.Name` property to get the name of the target pivot.

   If the active cell is not inside of a PivotTable, an error is thrown. This is why we use the `On Error Resume Next` statement. This tells Excel to continue with the macro if there is an error.

3. In Step 3, we check to see if the `pt` variable is filled with a PivotTable object. If the `pt` variable is set to `Nothing`, the active cell was not on a PivotTable, thus no PivotTable could be assigned to the variable. If this is the case, we tell the user in a message box, and then we exit the procedure.

4. If the macro reaches Step 4, it has successfully pointed to a PivotTable. The macro uses a `For Each` statement to iterate through each data field. Each time a new pivot field is selected, the macro changes the field name by setting the `Caption` property to match the field's `SourceName`. The `SourceName` property returns the name of the matching field in the original source data.

   To that name, the macro concatenates a non-breaking space character: `Chr(160)`.

   Every character has an underlying ASCII code, similar to a serial number. For instance, the lowercase letter *a* has an ASCII code of 97. The lowercase letter *c* has an ASCII code of 99. Likewise, invisible characters such as the space have a code. You can use invisible characters in your macro by passing their code through the CHR function.

   After the name has been changed, the macro moves to the next data field. After all the data fields have been evaluated, the macro ends.

How to use it

To implement this macro, you can copy and paste it into a standard module:

1. Activate the Visual Basic Editor by pressing ALT+F11.

2. Right-click the project/workbook name in the Project window.

3. Choose Insert➜Module.

4. Type or paste the code.

Macro 68: Set All Data Items to Sum

When creating a PivotTable, Excel, by default, summarizes your data by either counting or summing the items. The logic Excel uses to decide whether to sum or count the fields you add to your PivotTable is fairly simple. If all of the cells in a column contain numeric data, Excel chooses to `Sum`. If the field you are adding contains a blank or text, Excel chooses `Count`.

Although this seems to make sense, in many instances, a pivot field that should be summed legitimately contains blanks. In these cases, we are forced to manually go in after Excel and change the calculation type from `Count` back to `Sum`. That's if we're paying attention! It's not uncommon to miss the fact that a pivot field is being counted instead of summed up.

The macro in this section aims to help by automatically setting each data item's calculation type to `Sum`.

How it works

This macro loops through each data field in the PivotTable and changes the `Function` property to `xlSum`. You can alter this macro to use any one of the calculation choices: `xlCount`, `xlAverage`, `xlMin`, `xlMax`, and so on. When you go into the code window and type `pf.Function =`, you see a drop-down list showing you all your choices (see Figure 6-3).

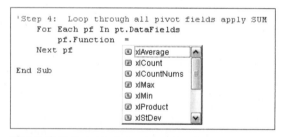

```
'Step 4:   Loop through all pivot fields apply SUM
    For Each pf In pt.DataFields
        pf.Function  =
    Next pf          ▣ xlAverage      ▲
                     ▣ xlCount
End Sub               ▣ xlCountNums   ▤
                     ▣ xlMax
                     ▣ xlMin
                     ▣ xlProduct
                     ▣ xlStDev       ▼
```

Figure 6-3: Excel helps out by showing you your enumeration choices.

```
Sub Macro68()


'Step 1: Declare your Variables
    Dim pt As PivotTable
    Dim pf As PivotField


'Step 2: Point to the PivotTable in the active cell
    On Error Resume Next
    Set pt = ActiveSheet.PivotTables(ActiveCell.PivotTable.Name)
```

```
'Step 3:  Exit if active cell is not in a PivotTable
    If pt Is Nothing Then
    MsgBox "You must place your cursor inside of a PivotTable."
    Exit Sub
    End If


'Step 4:  Loop through all pivot fields apply SUM
    For Each pf In pt.DataFields
        pf.Function = xlSum
    Next pf

End Sub
```

1. Step 1 declares two object variables. It uses `pt` as the memory container for the PivotTable and `pf` as a memory container for the data fields. This allows us to loop through all the data fields in the PivotTable.

2. This macro is designed so that we infer the active PivotTable based on the active cell. The active cell must be inside a PivotTable for this macro to run. The assumption is that when the cursor is inside a particular PivotTable, we want to perform the macro action on that pivot.

   Step 2 sets the `pt` variable to the name of the PivotTable on which the active cell is found. We do this by using the `ActiveCell.PivotTable.Name` property to get the name of the target pivot.

   If the active cell is not inside of a PivotTable, an error is thrown. This is why we use the `On Error Resume Next` statement. This tells Excel to continue with the macro if there is an error.

3. Step 3 checks to see if the `pt` variable is filled with a PivotTable object. If the `pt` variable is set to `Nothing`, the active cell was not on a PivotTable, thus no PivotTable could be assigned to the variable. If this is the case, we tell the user in a message box, and then we exit the procedure.

4. If the macro has reached Step 4, it has successfully pointed to a PivotTable. It uses a `For Each` statement to iterate through each data field. Each time a new pivot field is selected, it alters the `Function` property to set the calculation used by the field. In this case, we are setting all the data fields in the PivotTable to `Sum`.

   After the name has been changed, we move to the next data field. After all the data fields have been evaluated, the macro ends.

How to use it

To implement this macro, you can copy and paste it into a standard module:

1. Activate the Visual Basic Editor by pressing ALT+F11.

2. Right-click the project/workbook name in the Project window.

3. Choose Insert→Module.

4. Type or paste the code.

Macro 69: Apply Number Formatting for All Data Items

A PivotTable does not inherently store number formatting in its pivot cache. Formatting takes up memory; so in order to be as lean as possible, the pivot cache only contains data. Unfortunately, this results in the need to apply number formatting to every field you add to a PivotTable. This takes from eight to ten clicks of the mouse for every data field you add. When you have PivotTables that contain five or more data fields, you're talking about more than 40 clicks of the mouse!

Ideally, a PivotTable should be able to look back at its source data and adopt the number formatting from the fields there. The macro outlined in this section is designed to do just that. It recognizes the number formatting in the PivotTable's source data and applies the appropriate formatting to each field automatically.

How it works

Before running this code, you want to make sure that

➤ The source data for your PivotTable is accessible. The macro needs to see it in order to capture the correct number formatting.

➤ The source data is appropriately formatted. Money fields are formatted as currency, value fields are formatted as numbers, and so on.

This macro uses the PivotTable SourceData property to find the location of the source data. It then loops through each column in the source, capturing the header name and the number format of the first value under each column. After it has that information, the macro determines whether any of the data fields match the evaluated column. If it finds a match, the number formatting is applied to that data field.

```
Sub Macro69()


'Step 1: Declare your Variables
    Dim pt As PivotTable
    Dim pf As PivotField
    Dim SrcRange As Range
    Dim strFormat As String
    Dim strLabel As String
    Dim i As Integer

'Step 2: Point to the PivotTable in the activecell
    On Error Resume Next
    Set pt = ActiveSheet.PivotTables(ActiveCell.PivotTable.Name)
```

```
'Step 3:  Exit if active cell is not in a PivotTable
    If pt Is Nothing Then
    MsgBox "You must place your cursor inside of a PivotTable."
    Exit Sub
    End If

'Step 4: Capture the source range
    Set SrcRange = _
    Range(Application.ConvertFormula(pt.SourceData, xlR1C1, xlA1))


'Step 5: Start looping through the columns in source range
    For i = 1 To SrcRange.Columns.Count


'Step 6: Trap the source column name and number format
        strLabel = SrcRange.Cells(1, i).Value
        strFormat = SrcRange.Cells(2, i).NumberFormat


'Step 7: Loop through the fields PivotTable data area
        For Each pf In pt.DataFields


'Step 8: Check for match on SourceName then apply format
            If pf.SourceName = strLabel Then
            pf.NumberFormat = strFormat
            End If
        Next pf
    Next i

End Sub
```

1. Step 1 declares six variables. It uses `pt` as the memory container for our PivotTable and `pf` as a memory container for our data fields. The `SrcRange` variable holds the data range for the source data. The `strFormat` and `strLabel` variables are both text string variables used to hold the source column label and number formatting respectively. The `i` variable serves as a counter, helping us enumerate through the columns of the source data range.

2. The active cell must be inside a PivotTable for this macro to run. The assumption is that when the cursor is inside a particular PivotTable, we want to perform the macro action on that pivot.

   Step 2 sets the `pt` variable to the name of the PivotTable on which the active cell is found. We do this by using the `ActiveCell.PivotTable.Name` property to get the name of the target pivot.

If the active cell is not inside a PivotTable, an error is thrown. This is why the macro uses the `On Error Resume Next` statement. This tells Excel to continue with the macro if there is an error.

3. Step 3 checks to see whether the `pt` variable is filled with a PivotTable object. If the `pt` variable is set to `Nothing`, the active cell was not on a PivotTable, thus no PivotTable could be assigned to the variable. If this is the case, we tell the user in a message box, and then we exit the procedure.

4. If the macro reaches Step 4, it has successfully pointed to a PivotTable. We immediately fill our `SrcRange` object variable with the PivotTable's source data range.

   All PivotTables have a `SourceData` property that points to the address of its source. Unfortunately, the address is stored in the R1C1 reference style — like this: `'Raw Data'!R3C1:R59470C14`. Range objects cannot use the R1C1 style, so we need the address to be converted to `'Raw Data'!$A$3:$N$59470`.

   This is a simple enough fix. We simply pass the `SourceData` property through the `Application.ConvertFormula` function. This handy function converts ranges to and from the R1C1 reference style.

5. After the range is captured, the macro starts looping through the columns in the source range. In this case, we manage the looping by using the `i` integer as an index number for the columns in the source range. We start the index number at 1 and end it at the maximum number of rows in the source range.

6. As the macro loops through the columns in the source range, we capture the column header label and the column format.

   We do this with the aid of the `Cells` item. The `Cells` item gives us an extremely handy way of selecting ranges through code. It requires only relative row and column positions as parameters. `Cells(1,1)` translates to row 1, column 1 (or the header row of the first column). `Cells(2, 1)` translates to row 2, column 1 (or the first value in the first column).

   `strLabel` is filled by the header label taken from row 1 of the column that is selected. `strFormat` is filled with the number formatting from row 2 of the column that is selected.

7. At this point, the macro has connected with the PivotTable's source data and captured the first column name and number formatting for that column. Now it starts looping through the data fields in the PivotTable.

8. Step 8 simply compares each data field to see if its source matches the name in `strLabel`. If it does, that means the number formatting captured in `strFormat` belongs to that data field.

9. After all data fields have been evaluated, the macro increments `i` to the next column in the source range. After all columns have been evaluated, the macro ends.

How to use it

To implement this macro, you can copy and paste it into a standard module:

1. Activate the Visual Basic Editor by pressing ALT+F11.

2. Right-click project/workbook name in the Project window.

3. Choose Insert→Module.

4. Type or paste the code.

Macro 70: Sort All Fields in Alphabetical Order

If you frequently add data to your PivotTables, you may notice that new data doesn't automatically fall into the sort order of the existing pivot data. Instead, it gets tacked to the bottom of the existing data. This means that your drop-down lists show all new data at the very bottom, whereas existing data is sorted alphabetically.

How it works

This macro works to reset the sorting on all data fields, ensuring that any new data snaps into place. The idea is to run it each time you refresh your PivotTable. In the code, we enumerate through each data field in the PivotTable, sorting each one as we go.

```
Sub Macro70()

'Step 1: Declare your Variables
    Dim pt As PivotTable
    Dim pf As PivotField


'Step 2: Point to the PivotTable in the activecell
    On Error Resume Next
    Set pt = ActiveSheet.PivotTables(ActiveCell.PivotTable.Name)


'Step 3:  Exit if active cell is not in a PivotTable
    If pt Is Nothing Then
    MsgBox "You must place your cursor inside of a PivotTable."
    Exit Sub
    End If


'Step 4:  Loop through all pivot fields and sort
    For Each pf In pt.PivotFields
        pf.AutoSort xlAscending, pf.Name
    Next pf

End Sub
```

1. Step 1 declares two object variables, using `pt` as the memory container for the PivotTable and using `pf` as a memory container for our data fields. This allows the macro to loop through all the data fields in the PivotTable.

2. The active cell must be inside a PivotTable for this macro to run. The assumption is that when the cursor is inside a particular PivotTable, we want to perform the macro action on that pivot.

In Step 2, we set the `pt` variable to the name of the PivotTable on which the active cell is found. We do this by using the `ActiveCell.PivotTable.Name` property to get the name of the target pivot.

If the active cell is not inside of a PivotTable, an error is thrown. This is why we use the `On Error Resume Next` statement. This tells Excel to continue with the macro if there is an error.

3. Step 3 checks to see whether the `pt` variable is filled with a PivotTable object. If the `pt` variable is set to `Nothing`, the active cell was not on a PivotTable, thus no PivotTable could be assigned to the variable. If this is the case, the macro puts up a message box to notify the user, and then exits the procedure.

4. Finally, we use a `For Each` statement to iterate through each pivot field. Each time a new pivot field is selected, we use the `AutoSort` method to reset the automatic sorting rules for the field. In this case, we are sorting all fields in ascending order. After all the data fields have been evaluated, the macro ends.

How to use it

To implement this macro, you can copy and paste it into a standard module:

1. Activate the Visual Basic Editor by pressing ALT+F11.

2. Right-click the project/workbook name in the Project window.

3. Choose Insert➜Module.

4. Type or paste the code.

Macro 71: Apply Custom Sort to Data Items

On occasion, you may need to apply a custom sort to the data items in your PivotTable. For instance, if you work for a company in California, your organization may want the West region to come before the North and South. In these types of situations, neither the standard ascending nor descending sort order will work.

How it works

You can automate the custom sorting of your fields by using the `Position` property of the `PivotItems` object. With the `Position` property, you can assign a position number that specifies the order in which you would like to see each pivot item.

In this example code, we first point to the `Region` pivot field in the `Pvt1` PivotTable. Then we list each item along with the position number indicating the customer sort order we need.

```
Sub Macro71()

With Sheets("Sheet1").PivotTables("Pvt1").PivotFields("Region ")
    .PivotItems("West").Position = 1
    .PivotItems("North").Position = 2
    .PivotItems("South").Position = 3

End With

End Sub
```

Tip

The other solution is to set up a custom sort list. A custom sort list is a defined list that is stored in your instance of Excel. To create a custom sort list, go to the Excel Options dialog box and choose Edit Custom Lists. Here, you can type West, North, and South in the List Entries box and click Add. After setting up a custom list, Excel realizes that the Region data items in your PivotTable match a custom list and sorts the field to match your custom list.

As brilliant as this option is, custom lists do not travel with your workbook, so a macro helps in cases where it's impractical to expect your clients or team members to set up their own custom sort lists.

How to use it

You can implement this kind of a macro in a standard module:

1. Activate the Visual Basic Editor by pressing ALT+F11.

2. Right-click the project/workbook name in the Project window.

3. Choose Insert→Module.

4. Type or paste the code.

Macro 72: Apply PivotTable Restrictions

We often send PivotTables to clients, coworkers, managers, and other groups of people. In some cases, we'd like to restrict the types of actions our users can take on the PivotTable reports we send them. The macro outlined in this section demonstrates some of the protection settings available via VBA.

How it works

The `PivotTable` object exposes several properties that allow you (the developer) to restrict different features and components of a PivotTable:

> **EnableWizard:** Setting this property to `False` disables the PivotTable Tools context menu that normally activates when clicking inside of a PivotTable. In Excel 2003, this setting disables the PivotTable and Pivot Chart Wizard.

> **EnableDrilldown:** Setting this property to `False` prevents users from getting to detailed data by double-clicking a data field.

> **EnableFieldList:** Setting this property to `False` prevents users from activating the field list or moving pivot fields around.

> **EnableFieldDialog:** Setting this property to `False` disables the users' ability to alter the pivot field via the Value Field Settings dialog box.

> **PivotCache.EnableRefresh:** Setting this property to `False` disables the ability to refresh the PivotTable.

You can set any or all of these properties independently to either `True` or `False`. In this macro, we apply all of the restrictions to the target PivotTable.

```
Sub Macro72()

'Step 1: Declare your Variables
    Dim pt As PivotTable


'Step 2: Point to the PivotTable in the activecell
    On Error Resume Next
    Set pt = ActiveSheet.PivotTables(ActiveCell.PivotTable.Name)


'Step 3:  Exit if active cell is not in a PivotTable
    If pt Is Nothing Then
    MsgBox "You must place your cursor inside of a PivotTable."
    Exit Sub
    End If
```

```
'Step 4:  Apply PivotTable Restrictions
    With pt
       .EnableWizard = False
       .EnableDrilldown = False
       .EnableFieldList = False
       .EnableFieldDialog = False
       .PivotCache.EnableRefresh = False
    End With

End Sub
```

1. Step 1 declares the `pt` PivotTable object variable that serves as the memory container for our PivotTable.

2. Step 2 sets the `pt` variable to the name of the PivotTable on which the active cell is found. We do this by using the `ActiveCell.PivotTable.Name` property to get the name of the target pivot.

3. Step 3 checks to see if the `pt` variable is filled with a PivotTable object. If the `pt` variable is set to `Nothing`, the active cell was not on a PivotTable, thus no PivotTable could be assigned to the variable. If this is the case, the macro notifies the user in a message box, and then we exit the procedure.

4. In the last step of the macro, we are applying all PivotTable restrictions.

How to use it

You can implement this kind of a macro in a standard module:

1. Activate the Visual Basic Editor by pressing ALT+F11.

2. Right-click the project/workbook name in the Project window.

3. Choose Insert➜Module.

4. Type or paste the code.

Macro 73: Apply Pivot Field Restrictions

Like PivotTable restrictions, pivot field restrictions enable us to restrict the types of actions our users can take on the pivot fields in a PivotTable. The macro outlined in this section demonstrates some of the protection settings available via VBA.

How it works

The `PivotField` object exposes several properties that allow you (the developer) to restrict different features and components of a PivotTable.

> **DragToPage:** Setting this property to `False` prevents the users from dragging any pivot field into the Report Filter area of the PivotTable.

> **DragToRow:** Setting this property to `False` prevents the users from dragging any pivot field into the Row area of the PivotTable.

> **DragToColumn:** Setting this property to `False` prevents the users from dragging any pivot field into the Column area of the PivotTable.

> **DragToData:** Setting this property to `False` prevents the users from dragging any pivot field into the Data area of the PivotTable.

> **DragToHide:** Setting this property to `False` prevents the users from dragging pivot fields off the PivotTable. It also prevents the use of the right-click menu to hide or remove pivot fields.

> **EnableItemSelection:** Setting this property to `False` disables the drop-down lists on each pivot field.

You can set any or all of these properties independently to either `True` or `False`. In this macro, we apply all of the restrictions to the target PivotTable.

```
Sub Macro73()

'Step 1: Declare your Variables
    Dim pt As PivotTable
    Dim pf As PivotField


'Step 2: Point to the PivotTable in the activecell
    On Error Resume Next
    Set pt = ActiveSheet.PivotTables(ActiveCell.PivotTable.Name)


'Step 3:  Exit if active cell is not in a PivotTable
    If pt Is Nothing Then
    MsgBox "You must place your cursor inside of a PivotTable."
```

```
      Exit Sub
      End If


'Step 4:  Apply Pivot Field Restrictions
    For Each pf In pt.PivotFields
        pf.EnableItemSelection = False
        pf.DragToPage = False
        pf.DragToRow = False
        pf.DragToColumn = False
        pf.DragToData = False
        pf.DragToHide = False
    Next pf

End Sub
```

1. Step 1 declares two object variables, using `pt` as the memory container for our PivotTable and `pf` as a memory container for our pivot fields. This allows us to loop through all the pivot fields in the PivotTable.

2. Set the `pt` variable to the name of the PivotTable on which the active cell is found. We do this by using the `ActiveCell.PivotTable.Name` property to get the name of the target pivot.

3. Step 3 checks to see whether the `pt` variable is filled with a PivotTable object. If the `pt` variable is set to `Nothing`, the active cell was not on a PivotTable, thus no PivotTable could be assigned to the variable. If this is the case, the macro notifies the user via a message box, and then exits the procedure.

4. Step 4 of the macro uses a `For Each` statement to iterate through each pivot field. Each time a new pivot field is selected, we apply all of our pivot field restrictions.

How to use it

You can implement this kind of a macro in a standard module:

1. Activate the Visual Basic Editor by pressing ALT+F11.

2. Right-click the project/workbook name in the Project window.

3. Choose Insert➔Module.

4. Type or paste the code.

Macro 74: Automatically Delete Pivot Table Drill-Down Sheets

One of the coolest features of a PivotTable is that it gives you the ability to double-click on a number and drill into the details. The details are output to a new sheet that you can review. In most cases, you don't want to keep these sheets. In fact, they often become a nuisance, forcing you to take the time to clean them up by deleting them.

This is especially a problem when you distribute PivotTable reports to users who frequently drill into details. There is no guarantee they will remember to clean up the drill-down sheets. Although these sheets probably won't cause issues, they can clutter up the workbook.

Here is a technique you can implement to have your workbook automatically remove these drill-down sheets.

How it works

The basic premise of this macro is actually very simple. When the user clicks for details, outputting a drill-down sheet, the macro simply renames the output sheet so that the first ten characters are *PivotDrill*. Then before the workbook closes, the macro finds any sheet that starts with *PivotDrill* and deletes it.

The implementation does get a bit tricky because you essentially have to have two pieces of code. One piece goes in the `Worksheet_BeforeDoubleClick` event, whereas the other piece goes into the `Workbook_BeforeClose` event.

```
Private Sub Worksheet_BeforeDoubleClick(ByVal Target As Range, Cancel As
    Boolean)


'Step 1: Declare your Variables
    Dim pt As String


'Step 2: Exit if Double-Click did not occur on a PivotTable
    On Error Resume Next
    If IsEmpty(Target) And ActiveCell.PivotField.Name <> "" Then
    Cancel = True
    Exit Sub
    End If


'Step 3:  Set the PivotTable object
    pt = ActiveSheet.Range(ActiveCell.Address).PivotTable
```

```
'Step 4:  If Drilldowns are Enabled, Drill down
    If ActiveSheet.PivotTables(pt).EnableDrilldown Then
        Selection.ShowDetail = True

        ActiveSheet.Name = _
        Replace(ActiveSheet.Name, "Sheet", "PivotDrill")
    End If

End Sub
```

1. Step 1 starts by creating the `pt` object variable for our PivotTable.

2. Step 2 checks the double-clicked cell. If the cell is not associated with any PivotTable, we cancel the double-click event.

3. If a PivotTable is indeed associated with a cell, Step 3 fills the `pt` variable with the PivotTable.

4. Finally, Step 4 checks the `EnableDrillDown` property. If it is enabled, we trigger the `ShowDetail` method. This outputs the drill-down details to a new worksheet.

The macro follows the output and renames the output sheet so that the first ten characters are *PivotDrill*. We do this by using the `Replace` function. The `Replace` function replaces certain text in an expression with other text. In this case, we are replacing the word *Sheet* with *PivotDrill*: `Replace(ActiveSheet.Name, "Sheet", "PivotDrill")`.

Sheet1 becomes PivotDrill1; Sheet12 becomes PivotDrill12, and so on.

Next, the macro sets up the `Worksheet_BeforeDoubleClick` event. As the name suggests, this code runs when the workbook closes.

```
Private Sub Workbook_BeforeClose(Cancel As Boolean)


'Step 5:  Declare your Variables
    Dim ws As Worksheet


'Step 6:  Loop through worksheets
    For Each ws In ThisWorkbook.Worksheets


'Step 7:  Delete any sheet that starts with PivotDrill
        If Left(ws.Name, 10) = "PivotDrill" Then
            Application.DisplayAlerts = False
            ws.Delete
            Application.DisplayAlerts = True
        End If
```

```
    Next ws

End Sub
```

5. Step 5 declares the `ws` Worksheet variable. This is used to hold worksheet objects as we loop through the workbook.

6. Step 6 starts the looping, telling Excel we want to evaluate all worksheets in this workbook.

7. In the last step, we evaluate the name of the sheet that has focus in the loop. If the left ten characters of that sheet name are PivotDrill, we delete the worksheet. After all of the sheets have been evaluated, all drill-down sheets have been cleaned up and the macro ends.

How to use it

To implement the first part of the macro, you need to copy and paste it into the `Worksheet_BeforeDoubleClick` event code window. Placing the macro here allows it to run each time you double-click on the sheet:

1. Activate the Visual Basic Editor by pressing ALT+F11.

2. In the Project window, find your project/workbook name and click the plus sign next to it in order to see all the sheets.

3. Click on the sheet in which you want to trigger the code.

4. Select the `BeforeDoubleClick` event from the Event drop-down list box (see Figure 6-4).

5. Type or paste the code.

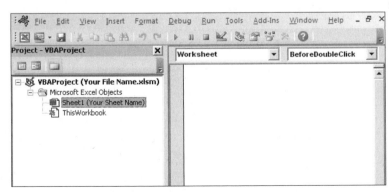

Figure 6-4: Type or paste your code in the Worksheet_BeforeDoubleClick event code window.

To implement this macro, you need to copy and paste it into the `Workbook_BeforeClose` event code window. Placing the macro here allows it to run each time you try to close the workbook.

1. Activate the Visual Basic Editor by pressing ALT+F11.

2. In the Project window, find your project/workbook name and click the plus sign next to it in order to see all the sheets.

3. Click ThisWorkbook.

4. Select the `BeforeClose` event in the Event drop-down list (see Figure 6-5).

5. Type or paste the code.

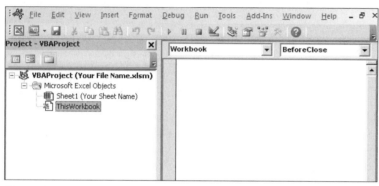

Figure 6-5: Enter or paste your code in the Workbook_BeforeClose event code window.

Macro 75: Print Pivot Table for Each Report Filter Item

Pivot tables provide an excellent mechanism to parse large data sets into printable files. You can build a PivotTable report, complete with aggregations and analysis, and then place a field (like Region) into the report filter. With the report filter, you can select each data item one at a time, and then print the PivotTable report.

The macro in this section demonstrates how to automatically iterate through all the values in a report filter and print.

How it works

In the Excel object model, the Report Filter drop-down list is known as the `PageField`. To print a PivotTable for each data item in a report filter, we need to loop through the `PivotItems` collection of the `PageField` object. As we loop, we dynamically change the selection in the report filter, and then use the `ActiveSheet.PrintOut` method to print the target range.

```
Sub Macro75()

'Step 1: Declare your Variables
    Dim pt As PivotTable
    Dim pf As PivotField
    Dim pi As PivotItem


'Step 2: Point to the PivotTable in the activecell
    On Error Resume Next
    Set pt = ActiveSheet.PivotTables(ActiveCell.PivotTable.Name)


'Step 3:  Exit if active cell is not in a PivotTable
    If pt Is Nothing Then
    MsgBox "You must place your cursor inside of a PivotTable."
    Exit Sub
    End If


'Step 4:  Exit if more than one page field
    If pt.PageFields.Count > 1 Then
    MsgBox "Too many Report Filter Fields. Limit 1."
    Exit Sub
    End If
```

```
'Step 5:  Start looping through the page field and its pivot items
    For Each pf In pt.PageFields
        For Each pi In pf.PivotItems


'Step 6:  Change the selection in the report filter
        pt.PivotFields(pf.Name).CurrentPage = pi.Name


'Step 7: Set Print Area and print
        ActiveSheet.PageSetup.PrintArea = pt.TableRange2.Address
        ActiveSheet.PrintOut Copies:=1


'Step 8: Get the next page field item
        Next pi
    Next pf

End Sub
```

1. For this macro, Step 1 declares three variables: `pt` as the memory container for our PivotTable, `pf` as a memory container for our page fields, and `pi` to hold each pivot item as we loop through the `PageField` object.

2. The active cell must be inside a PivotTable for this macro to run. The assumption is that when the cursor is inside a particular PivotTable, we want to perform the macro action on that pivot.

   Step 2 sets the `pt` variable to the name of the PivotTable on which the active cell is found. We do this by using the `ActiveCell.PivotTable.Name` property to get the name of the target pivot.

   If the active cell is not inside of a PivotTable, the macro throws an error. This is why we use the `On Error Resume Next` statement. This tells Excel to continue with the macro if there is an error.

3. Step 3 checks to see whether the `pt` variable is filled with a PivotTable object. If the `pt` variable is set to `Nothing`, the active cell was not on a PivotTable, thus no PivotTable could be assigned to the variable. If this is the case, the user is notified via a message box, and then we exit the procedure.

4. Step 4 determines whether there is more than one report filter field. (If the count of `PageFields` is greater than one, there is more than one report filter.) We do this check for a simple reason: We want to avoid printing reports for filters that just happen to be there. Without this check, you might wind up printing hundreds of pages. The macro stops with a message box if the field count is greater than 1.

   You can remove this limitation should you need to simply by deleting or commenting out Step 4 in the macro.

5. Step 5 starts two loops. The outer loop tells Excel to iterate through all the report filters. The inner loop tells Excel to loop through all the pivot items in the report filter that currently has focus.

6. For each pivot item, the macro captures the item name and uses it to change the report filter selection. This effectively alters the PivotTable report to match the pivot item.

7. Step 7 prints the active sheet, and then moves to the next pivot item. After we have looped through all pivot items in the report filter, the macro moves to the next `PageField`. After all `PageFields` have been evaluated, the macro ends.

How to use it

You can implement this kind of a macro in a standard module:

1. Activate the Visual Basic Editor by pressing ALT+F11.

2. Right-click the project/workbook name in the Project window.

3. Choose Insert➜Module.

4. Type or paste the code.

Macro 76: Create New Workbook for Each Report Filter Item

Pivot tables provide an excellent mechanism to parse large data sets into separate files. You can build a PivotTable report, complete with aggregations and analysis, and then place a field (like Region) into the report filter. With the report filter, you can select each data item one at a time, and then export the PivotTable data to a new workbook.

The macro in this section demonstrates how to automatically iterate through all the values in a report filter and export to a new workbook.

How it works

In the Excel object model, the Report Filter drop-down list is known as the `PageField`. To print a PivotTable for each data item in a report filter, the macro needs to loop through the `PivotItems` collection of the `PageField` object. As the macro loops, it must dynamically change the selection in the report filter, and then export the PivotTable report to a new workbook.

```
Sub Macro76()

'Step 1: Declare your Variables
    Dim pt As PivotTable
    Dim pf As PivotField
    Dim pi As PivotItem


'Step 2: Point to the PivotTable in the activecell
    On Error Resume Next
    Set pt = ActiveSheet.PivotTables(ActiveCell.PivotTable.Name)


'Step 3:  Exit if active cell is not in a PivotTable
    If pt Is Nothing Then
    MsgBox "You must place your cursor inside of a PivotTable."
    Exit Sub
    End If


'Step 4:  Exit if more than one page field
    If pt.PageFields.Count > 1 Then
    MsgBox "Too many Report Filter Fields. Limit 1."
    Exit Sub
    End If
```

```
'Step 5:  Start looping through the page field and its pivot items
    For Each pf In pt.PageFields
        For Each pi In pf.PivotItems


'Step 6:  Change the selection in the report filter
        pt.PivotFields(pf.Name).CurrentPage = pi.Name


'Step 7: Copy the data area to a new workbook
        pt.TableRange1.Copy

        Workbooks.Add.Worksheets(1).Paste
        Application.DisplayAlerts = False

        ActiveWorkbook.SaveAs _
        Filename:="C:\Temp\" & pi.Name & ".xlsx"
        ActiveWorkbook.Close
        Application.DisplayAlerts = True


'Step 8: Get the next page field item
        Next pi
    Next pf

End Sub
```

1. Step 1 declares three variables, `pt` as the memory container for our PivotTable, `pf` as a memory container for our page fields, and `pi` to hold each pivot item as the macro loops through the `PageField` object.

2. The active cell must be inside a PivotTable for this macro to run. The assumption is that when the cursor is inside a particular PivotTable, we will want to perform the macro action on that pivot.

   Step 2 sets the `pt` variable to the name of the PivotTable on which the active cell is found. The macro does this by using the `ActiveCell.PivotTable.Name` property to get the name of the target pivot.

   If the active cell is not inside of a PivotTable, an error is thrown. This is why we use the `On Error Resume Next` statement. This tells Excel to continue with the macro if there is an error.

3. Step 3 checks to see whether the `pt` variable is filled with a PivotTable object. If the `pt` variable is set to `Nothing`, the active cell was not on a PivotTable, thus no PivotTable could be assigned to the variable. If this is the case, the macro notifies the user via a message box, and then we exit the procedure.

4. Step 4 determines whether there is more than one report filter field. If the count of `PageFields` is greater than one, there is more than one report filter. The reason we do this check is simple. We want to avoid printing reports for filters that just happen to be there. Without this check, you might wind up printing hundreds of pages. The macro stops and displays a message box if the field count is greater than 1.

    You can remove the one report filter limitation if you need to simply by deleting or commenting out Step 4 in the macro.

5. Step 5 starts two loops. The outer loop tells Excel to iterate through all the report filters. The inner loop tells Excel to loop through all the pivot items in the report filter that currently has focus.

6. For each pivot item, Step 6 captures the item name and uses it to change the report filter selection. This effectively alters the PivotTable report to match the pivot item.

7. Step 7 copies `TableRange1` of the PivotTable object. `TableRange1` is a built-in range object that points to the range of the main data area for the PivotTable. We then paste the data to a new workbook and save it. Note that you need to change the save path to one that works in your environment.

8. Step 8 moves to the next pivot item. After the macro has looped through all pivot items in the report filter, the macro moves to the next `PageField`. After all `PageFields` have been evaluated, the macro ends.

How to use it

You can implement this kind of a macro in a standard module:

1. Activate the Visual Basic Editor by pressing ALT+F11.

2. Right-click the project/workbook name in the Project window.

3. Choose Insert➜Module.

4. Type or paste the code.

Macro 77: Transpose Entire Data Range with a PivotTable

You may often encounter matrix-style data tables like the one shown in Figure 6-6. The problem is that the month headings are spread across the top of the table, pulling double duty as column labels and actual data values. In a PivotTable, this format would force you to manage and maintain 12 fields, each representing a different month.

Ideally, the data would be formatted in a more tabular format, as shown in Figure 6-7.

Market; Category	Jan	Feb	Mar
BUFFALO; Cleaning & Housekeeping Services	6,220	4,264	5,386
BUFFALO; Facility Maint and Repair	3,256	9,490	4,409
BUFFALO; Fleet Maint	5,350	8,925	6,394
BUFFALO; Green Plants and Foliage Care	2,415	2,580	2,402
BUFFALO; Landscaping/Grounds Care	5,474	4,501	5,324
BUFFALO; Predictive Maint/Preventative Main	9,811	10,180	9,626
CALIFORNIA; Cleaning & Housekeeping Service	2,841	2,997	2,097
CALIFORNIA; Facility Maint and Repair	16,251	35,879	18,369
CALIFORNIA; Fleet Maint	22,575	36,895	22,016
CALIFORNIA; Green Plants and Foliage Care	48,251	90,013	51,130
CALIFORNIA; Landscaping/Grounds Care	19,401	21,191	21,292
CALIFORNIA; Predictive Maint/Preventative M	38,712	46,073	43,950
CANADA; Facility Maint and Repair	20,308	30,149	23,963
CANADA; Fleet Maint	15,904	25,313	23,207

Figure 6-6: Matrix-style reports are often problematic in PivotTables.

	A	B	C
1	Market; Category	Month	Value
2	BUFFALO; Cleaning & Housekeeping Services	Jan	6,220
3	BUFFALO; Cleaning & Housekeeping Services	Feb	4,264
4	BUFFALO; Cleaning & Housekeeping Services	Mar	5,386
5	BUFFALO; Cleaning & Housekeeping Services	Apr	6,444
6	BUFFALO; Cleaning & Housekeeping Services	May	4,360
7	BUFFALO; Cleaning & Housekeeping Services	Jun	5,097
8	BUFFALO; Cleaning & Housekeeping Services	Jul	7,566
9	BUFFALO; Cleaning & Housekeeping Services	Aug	4,264
10	BUFFALO; Cleaning & Housekeeping Services	Sep	7,246
11	BUFFALO; Cleaning & Housekeeping Services	Oct	3,847
12	BUFFALO; Cleaning & Housekeeping Services	Nov	6,540
13	BUFFALO; Cleaning & Housekeeping Services	Dec	5,610

Figure 6-7: Tabular data sets are ideal when working with data.

There are countless methods you can use to transpose an entire data range. The macro in this section provides an easy way to automate this task.

Note

Multiple consolidation ranges can only output three base fields: Row, Column, and Value. The Row field is always made up of the first column in your data source. The Column field is made up of all the column headers after the first column in your data source. The Value field is made up of the values in your data source.

Because of this, you can only have one dimension column. To understand this, take a look at Figure 6-6. Note that the first column is essentially a concatenated column consisting of two data dimensions: Market and Category. This is because a multiple consolidation range pivot table can handle only one dimension field.

How it works

You can transpose a dataset with a multiple consolidation range PivotTable. The manual steps to do so are

1. Press Alt+D+P to call up the Excel 2003 PivotTable Wizard.

2. Click the option for Multiple Consolidation Ranges, and then click Next.

3. Select the I Will Create the Page Fields option, and then click Next.

4. Define the range you are working with and click Finish to create the PivotTable.

5. Double-click on the intersection of the Grand Total row and column.

This macro duplicates the steps above, allowing you to transpose your data set in a fraction of the time.

```
Sub Macro77()

'Step 1: Declare your Variables
    Dim SourceRange As Range
    Dim GrandRowRange As Range
    Dim GrandColumnRange As Range


'Step 2:  Define your data source range
    Set SourceRange = Sheets("Sheet1").Range("A4:M87")


'Step 3: Build Multiple Consolidation Range Pivot Table
    ActiveWorkbook.PivotCaches.Create(SourceType:=xlConsolidation, _
    SourceData:=SourceRange.Address(ReferenceStyle:=xlR1C1), _
    Version:=xlPivotTableVersion14).CreatePivotTable _
    TableDestination:="", _
    TableName:="Pvt2", _
    DefaultVersion:=xlPivotTableVersion14
```

```
'Step 4: Find the Column and Row Grand Totals
    ActiveSheet.PivotTables(1).PivotSelect "'Row Grand Total'"
    Set GrandRowRange = Range(Selection.Address)

    ActiveSheet.PivotTables(1).PivotSelect "'Column Grand Total'"
    Set GrandColumnRange = Range(Selection.Address)


'Step 5:  Drill into the intersection of Row and Column
    Intersect(GrandRowRange, GrandColumnRange).ShowDetail = True

End Sub
```

How to use it

You can implement this kind of a macro in a standard module:

1. Activate the Visual Basic Editor by pressing ALT+F11.

2. Right-click the project/workbook name in the Project window.

3. Choose Insert→Module.

4. Type or paste the code.

PART VII

Manipulating Charts with Macros

Charts are the topic of this Part. We show you how to resize them, label them, format them, and more.

In This Part

For those of us tasked with building dashboards and reports, charts are a daily part of our work life. However, few of us have had the inclination to automate any aspect of our chart work with macros. Many of us would say that there are too many scope changes and iterative adjustments in the normal reporting environment to automate charting.

On many levels, that is true, but some aspects of our work lend themselves to a bit of automation. In this Part, we explore a handful of charting macros that can help you save time and become a bit more efficient.

Tip

The code for this Part can be found on this book's companion website. See this book's Introduction for more on the companion website.

Macro 78: Resize All Charts on a Worksheet

When building a dashboard, you often want to achieve some level of symmetry and balance. This sometimes requires some level of chart size standardization. The macro in this section gives you an easy way to set a standard height and width for all your charts at once.

How it works

All charts belong to the `ChartObjects` collection. To take an action on all charts at one time, you simply iterate through all the charts in `ChartObjects`. Each chart in the `ChartObjects` collection has an index number that you can use to bring it into focus. For example, `ChartObjects(1)` points to the first chart in the sheet.

In this macro, we use this concept to loop through the charts on the active sheet with a simple counter. Each time a new chart is brought into focus, we change its height and width to the size we've defined.

```
Sub Macro78()

'Step 1: Declare your variables
    Dim i As Integer


'Step 2:  Start Looping through all the charts
    For i = 1 To ActiveSheet.ChartObjects.Count


'Step 3: Activate each chart and size
    With ActiveSheet.ChartObjects(i)
    .Width = 300
    .Height = 200
    End With
```

```
'Step 4:  Increment to move to next chart
     Next i

End Sub
```

1. Step 1 declares an integer object that is used as a looping mechanism. We call the variable `i`.

2. Step 2 starts the looping by setting `i` to count from 1 to the maximum number of charts in the `ChartObjects` collection on the active sheet. When the code starts, `i` initiates with the number 1. As we loop, the variable increments up one number until it reaches a number equal to the maximum number of charts on the sheet.

3. Step 3 passes `i` to the `ChartObjects` collection as the index number. This brings a chart into focus. We then set the width and height of the chart to the number we specify here in the code. You can change these numbers to suit your needs.

4. In Step 4, the macro loops back around to increment `i` up one number and get the next chart. After all charts have been evaluated, the macro ends.

How to use it

To implement this macro, you can copy and paste it into a standard module:

1. Activate the Visual Basic Editor by pressing ALT+F11.

2. Right-click the project/workbook name in the Project window.

3. Choose Insert→Module.

4. Type or paste the code into the newly created blank module.

Macro 79: Align a Chart to a Specific Range

Along with adjusting the size of our charts, many of us spend a good bit of time positioning them so that they align nicely in our dashboards. This macro helps easily snap your charts to defined ranges, getting perfect positioning every time.

How it works

Every chart has four properties that dictate its size and position. These properties are `Width`, `Height`, `Top`, and `Left`. Interestingly enough, every `Range` object has these same properties. So if you set a chart's `Width`, `Height`, `Top`, and `Left` properties to match that of a particular range, the chart essentially snaps to that range.

The idea is that after you have decided how you want your dashboard to be laid out, you take note of the ranges that encompass each area of your dashboard. You then use those ranges in this macro to snap each chart to the appropriate range. In this example, we adjust four charts so that their `Width`, `Height`, `Top`, and `Left` properties match a given range.

Note that we are identifying each chart with a name. Charts are, by default, named "Chart" and the order number they were added (Chart 1, Chart 2, Chart 3, and so on). You can see what each of your charts is named by clicking any chart, and then going up to the Ribbon and selecting Format➜Selection Pane. This activates a task pane (seen here in Figure 7-1) that lists all the objects on your sheet with their names.

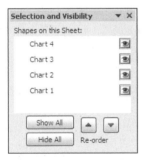

Figure 7-1: The Selection Pane allows you to see all of your chart objects and their respective names.

You can use it to get the appropriate chart names for your version of this macro.

```
Sub Macro79()

Dim SnapRange As Range

Set SnapRange = ActiveSheet.Range("B6:G19")
    With ActiveSheet.ChartObjects("Chart 1")
     .Height = SnapRange.Height
     .Width = SnapRange.Width
```

```
         .Top = SnapRange.Top
         .Left = SnapRange.Left
      End With


   Set SnapRange = ActiveSheet.Range("B21:G34")
      With ActiveSheet.ChartObjects("Chart 2")
         .Height = SnapRange.Height
         .Width = SnapRange.Width
         .Top = SnapRange.Top
         .Left = SnapRange.Left
      End With


   Set SnapRange = ActiveSheet.Range("I6:Q19")
      With ActiveSheet.ChartObjects("Chart 3")
         .Height = SnapRange.Height
         .Width = SnapRange.Width
         .Top = SnapRange.Top
         .Left = SnapRange.Left
      End With


   Set SnapRange = ActiveSheet.Range("I21:Q34")
      With ActiveSheet.ChartObjects("Chart 4")
         .Height = SnapRange.Height
         .Width = SnapRange.Width
         .Top = SnapRange.Top
         .Left = SnapRange.Left
      End With

End Sub
```

How to use it

To implement this macro, you can copy and paste it into a standard module:

1. Activate the Visual Basic Editor by pressing ALT+F11.

2. Right-click the project/workbook name in the Project window.

3. Choose Insert➜Module.

4. Type or paste the code into the newly created Module.

Macro 80: Create a Set of Disconnected Charts

When you need to copy charts from a workbook and paste them elsewhere (another workbook, PowerPoint, Outlook, and so on), it's often best to disconnect them from the original source data. This way, you won't get any of the annoying missing link messages that Excel throws. This macro copies all of the charts in the active sheet, pastes them into a new workbook, and disconnects them from the original source data.

How it works

This macro uses the `ShapeRange.Group` method to group all the charts on the active sheet into one shape. This is similar to what you would do if you were to group a set of shapes manually. After the charts are grouped, we copy the group and paste it to a new workbook. We then use the `BreakLink` method to remove references to the original source data. When we do this, Excel hard-codes the chart data into array formulas.

```
Sub Macro80()

'Step 1:  Declare your variables
Dim wbLinks As Variant

'Step 2:  Group the charts, copy the group, and then ungroup
    With ActiveSheet.ChartObjects.ShapeRange.Group
    .Copy
    .Ungroup
    End With

'Step 3:  Paste into a new workbook and ungroup
    Workbooks.Add.Sheets(1).Paste
    Selection.ShapeRange.Ungroup


'Step 4: Break the links
    wbLinks = ActiveWorkbook.LinkSources(Type:=xlLinkTypeExcelLinks)
    ActiveWorkbook.BreakLink Name:=wbLinks(1), _
                        Type:=xlLinkTypeExcelLinks

End Sub
```

1. Step 1 declares the `wbLinks` variant variable. The macro uses this in Step 4 to pass the link source when breaking the links.

2. Step 2 uses `ChartObjects.ShapeRange.Group` to group all the charts into a single shape. The macro then copies the group to the clipboard. After the group is copied, the macro ungroups the charts.

3. Step 3 creates a new workbook and pastes the copied group to Sheet 1. After the group has been pasted, we can ungroup so that each chart is separate again. Note that the newly created workbook is now the active object, so all references to ActiveWorkbook point back to this workbook.

4. Step 4 captures the link source in the `wbLinks` variable. The macro then tells Excel to break the links.

Note

Note that because this technique converts the chart source links to an array formula, this technique can fail if your chart contains too many data points. How many is too many? It can be different for every PC because it's limited by memory.

How to use it

To implement this macro, you can copy and paste it into a standard module:

1. Activate the Visual Basic Editor by pressing ALT+F11.

2. Right-click the project/workbook name in the Project window.

3. Choose Insert→Module.

4. Type or paste the code into the newly created Module.

Macro 81: Print All Charts on a Worksheet

To print a chart, you can click any embedded chart in your worksheet and then click Print. This prints the chart on its own sheet without any of the other data on the sheet. This sounds easy enough, but it can become a chore if you've got to do this for many charts. This macro makes short work of this task.

How it works

All charts belong to the `ChartObjects` collection. To take an action on all charts at one time, you simply iterate through all the charts in `ChartObjects`. Each chart in the `ChartObjects` collection has an index number that you can use to bring it into focus. For example, `ChartObjects(1)` points to the first chart in the sheet.

In this macro, we use this concept to loop through the charts on the active sheet with a simple counter. Each time a new chart is brought into focus, print it.

```
Sub Macro81()

'Step 1: Declare your variables
    Dim ChartList As Integer
    Dim i As Integer


'Step 2:  Start Looping through all the charts
    For i = 1 To ActiveSheet.ChartObjects.Count


'Step 3: Activate each chart and print
        ActiveSheet.ChartObjects(i).Activate
        ActiveChart.PageSetup.Orientation = xlLandscape
        ActiveChart.PrintOut Copies:=1


'Step 4:  Increment to move to next chart
    Next i

End Sub
```

1. Step 1 declares an integer object that is used as a looping mechanism. We call the variable `i`.

2. Step 2 starts the looping by setting `i` to count from 1 to the maximum number of charts in the `ChartObjects` collection on the active sheet. When the code starts, `i` initiates with the number 1. As we loop, the variable increments up one number until it reaches a number equal to the maximum number of charts on the sheet.

3. Step 3 passes i to the ChartObjects collection as the index number. This brings a chart into focus. We then use the ActiveChart.Printout method to trigger the print. Note that you can adjust the Orientation property to either xlLandscape or xlPortrait depending on what you need.

4. Step 4 loops back around to increment i up one number and get the next chart. After all charts have been evaluated, the macro ends.

How to use it

To implement this macro, you can copy and paste it into a standard module:

1. Activate the Visual Basic Editor by pressing ALT+F11.

2. Right-click the project/workbook name in the Project window.

3. Choose Insert→Module.

4. Type or paste the code into the newly created module.

Macro 82: Label First and Last Chart Points

One of the best practices for dashboard building is to avoid overwhelming your customers with too much data at one time — especially in a chart, where they can lose sight of the primary message if focusing on inconsequential data.

One of the common ways dashboard designers help focus the message of a chart is to limit the data labels to only the key points — typically, the first and last data points.

That being said, it is a bit arduous to continuously adjust labels every time data is added or when a new chart is needed. The macro outlined in this section automates the adding of labels to the first and last data points.

How it works

All charts have a `SeriesCollection` object that holds the various data series. This macro loops through all the series, bringing each one into focus one at a time. With the series in focus, we can use any of its many properties to manipulate it. Here, we are activating the data labels for the first and last data point in the series.

```
Sub Macro82()

'Step 1:  Declare your variables
    Dim oChart As Chart
    Dim MySeries As Series


'Step 2: Point to the active chart
    On Error Resume Next
    Set oChart = ActiveChart


'Step 3:  Exit no chart has been selected
    If oChart Is Nothing Then
    MsgBox "You select a chart first."
    Exit Sub
    End If


'Step 4: Loop through the chart series
    For Each MySeries In oChart.SeriesCollection


'Step 5: Clear ExistingData Labels
    MySeries.ApplyDataLabels (xlDataLabelsShowNone)
```

```
'Step 6:  Add labels to the first and last data point
   MySeries.Points(1).ApplyDataLabels
   MySeries.Points(MySeries.Points.Count).ApplyDataLabels
   MySeries.DataLabels.Font.Bold = True


'Step 7:  Move to the next series
   Next MySeries

End Sub
```

1. Step 1 declares two variables. We use `oChart` as the memory container for our chart. We use `MySeries` as a memory container for each series in our chart.

2. This macro is designed so that we infer the target chart based on the chart selection. That is to say, a chart must be selected for this macro to run. The assumption is that we want to perform the macro action on the chart we clicked on.

   Step 2 sets the `oChart` variable to the ActiveChart. If a chart is not selected, an error is thrown. This is why we use the `On Error Resume Next` statement. This tells Excel to continue with the macro if there is an error.

3. Step 3 checks to see if the `oChart` variable is filled with a chart object. If the `oChart` variable is set to `Nothing`, no chart was selected before running the macro. If this is the case, we tell the user in a message box, and then we exit the procedure.

4. Step 4 uses the `For...Each` statement to start looping through the series in the active charts `SeriesCollection`.

5. If data labels already exist, we need to clear them out. We can do this by using `xlDataLabelsShowNone`.

6. Each data series has a `Points` collection, which holds all the data points for the chart. Like most collections in the Excel object model, data points have index numbers.

   Step 6 of the macro uses index numbers to get to the first and last data points. The first data point is easy; we capture it by using `MySeries.Points(1)`. After we have it in focus, we can use the `ApplyDataLabels` method to turn on data labels for that one point.

   The last data label is a bit trickier. We use `MySeries.Points.Count` to get the maximum number of data points in the series. That is the index number of the last data point. We place the last data point in focus, and then we apply labels to it.

   Finally, we adjust the formatting on the data labels so they have bold font.

7. Step 7 loops back around to get the next series. After we have gone through all the data series in the chart, the macro ends.

How to use it

The best place to store this macro is in your Personal Macro Workbook. This way, the macro is always available to you. The Personal Macro Workbook is loaded whenever you start Excel. In the VBE Project window, it will be named **personal.xlsb**.

1. Activate the Visual Basic Editor by pressing ALT+F11.

2. Right-click personal.xlb in the Project window.

3. Choose Insert→Module.

4. Type or paste the code into the newly created module.

If you don't see personal.xlb in your project window, it doesn't exist yet. You'll have to record a macro, using Personal Macro Workbook as the destination.

To record the macro in your Personal Macro Workbook, select the Personal Macro Workbook option in the Record Macro dialog box before you start recording. This option is in the Store Macro In drop-down list box. Simply record a couple of cell clicks and then stop recording. You can discard the recorded macro and replace it with this one.

Macro 83: Color Chart Series to Match Source Cell Colors

When you create a dashboard, you may have specific color schemes for various types of data. For example, you may want the North region to always appear in a certain color, or you may want certain products to have a trademark color. This gives your dashboards a familiarity and consistency that makes it easier for your audience to consume.

The macro in this section allows the series in your charts to automatically adopt colors in their source range. The idea is that you can color code the cells in the source range, and then fire this macro to force the chart to apply the same colors to each respective chart series. Although it's in black and white, Figure 7-2 gives you an idea of how it works.

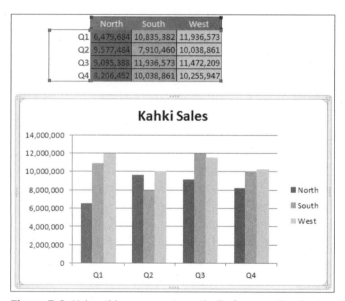

Figure 7-2: Using this macro automatically formats the chart series to match the source cells.

Note This macro cannot capture colors that have been applied via conditional formatting or table color banding. This is because conditional format coloring and table color banding are not applied directly to the cell. They are applied to objects that are separate but sit on top of the cells.

How it works

All charts have a `SeriesCollection` object that holds the various data series. In this macro, we loop through all the series, bringing each one into focus one at a time. With the series in focus, we can use any of its many properties to manipulate it.

In this case, we are setting the color to the color of the source range. We identify the source range for each series by evaluating its series formula. The series formula contains the range address of the source data. Passing that address to a range object, we can capture the exact color of cells, and then use that to color the series.

```vba
Sub Macro83()

'Step 1:  Declare your variables
    Dim oChart As Chart
    Dim MySeries As Series
    Dim FormulaSplit As Variant
    Dim SourceRangeColor As Long


'Step 2: Point to the active chart
    On Error Resume Next
    Set oChart = ActiveChart


'Step 3:  Exit no chart has been selected
    If oChart Is Nothing Then
    MsgBox "You must select a chart first."
    Exit Sub
    End If
'Step 4: Loop through the chart series
    For Each MySeries In oChart.SeriesCollection


'Step 5: Get Source Data Range for the target series
    FormulaSplit = Split(MySeries.Formula, ",")(2)


'Step 6: Capture the color in the first cell
    SourceRangeColor = Range(FormulaSplit).Item(1).Interior.Color


'Step 7: Apply Coloring
        On Error Resume Next
        MySeries.Format.Line.ForeColor.RGB = SourceRangeColor
        MySeries.Format.Line.BackColor.RGB = SourceRangeColor
        MySeries.Format.Fill.ForeColor.RGB = SourceRangeColor

        If Not MySeries.MarkerStyle = xlMarkerStyleNone Then
            MySeries.MarkerBackgroundColor = SourceRangeColor
            MySeries.MarkerForegroundColor = SourceRangeColor
        End If
```

```
'Step 8:   Move to the next series
    Next MySeries

End Sub
```

1. Step 1 declares four variables. We use `oChart` as the memory container for our chart, `MySeries` as a memory container for each series in our chart, `FormulaSplit` to capture and store the source data range, and `SourceRangeColor` to capture and store the color index for the source range.

2. This macro is designed so that we infer the target chart based on the chart selection. In other words, a chart must be selected for this macro to run. The assumption is that we will want to perform the macro action on the chart we clicked on.

   In Step 2, we set the `oChart` variable to the ActiveChart. If a chart is not selected, an error is thrown. This is why we use the `On Error Resume Next` statement. This tells Excel to continue with the macro if there is an error.

3. Step 3 checks to see whether the `oChart` variable is filled with a chart object. If the `oChart` variable is set to `Nothing`, no chart was selected before running the macro. If this is the case, we tell the user in a message box, and then we exit the procedure.

4. Step 4 uses the `For…Each` statement to start looping through the series in the active charts `SeriesCollection`.

5. Every chart series has a series formula. The series formula contains references back to the spreadsheet, pointing to the cells used to create it. A typical series formula looks something like this:

   `=SERIES(Sheet1!$F$6,Sheet1!$D$7:$D$10,Sheet1!$F$7:$F$10,2)`

   Note that there are three distinct ranges in the formula. The first range points to the series name, the second range points to the series data labels, and the third range points to the series data values.

   Step 5 uses the `Split` function to parse this formula in order to extract out the range for the series data values.

6. Step 6 captures the color index of the first cell (item) in the source data range. We assume that the first cell will be formatted the same as the rest of the range.

7. After we have the color index, we can apply the color to the various series properties.

8. In the last step, we loop back around to get the next series. After we have gone through all the data series in the chart, the macro ends.

How to use it

The best place to store this macro is in your Personal Macro Workbook. This way, the macro is always available to you. The Personal Macro Workbook is loaded whenever you start Excel. In the VBE Project window, it will be named **personal.xlsb**.

1. Activate the Visual Basic Editor by pressing ALT+F11.

2. Right-click personal.xlb in the Project window.

3. Choose Insert→Module.

4. Type or paste the code into the newly created module.

If you don't see personal.xlb in your project window, it means it doesn't exist yet. You'll have to record a macro, using Personal Macro Workbook as the destination.

To record the macro in your Personal Macro Workbook, select the Personal Macro Workbook option in the Record Macro dialog box before you start recording. This option is in the Store Macro In drop-down list box. Simply record a couple of cell clicks and then stop recording. You can discard the recorded macro and replace it with this one.

Macro 84: Color Chart Data Points to Match Source Cell Colors

In the previous macro, we force each chart series to apply the same colors as their respective source data ranges. This macro works the same way, but with data points. You would use this macro if you wanted to force a pie chart to adopt the color of each data point's source range.

Note   **This macro cannot capture colors that have been applied via conditional formatting or table color banding. This is because conditional format coloring and table color banding are not applied directly to the cell. They are applied to objects that are separate but sit on top of the cells.**

How it works

In this case, we are setting the color to the color of the source range. We identify the source range for each series by evaluating its series formula. The series formula contains the range address of the source data. Passing that address to a range object, we can capture the exact color of cells, and then use that to color the series.

```
Sub Macro84()

'Step 1:  Declare your variables
    Dim oChart As Chart
    Dim MySeries As Series
    Dim i As Integer
    Dim dValues As Variant
    Dim FormulaSplit As String


'Step 2: Point to the active chart
    On Error Resume Next
    Set oChart = ActiveChart


'Step 3:  Exit no chart has been selected
    If oChart Is Nothing Then
    MsgBox "You must select a chart first."
    Exit Sub
    End If


'Step 4: Loop through the chart series
    For Each MySeries In oChart.SeriesCollection
```

```
'Step 5: Get Source Data Range for the target series
    FormulaSplit = Split(MySeries.Formula, ",")(2)


'Step 6: Capture Series Values
    dValues = MySeries.Values


'Step 7:  Loop through series values and set color
    For i = 1 To UBound(dValues)
        MySeries.Points(i).Interior.Color = _
        Range(FormulaSplit).Cells(i).Interior.Color
    Next i


'Step 8:  Move to the next series
    Next MySeries

End Sub
```

1. Step 1 declares five variables. We use `oChart` as the memory container for our chart, `MySeries` as a memory container for each series in our chart, `dValues` in conjunction with `i` to loop through the values in the series, and `FormulaSplit` to capture and store the source data range.

2. This macro is designed so that we infer the target chart based on the chart selection. A chart must be selected for this macro to run. The assumption is that we want to perform the macro action on the chart we clicked on.

    In Step 2, we set the `oChart` variable to the ActiveChart. If a chart is not selected, an error is thrown. This is why we use the `On Error Resume Next` statement. This tells Excel to continue with the macro if there is an error.

3. In Step 3, we check to see whether the `oChart` variable is filled with a chart object. If the `oChart` variable is set to `Nothing`, no chart was selected before running the macro. If this is the case, we tell the user in a message box, and then we exit the procedure.

4. Step 4 uses the `For…Each` statement to start looping through the series in the active charts `SeriesCollection`.

5. Every chart series has a series formula. The series formula contains references back to the spreadsheet, pointing to the cells used to create it. A typical series formula looks something like this:

    `=SERIES(Sheet1!$F$6,Sheet1!$D$7:$D$10,Sheet1!$F$7:$F$10,2)`

Note that there are three distinct ranges in the formula. The first range points to the series name, the second range points to the series data labels, and the third range points to the series data values.

Step 5 uses the `Split` function to parse this formula in order to extract the range for the series data values.

6. Step 6 uses the `dValues` variant variable to capture the array of data values in the active series.

7. Step 7 starts the looping through the data points in the series. It does this by setting `i` to count from 1 to the number of data points in dValues. When the loop begins, `i` initiates with the number 1. As the macro loops, the variable increments up one number until it reaches a number equal to the maximum number of data points in the series.

   As the macro loops, it uses `i` as the index number for the Points collection, effectively exposing the properties for each data point. We then set the color index of the data point to match the color index for its corresponding source cell.

8. In the last step, the macro loops back around to get the next series. After we have gone through all the data series in the chart, the macro ends.

How to use it

The best place to store this macro is in your Personal Macro Workbook. This way, the macro is always available to you. The Personal Macro Workbook is loaded whenever you start Excel. In the VBE Project window, it will be named **personal.xlsb**.

1. Activate the Visual Basic Editor by pressing ALT+F11.

2. Right-click personal.xlb in the Project window.

3. Choose Insert➜Module.

4. Type or paste the code into the newly created module.

If you don't see personal.xlb in your project window, it doesn't exist yet. You'll have to record a macro, using Personal Macro Workbook as the destination.

To record the macro in your Personal Macro Workbook, select the Personal Macro Workbook option in the Record Macro dialog box before you start recording. This option is in the Store Macro In drop-down list box. Simply record a couple of cell clicks and then stop recording. You can discard the recorded macro and replace it with this one.

PART VIII

E-Mailing from Excel

This Part covers e-mailing from Excel: converting ranges or worksheets to attachments, saving attachments to a folder, and more.

In This Part

Did you know that you probably integrate Excel and Outlook all the time? It's true. If you've sent or received an Excel workbook through Outlook, you've integrated the two programs; albeit manually. In this Part, we show you a few examples of how you can integrate Excel and Outlook in a more automated fashion.

Note

Note that the macros in this Part automate Microsoft Outlook. For these macros to work, you need to have Microsoft Outlook installed on your system.

Tip

The code for this Part can be found on this book's companion website. See this book's Introduction for more on the companion website.

Macro 85: Mailing the Active Workbook as an Attachment

The most fundamental Outlook task you can perform through automation is sending an e-mail. In the sample code shown here, the active workbook is sent to two e-mail recipients as an attachment.

Note

Some of you may notice that we are not using the `SendMail` command native to Excel. With the `SendMail` command, you can send simple e-mail messages directly from Excel. However, the `SendMail` command is not as robust as Outlook automation. `SendMail` does not allow you to attach files, or use the CC and BCC fields in the e-mail. This makes the technique used by this macro a superior method.

How it works

Because this code will be run from Excel, we need to set a reference to the Microsoft Outlook Object Library. We can set the reference by opening the Visual Basic Editor in Excel and selecting Tools➜References. Scroll down until you find the entry Microsoft Outlook *XX* Object Library, where the *XX* is your version of Outlook. Select the check box next to the entry.

```
Sub Macro85()

'Step 1:  Declare our variables
    Dim OLApp As Outlook.Application
    Dim OLMail As Object


'Step 2:  Open Outlook start a new mail item
    Set OLApp = New Outlook.Application
```

```
    Set OLMail = OLApp.CreateItem(0)
    OLApp.Session.Logon


'Step 3:  Build our mail item and send
    With OLMail
    .To = "admin@datapigtechnologies.com; mike@datapigtechnologies.com"
    .CC = ""
    .BCC = ""
    .Subject = "This is the Subject line"
    .Body = "Sample File Attached"
    .Attachments.Add ActiveWorkbook.FullName
    .Display
    End With


'Step 4:  Memory cleanup
    Set OLMail = Nothing
    Set OLApp = Nothing

End Sub
```

1. Step 1 first declares two variables. OLApp is an object variable that exposes the Outlook Application object. OLMail is an object variable that holds a mail item.

2. Step 2 activates Outlook and starts a new session. Note that we use OLApp.Session. Logon to log on to the current MAPI (Messaging Application Programming Interface) session with default credentials. It also creates a mail item. This is equivalent to selecting the New Message button in Outlook.

3. Step 3 builds the profile of our mail item. This includes the To recipients, the CC recipients, the BCC recipients, the Subject, the Body, and the Attachments. This step notes that the recipients are entered in quotes and separates recipients with a semicolon. The standard syntax for an attachment is .Attachments.Add "File Path". Here in this code, we specify the current workbook's file path with the syntax ActiveWorkbook. Fullname. This sets the current workbook as the attachment for the e-mail. When the message has been built, we use the .Display method to review the e-mail. We can replace .Display with .Send to automatically fire the e-mail without reviewing.

4. Releasing the objects assigned to our variables is generally good practice. This reduces the chance of any problems caused by rouge objects that may remain open in memory. As we can see in the code, we simply set variable to Nothing.

How to use it

To implement this macro, we can copy and paste it into a standard module:

1. Activate the Visual Basic Editor by pressing ALT+F11.

2. Right-click the project/workbook name in the Project window.

3. Choose Insert➜Module.

4. Type or paste the code into the newly created module.

Macro 86: Mailing a Specific Range as Attachment

You may not always want to send your entire workbook through e-mail. This macro demonstrates how to send a specific range of data rather than the entire workbook.

How it works

Because this code is run from Excel, we need to set a reference to the Microsoft Outlook Object Library. We can set the reference by opening the Visual Basic Editor in Excel and selecting Tools→References. Scroll down until you find the entry Microsoft Outlook *XX* Object Library, where the *XX* is your version of Outlook. Select the check box next to the entry.

```vb
Sub Macro86()

'Step 1:  Declare our variables
    Dim OLApp As Outlook.Application
    Dim OLMail As Object


'Step 2:  Copy range, paste to new workbook, and save it
    Sheets("Revenue Table").Range("A1:E7").Copy
    Workbooks.Add
    Range("A1").PasteSpecial xlPasteValues
    Range("A1").PasteSpecial xlPasteFormats
    ActiveWorkbook.SaveAs ThisWorkbook.Path & "\TempRangeForEmail.xlsx"


'Step 3:  Open Outlook start a new mail item
    Set OLApp = New Outlook.Application
    Set OLMail = OLApp.CreateItem(0)
    OLApp.Session.Logon


'Step 4:  Build our mail item and send
    With OLMail
    .To = "admin@datapigtechnologies.com; mike@datapigtechnologies.com"
    .CC = ""
    .BCC = ""
    .Subject = "This is the Subject line"
    .Body = "Sample File Attached"
    .Attachments.Add (ThisWorkbook.Path & "\TempRangeForEmail.xlsx")
    .Display
    End With


'Step 5:  Delete the temporary Excel file
    ActiveWorkbook.Close SaveChanges:=True
```

```
    Kill ThisWorkbook.Path & "\TempRangeForEmail.xlsx"


'Step 6:  Memory cleanup
    Set OLMail = Nothing
    Set OLApp = Nothing

End Sub
```

1. Step 1 declares two variables. `OLApp` is an object variable that exposes the Outlook Application object. `OLMail` is an object variable that holds a mail item.

2. Step 2 copies a specified range and pastes the values and formats to a temporary Excel file. The macro then saves that temporary file, giving it a file path and filename.

3. Step 3 activates Outlook and starts a new session. Note that we use `OLApp.Session.Logon` to log on to the current MAPI session with default credentials. We also create a mail item. This is equivalent to selecting the New Message button in Outlook.

4. Step 4 builds the profile of the mail item. This includes the To recipients, the CC recipients, the BCC recipients, the Subject, the Body, and the Attachments. This step notes that the recipients are entered in quotes and separates recipients by a semicolon.

   Here in this code, we specify our newly created temporary Excel file path as the attachment for the e-mail. When the message has been built, we use the `.Display` method to review the e-mail. We can replace `.Display` with `.Send` to automatically fire the e-mail without reviewing.

5. We don't want to leave temporary files hanging out there, so after the e-mail has been sent, Step 5 deletes the temporary Excel file we created.

6. It is generally good practice to release the objects assigned to our variables. This reduces the chance of any problems caused by rouge objects that may remain open in memory. In Step 6, we simply set variable to `Nothing`.

How to use it

To implement this macro, we can copy and paste it into a standard module:

1. Activate the Visual Basic Editor by pressing ALT+F11.

2. Right-click the project/workbook name in the Project window.

3. Choose Insert➜Module.

4. Type or paste the code into the newly created module.

Macro 87: Mailing a Single Sheet as an Attachment

This example demonstrates how we would send a specific worksheet of data rather than the entire workbook.

How it works

Because this code is run from Excel, we need to set a reference to the Microsoft Outlook Object Library. We can set the reference by opening the Visual Basic Editor in Excel and selecting Tools→References. Scroll down until we find the entry Microsoft Outlook *XX* Object Library, where the *XX* is your version of Outlook. Place a check in the check box next to the entry.

```vba
Sub Macro87()

'Step 1:  Declare our variables
    Dim OLApp As Outlook.Application
    Dim OLMail As Object


'Step 2:  Copy Worksheet, paste to new workbook, and save it
    Sheets("Revenue Table").Copy
    ActiveWorkbook.SaveAs ThisWorkbook.Path & "\TempRangeForEmail.xlsx"


'Step 3:  Open Outlook start a new mail item
    Set OLApp = New Outlook.Application
    Set OLMail = OLApp.CreateItem(0)
    OLApp.Session.Logon


'Step 4:  Build our mail item and send
    With OLMail
    .To = "admin@datapigtechnologies.com; mike@datapigtechnologies.com"
    .CC = ""
    .BCC = ""
    .Subject = "This is the Subject line"
    .Body = "Sample File Attached"
    .Attachments.Add (ThisWorkbook.Path & "\TempRangeForEmail.xlsx")
    .Display
    End With


'Step 5:  Delete the temporary Excel file
    ActiveWorkbook.Close SaveChanges:=True
    Kill ThisWorkbook.Path & "\TempRangeForEmail.xlsx"
```

```
'Step 6:  Memory cleanup
    Set OLMail = Nothing
    Set OLApp = Nothing

End Sub
```

1. Step 1 first declares two variables. `OLApp` is an object variable that exposes the Outlook Application object. `OLMail` is an object variable that holds a mail item.

2. Step 2 copies a specified range and pastes the values and formats to a temporary Excel file. We then save that temporary file, giving it a file path and filename.

3. Step 3 activates Outlook and starts a new session. Note that we use `OLApp.Session.Logon` to log on to the current MAPI session with default credentials. We also create a mail item. This is equivalent to selecting the New Message button in Outlook.

4. Step 4 builds the profile of the mail item. This includes the To recipients, the CC recipients, the BCC recipients, the Subject, the Body, and the Attachments. The recipients are entered in quotes and separated by a semicolon.

   In this code, we specify our newly created temporary Excel file path as the attachment for the e-mail. When the message has been built, we use the `.Display` method to review the e-mail. We can replace `.Display` with `.Send` to automatically fire the e-mail without reviewing.

5. We don't want to leave temporary files hanging out there, so after the e-mail has been sent, we delete the temporary Excel file we created.

6. It is generally good practice to release the objects assigned to our variables. This reduces the chance of any problems caused by rouge objects that may remain open in memory. As we can see in the code, we simply set variable to `Nothing`.

How to use it

To implement this macro, we can copy and paste it into a standard module:

1. Activate the Visual Basic Editor by pressing ALT+F11.

2. Right-click the project/workbook name in the Project window.

3. Choose Insert➡Module.

4. Type or paste the code into the newly created module.

Macro 88: Send Mail with a Link to Our Workbook

Sometimes, you don't need to send an attachment at all. Instead, you simply want to send an automated e-mail with a link to a file. This macro does just that.

Note

Note that your users or customers will have to have at least read access to the network or location that is tied to the link.

How it works

Keep in mind that because this code will be run from Excel, we need to set a reference to the Microsoft Outlook Object Library. We can set the reference by opening the Visual Basic Editor in Excel and selecting Tools➜References. Scroll down until we find the entry Microsoft Outlook *XX* Object Library, where the *XX* is your version of Outlook. Select the check box next to the entry.

```
Sub Macro88()

'Step 1:  Declare our variables
    Dim OLApp As Outlook.Application
    Dim OLMail As Object


'Step 2:  Open Outlook start a new mail item
    Set OLApp = New Outlook.Application
    Set OLMail = OLApp.CreateItem(0)
    OLApp.Session.Logon


'Step 3:  Build our mail item and send
    With OLMail
    .To = "admin@datapigtechnologies.com; mike@datapigtechnologies.com"
    .CC = ""
    .BCC = ""
    .Subject = "Monthly Report Email with Link"
    .HTMLBody = _
    "<p>Monthly report is ready.  Click to Link to get it.</p>" & _
    "<p><a href=" & Chr(34) & "Z:\Downloads\MonthlyReport.xlsx" & _
    Chr(34) & ">Download Now</a></p>"
    .Display
    End With


'Step 4:  Memory cleanup
    Set OLMail = Nothing
    Set OLApp = Nothing

End Sub
```

1. Step 1 declares two variables. `OLApp` is an object variable that exposes the Outlook Application object. `OLMail` is an object variable that holds a mail item.

2. Step 2 activates Outlook and starts a new session. Note that we use `OLApp.Session.Logon` to log on to the current MAPI session with default credentials. This step also creates a mail item. This is equivalent to selecting the New Message button in Outlook.

3. Step 3 builds the profile of our mail item. This includes the To recipients, the CC recipients, the BCC recipients, the Subject, and the HTMLBody.

   To create the hyperlink, we need to use the `HTMLBody` property to pass HTML tags. We can replace the file path address shown in the macro with the address for our file. Note this macro is using the `.Display` method, which opens the e-mail for our review. We can replace `.Display` with `.Send` to automatically fire the e-mail without reviewing.

4. It is generally good practice to release the objects assigned to our variables. This reduces the chance of any problems caused by rouge objects that may remain open in memory. In Step 4, we simply set variable to `Nothing`.

How to use it

To implement this macro, we can copy and paste it into a standard module:

1. Activate the Visual Basic Editor by pressing ALT+F11 on our keyboard.

2. Right-click the project/workbook name in the Project window.

3. Choose Insert→Module.

4. Type or paste the code into the newly created module.

Macro 89: Mailing All E-Mail Addresses in Our Contact List

Ever need to send out a mass mailing such as a newsletter or a memo? Instead of manually entering each of our contacts' e-mail address, we can run the following procedure. In this procedure, we send out one e-mail, automatically adding all the e-mail addresses in our contact list to our e-mail.

How it works

Because this code will be run from Excel, we need to set a reference to the Microsoft Outlook Object Library. We can set the reference by opening the Visual Basic Editor in Excel and selecting Tools➜References. Scroll down until we find the entry Microsoft Outlook *XX* Object Library, where the *XX* is your version of Outlook. Select the check box next to the entry.

```
Sub Macro89()

'Step 1:  Declare our variables
    Dim OLApp As Outlook.Application
    Dim OLMail As Object
    Dim MyCell As Range
    Dim MyContacts As Range


'Step 2:  Define the range to loop through
    Set MyContacts = Sheets("Contact List").Range("H2:H21")


'Step 3:  Open Outlook
    Set OLApp = New Outlook.Application
    Set OLMail = OLApp.CreateItem(0)
    OLApp.Session.Logon


'Step 4:  Add each address in the contact list
    With OLMail

        For Each MyCell In MyContacts
         .BCC = .BCC & Chr(59) & MyCell.Value
        Next MyCell

     .Subject = "Sample File Attached"
     .Body = "Sample file is attached"
     .Attachments.Add ActiveWorkbook.FullName
     .Display
```

```
    End With


'Step 5:  Memory cleanup
    Set OLMail = Nothing
    Set OLApp = Nothing


End Sub
```

1. Step 1 declares four variables: `OLApp` is an object variable that exposes the Outlook Application object. `OLMail` is an object variable that holds a mail item. `MyCell` is an object variable that holds an Excel range. `MyContacts` is an object variable that holds an Excel range.

2. Step 2 points to the `MyContacts` variable to the range of cells that contains our e-mail addresses. This is the range of cells we loop through to add e-mail addresses to our e-mail.

3. Step 3 activates Outlook and starts a new session. Note that we use `OLApp.Session.Logon` to log on to the current MAPI session with default credentials. We also create a mail item. This is equivalent to selecting the New Message button in Outlook.

4. Step 4 builds the profile of our mail item. We note that we are looping through each cell in the `MyContacts` range and adding the contents (which are e-mail addresses) to the BCC. Here, we are using the BCC property instead of To or CC so that each recipient gets an e-mail that looks as though it was sent only to him. Our recipients won't be able to see any of the other e-mail addresses because they have been sent with BCC (Blind Courtesy Copy). Note this macro is using the `.Display` method, which opens the e-mail for our review. We can replace `.Display` with `.Send` to automatically fire the e-mail without reviewing.

5. It is generally good practice to release the objects assigned to our variables. This reduces the chance of any problems caused by rouge objects that may remain open in memory. In Step 5, we simply set the variable to `Nothing`.

How to use it

To implement this macro, we can copy and paste it into a standard module:

1. Activate the Visual Basic Editor by pressing ALT+F11 on our keyboard.

2. Right-click project/workbook name in the Project window.

3. Choose Insert➔Module.

4. Type or paste the code into the newly created module.

Macro 90: Saving All Attachments to a Folder

You may often find that certain processes lend themselves to the exchange of data via e-mail. For example, you may send a budget template out for each branch manager to fill out and send back to you via e-mail. Well, if there are 150 branch members, it could be a bit of a pain to bring down all those e-mail attachments.

The following procedure demonstrates one solution to this problem. In this procedure, we use automation to search for all attachments in the inbox and save them to a specified folder.

How it works

Because this code will be run from Excel, we need to set a reference to the Microsoft Outlook Object Library. You can set the reference by opening the Visual Basic Editor in Excel and selecting Tools➜References. Scroll down until you find the entry Microsoft Outlook *XX* Object Library, where the *XX* is your version of Outlook. Select the check box next to the entry.

```
Sub Macro90()

'Step 1:  Declare our variables
    Dim ns As Namespace
    Dim MyInbox As MAPIFolder
    Dim MItem As MailItem
    Dim Atmt As Attachment
    Dim FileName As String


'Step 2:  Set a reference to our inbox
    Set ns = GetNamespace("MAPI")
    Set MyInbox = ns.GetDefaultFolder(olFolderInbox)


'Step 3:  Check for messages in our inbox; exit if none
    If MyInbox.Items.Count = 0 Then
    MsgBox "No messages in folder."
    Exit Sub
    End If


'Step 4:  Create directory to hold attachments
    On Error Resume Next
    MkDir "C:\Temp\MyAttachments\"


'Step 5:  Start to loop through each mail item
    For Each MItem In MyInbox.Items
```

```
'Step 6:  Save each attachment then go to the next attachment
    For Each Atmt In MItem.Attachments
    FileName = "C:\Temp\MyAttachments\" & Atmt.FileName
    Atmt.SaveAsFile FileName
    Next Atmt


'Step 7:  Move to the next mail item
    Next MItem


'Step 8:  Memory cleanup
    Set ns = Nothing
    Set MyInbox = Nothing


End Sub
```

1. Step 1 declares five variables. `ns` is an object used to expose the MAPI namespace. `MyInbox` is used to expose the target mail folder. `MItem` is used to expose the properties of a mail item. `Atmt` is an object variable that holds an Attachment object. `FileName` is a string variable that holds the name of the attachment.

2. Step 2 sets the `MyInbox` variable to point to the inbox for the default mail client.

3. Step 3 performs a quick check to make sure there are actually messages in the inbox. If there are no messages, the macro exits the procedure with a message box stating that there are no messages.

4. Step 4 creates a directory to hold the attachments we find. Although you could use an existing directory, using a directory dedicated specifically for the attachments you bring down is usually best. Here, we are creating that directory on the fly. Note we are using `On Error Resume Next`. This ensures that the code does not error out if the directory we are trying to create already exists.

5. Step 5 starts the loop through each mail item in the target mail folder.

6. Step 6 ensures that each mail item we loop through gets checked for attachments. As we loop, we save each attachment we find into the specified directory we created.

7. Step 7 loops back to Step 5 until there are no more mail items to go through.

8. Releasing the objects assigned to our variables is good general practice. This reduces the chance of any problems caused by rogue objects that may remain open in memory. Step 8 simply sets the variable to `Nothing`.

How to use it

To implement this macro, we can copy and paste it into a standard module:

1. Activate the Visual Basic Editor by pressing ALT+F11.

2. Right-click the project/workbook name in the Project window.

3. Choose Insert→Module.

4. Type or paste the code into the newly created module.

Macro 91: Saving Certain Attachments to a Folder

In the previous procedure, we showed you how to use automation to search for all attachments in your inbox and save them to a specified folder. However, in most situations, you probably only want to save certain attachments; for example, those attachments attached to e-mails that contain a certain Subject. In this example, we get a demonstration of how to check for certain syntax and selectively bring down attachments.

How it works

Because this code will be run from Excel, we need to set a reference to the Microsoft Outlook Object Library. We can set the reference by opening the Visual Basic Editor in Excel and selecting Tools➜References. Scroll down until we find the entry Microsoft Outlook *XX* Object Library, where the *XX* is your version of Outlook. Select the check box next to the entry.

```
Sub Macro91()

'Step 1:  Declare our variables
    Dim ns As Namespace
    Dim MyInbox As MAPIFolder
    Dim MItem As Object
    Dim Atmt As Attachment
    Dim FileName As String
    Dim i As Integer


'Step 2:  Set a reference to our inbox
    Set ns = GetNamespace("MAPI")
    Set MyInbox = ns.GetDefaultFolder(olFolderInbox)


'Step 3:  Check for messages in our inbox; exit if none
    If MyInbox.Items.Count = 0 Then
    MsgBox "No messages in folder."
    Exit Sub
    End If


'Step 4:  Create directory to hold attachments
    On Error Resume Next
    MkDir "C:\OffTheGrid\MyAttachments\"


'Step 5:  Start to loop through each mail item
    For Each MItem In MyInbox.Items
```

```
'Step 6:  Check for the words Data Submission in Subject line
    If InStr(1, MItem.Subject, "Data Submission") < 1 Then
    GoTo SkipIt
    End If


'Step 7:  Save each with a log number; go to the next attachment
    i = 0
    For Each Atmt In MItem.Attachments
    FileName = _
    "C:\Temp\MyAttachments\Attachment-" & i & "-" & Atmt.FileName
    Atmt.SaveAsFile FileName
    i = i + 1
    Next Atmt


'Step 8:  Move to the next mail item
SkipIt:
    Next MItem


'Step 9:  Memory cleanup
    Set ns = Nothing
    Set MyInbox = Nothing


End Sub
```

1. Step 1 first declares six variables. `ns` is an object used to expose the MAPI namespace. `MyInbox` is used to expose the target mail folder. `MItem` is used to expose the properties of a mail item. `Atmt` is an object variable that holds an `Attachment` object. `FileName` is a string variable that holds the name of the attachment. `i` is an integer variable used to ensure each attachment is saved as a unique name.

2. Step 2 sets the `MyInbox` variable to point to the inbox for our default mail client.

3. Step 3 performs a quick check to make sure there are actually messages in our inbox. If there are no messages, it exits the procedure with a message box stating that there are no messages.

4. Step 4 creates a directory to hold the attachments we find. Note that it uses `On Error Resume Next`. This ensures that the code does not error out if the directory we are trying to create already exists.

5. Step 5 starts the loop through each mail item in the target mail folder.

6. In Step 6, we use the `Instr` function to check whether the string `Data Submission` is in the Subject line of the e-mail. If that string does not exist, we don't care about any attachments to that message. Therefore, we force the code to go to the `SkipIt` reference (in Step 8). Because the line of code immediately following the `SkipIt` reference is essentially a `Move Next` command, this has the effect of telling the procedure to move to the next mail item.

7. Step 7 loops through and saves each attachment into the specified directory we created. Note that we are adding a running integer to the name of each attachment. This is to ensure that each attachment is saved as a unique name, helping us to avoid overwriting attachments.

8. Step 8 loops back to Step 5 until there are no more mail items to go through.

9. Releasing the objects assigned to our variables is generally good practice. This reduces the chance of any problems caused by rouge objects that may remain open in memory. In Step 9, we simply set variable to `Nothing`.

How to use it

To implement this macro, we can copy and paste it into a standard module:

1. Activate the Visual Basic Editor by pressing ALT+F11.

2. Right-click the project/workbook name in the Project window.

3. Choose Insert➜Module.

4. Type or paste the code into the newly created module.

Integrating Excel and Other Office Applications

This Part contains macros for making Excel work with PowerPoint, Word, and Access.

In This Part

Every data-oriented process has an application flow — a succession of applications that take the data from creation to end-user. Sometimes a dataset is touched by only one application, such as when you're creating a report and presenting it in Excel. In many cases, however, data is moved from a database such as Microsoft Access, analyzed and aggregated in Excel, and then distributed via a Word document, PowerPoint presentation, or even e-mail. In this Part, we look at some of the useful macros you can implement to have Excel integrate with other Office applications.

Tip

The code for this Part can be found on this book's companion website. See this book's Introduction for more on the companion website.

Macro 92: Running an Access Query from Excel

Here's a nifty macro for those of you who often copy and paste the results of your Microsoft Access queries to Excel. In this macro, you use DAO (Data Access Object) to open and run an Access query in the background and output the results into Excel.

How it works

In this macro, you point Excel to an Access database and pull data from an existing Access query. You then store that query in a `Recordset` object, which you can use to populate your Excel spreadsheet.

Because you are automating Access, you need to set a reference to the Microsoft Access Object Library. To do so, open the VBE in Excel and select Tools➜References. The Reference dialog box opens. Scroll down until you find the entry Microsoft Access *XX* Object Library, where the *XX* is your version of Access. Select the check box next to the entry.

In addition to the Access Object Library, you need to set a reference to Microsoft DAO *XX* Object Library, where the *XX* is the version number. Note that you may see multiple versions of this library in the Reference dialog box. You should generally select the latest version of the Microsoft DAO Library available. While still in the Reference dialog box, select the check box next to the entry.

```
Sub Macro92()

'Step 1:  Declare your variables
    Dim MyDatabase As DAO.Database
    Dim MyQueryDef As DAO.QueryDef
    Dim MyRecordset As DAO.Recordset
    Dim i As Integer
```

```
'Step 2:  Identify the database and query
    Set MyDatabase = DBEngine.OpenDatabase _
                      ("C:\Temp\YourAccessDatabse.accdb")

    Set MyQueryDef = MyDatabase.QueryDefs("Your Query Name")


'Step 3:  Open the query
    Set MyRecordset = MyQueryDef.OpenRecordset


'Step 4:  Clear previous contents
        Sheets("Sheet1").Select
        ActiveSheet.Range("A6:K10000").ClearContents


'Step 5:  Copy the recordset to Excel
        ActiveSheet.Range("A7").CopyFromRecordset MyRecordset


'Step 6: Add column heading names to the spreadsheet
    For i = 1 To MyRecordset.Fields.Count
    ActiveSheet.Cells(6, i).Value = MyRecordset.Fields(i - 1).Name
    Next i

End Sub
```

1. Step 1 declares the necessary variables. The `MyDatabase` object variable exposes your Access database application via the DAO Object Library. `MyQueryDef` is also an object variable that serves as a memory container for the target query. `MyRecordset` is a `Recordset` object that holds the results of the data pull. In addition to these, the `i` integer variable is used to add column headings.

2. Step 2 specifies the database that holds your target query as well as which query will be run. Assigning the query to a `QueryDef` object allows you to essentially open the query in memory.

3. Step 3 literally runs the query in memory. The results of the query are then stored into the `MyRecordset` object. After the results are in a recordset, you can output the data to Excel.

4. Step 4 prepares for the recordset output by clearing the output area. This ensures no residual data is left from previous data pulls.

5. This step uses Excel's `CopyFromRecordset` method to get the returned dataset into the spreadsheet. In this example, the macro copies the data in the `MyRecordset` object onto Sheet1 at cell A7.

6. Finally, you enumerate through each field in the recordset to automatically get the name of each header and enter it into Excel.

How to use it

To implement this macro, you can copy and paste it into a standard module:

1. Activate the Visual Basic Editor by pressing ALT+F11.

2. Right-click the project/workbook name in the Project window.

3. Choose Insert→Module.

4. Type or paste the code into the newly created module.

Macro 93: Running an Access Macro from Excel

You can run Access macros from Excel, using automation to fire the macro without opening Access. This technique can be useful not only for running those epic macros that involve a multi-step series of 20 queries, but can also come in handy for everyday tasks like outputting a Access data to an Excel file.

How it works

The following macro is a simple way to trigger an Access macro programmatically.

Note that you will need to set a reference to the Microsoft Access Object Library. To do so, open the VBE in Excel and select Tools➜References. The Reference dialog box opens. Scroll down until you find the entry Microsoft Access *XX* Object Library, where the *XX* is your version of Access. Select the check box next to the entry.

```
Sub Macro93()

'Step 1:  Declare your variables
    Dim AC As Access.Application


'Step 2:  Start Access and open the target database
    Set AC = New Access.Application
            AC.OpenCurrentDatabase _
          ("C:\Temp\YourAccessDatabse.accdb")


'Step 3:  Open the target report and send to Word
    With AC
        .DoCmd.RunMacro "MyMacro"
        .Quit
    End With

End Sub
```

1. The first thing the macro does is declare the AC object variable. This variable exposes the Access database application library.

2. Step 2 uses the AC variable to start a new instance of Microsoft Access and open the database that houses the target macro.

3. Step 3 runs the appropriate macro and closes the database.

How to use it

To implement this macro, you can copy and paste it into a standard module:

1. Activate the Visual Basic Editor by pressing ALT+F11.

2. Right-click the project/workbook name in the Project window.

3. Choose Insert→Module.

4. Type or paste the code into the newly created module.

Macro 94: Opening an Access Report from Excel

Access reports allow you to build professional looking reports that have a clean PDF-style look and feel. If you run and distribute a great deal of Access reports, the following macro can help automate your processes.

How it works

This macro demonstrates how you can open your Access reports right from Excel. The appealing thing about this technique is that you don't see Access at all; the report goes straight to a Word rich text file.

Note that you will need to set a reference to the Microsoft Access Object Library. To do so, open the VBE in Excel and select Tools➔References. The Reference dialog box opens. Scroll down until you find the entry Microsoft Access *XX* Object Library, where *XX* is your version of Access. Select the check box next to the entry.

```
Sub Macro94()

'Step 1:  Declare your variables
    Dim AC As Access.Application


'Step 2:  Start Access and open the target database
    Set AC = New Access.Application
            AC.OpenCurrentDatabase _
        ("C:\Temp\YourAccessDatabase.accdb")


'Step 3:  Open the target report as a Word rich text file
    With AC
        .DoCmd.OpenReport "Revenue Report", acViewPreview
        .DoCmd.RunCommand acCmdOutputToRTF
        .Quit
    End With

End Sub
```

1. Step 1 declares the `AC` object variable. This variable exposes the Access database application library.

2. In Step 2, the `AC` variable starts a new instance of Microsoft Access and opens the database that houses the target report.

3. Step 3 simply runs the appropriate report, sending the output to a Microsoft Word rich text file. After the file is output, the database closes.

How to use it

To implement this macro, you can copy and paste it into a standard module

1. Activate the Visual Basic Editor by pressing ALT+F11.

2. Right-click project/workbook name in the Project window.

3. Choose Insert→Module.

4. Type or paste the code into the newly created module.

Macro 95: Opening an Access Form from Excel

In some instances, you or your clients may need to switch focus to an Access form. This example demonstrates how you can open an Access form from Excel.

How it works

With this macro, you point Excel to an Access database and trigger a specific Access form to open.

Because you are automating Access, you need to set a reference to the Microsoft Access Object Library. To do so, open the VBE in Excel and select Tools➜References. The Reference dialog box activates. Scroll down until you find the entry Microsoft Access *XX* Object Library, where the *XX* is your version of Access. Select the check box next to the entry.

```vba
Sub Macro95()

'Step 1:  Declare your variables
    Dim AC As Access.Application


'Step 2:  Start Access and open the target database
    Set AC = New Access.Application
            AC.OpenCurrentDatabase _
        ("C:\Temp\YourAccessDatabase.accdb")


'Step 3:  Open the target form and make Access visible
    With AC
        .DoCmd.OpenForm "MainForm", acNormal
        .Visible = True
    End With

End Sub
```

1. Step 1 declares the AC object variable. This variable exposes the Access database application library.

2. Step 2 uses the AC variable to start a new instance of Microsoft Access and opens the database that houses the target form.

3. Step 3 opens the appropriate form. The Access form opens in a new Microsoft Access window. Note that you are not closing the database in the last line of Step 3 (as with the previous macros). Instead, you make the Access application visible.

How to use it

To implement this macro, you can copy and paste it into a standard module:

1. Activate the Visual Basic Editor by pressing ALT+F11.

2. Right-click project/workbook name in the Project window

3. Choose Insert→Module.

4. Type or paste the code into the newly created module.

Macro 96: Compacting an Access Database from Excel

During your integrated processes, you may routinely increase or decrease the number of records and tables in your database. As time goes on, you may notice that your Access database gets bigger. This is because Access does not release file space. All the space needed for the data you move in and out of your database is held by your Access file, regardless of whether the data is still there. In that light, it's critical that you run Compact and Repair on your Access database regularly. Among other things, running Compact and Repair defragments your database, releasing any unused space and ensuring your database does not grow to an unmanageable size. Office automation enables you to Compact and Repair your databases right from code.

How it works

When you compact and repair an Access database manually, it seems as though Access compresses your original database; this is not the case. Access is really doing nothing more than creating a copy of your Access database (minus the empty file space) and deleting the old file.

This macro essentially mimics those actions in order to programmatically Compact and Repair an Access application.

Note that in order to use this code, you need to set a reference to the Microsoft Access Object Library. To do so, open the VBE in Excel and select Tools→References. The Reference dialog box opens. Scroll down until you find the entry Microsoft Access *XX* Object Library, where the *XX* is your version of Access. Select the check box next to the entry.

```
Sub Macro96()

'Step 1:  Declare your variables
    Dim OriginalFile As String
    Dim BackupFile As String
    Dim TempFile As String


'Step 2:  Identify the target database assign file paths
    OriginalFile = "C:\Temp\MyDatabase.accdb"
    BackupFile = "C:\Temp\MyDatabaseBackup.accdb"
    TempFile = "C:\Temp\MyDatabaseTemporary.accdb"


'Step 3:  Make a backup copy of database
    FileCopy OriginalFile, BackupFile


'Step 4:  Perform the compact and repair
    DBEngine.CompactDatabase OriginalFile, TempFile
```

```
'Step 5:   Delete the old database
    Kill OriginalFile


'Step 6:   Rename the temporary database to the old database name
    Name TempFile As OriginalFile

End Sub
```

1. Step 1 declares three string variables that hold filenames.

2. Step 2 then assigns each of the string variables a filename. The `OriginalFile` variable is assigned the file path and name of the target database. The `BackupFile` variable is assigned the file path and name of a backup file we will create during this procedure. The `TempFile` variable is assigned the file path and name of a temporary file we create during this procedure.

3. Step 3 uses the `FileCopy` function to make a backup of the `OriginalFile` (the target database). Although this step is not necessary for the Compact and Repair procedure, it's generally a good practice to make a backup of your database before running this level of VBA on it.

4. Step 4 executes the Compact and Repair, specifying the original database and specifying the file path of the temporary database.

5. At this point, you have two copies of your database: the original database and a second database, which is a copy of your original without the empty file space. Step 5 deletes the original database, leaving you with the copy.

6. Step 6 simply renames the temporary file, giving it the name of your original database. This leaves you with a database that is compact and optimized.

How to use it

To implement this macro, you can copy and paste it into a standard module:

1. Activate the Visual Basic Editor by pressing ALT+F11.

2. Right-click the project/workbook name in the Project window.

3. Choose Insert→Module.

4. Type or paste the code.

Macro 97: Sending Excel Data to a Word Document

If you find that you are constantly copying and pasting data into Microsoft Word, you can use a macro to automate this task.

How it works

Before walking through the macro, it's important to go over a few set-up steps.

To get ready for a process like this, you must have a template Word document already created. In that document, create a bookmark tagging the location where you want your Excel data to be copied.

To create a bookmark in a Word document, place your cursor where you want the bookmark, select the Insert tab, and select Bookmark (found under the Links group). This activates the Bookmark dialog box where you assign a name for your bookmark. After the name has been assigned, click the Add button.

Tip

One of the sample files for this Part is a document called PasteTable.docx. This document is a simple template that contains one bookmark called DataTableHere. In this sample code, you copy a range to that PasteTable.docx template, using the DataTableHere bookmark to specify where to paste the copied range.

You also need to set a reference to the Microsoft Word Object Library. To do so, open the Visual Basic Editor in Excel and select Tools→References. The Reference dialog box opens. Scroll down until you find the entry Microsoft Word *XX* Object Library, where the *XX* is your version of Word. Select the check box next to the entry.

```
Sub Macro97()

'Step 1:  Declare your variables
    Dim MyRange As Excel.Range
    Dim wd As Word.Application
    Dim wdDoc As Word.Document
    Dim WdRange As Word.Range


'Step 2:  Copy the defined range
    Sheets("Revenue Table").Range("B4:F10").Copy


'Step 3:  Open the target Word document
    Set wd = New Word.Application
    Set wdDoc = wd.Documents.Open _
```

```
    (ThisWorkbook.Path & "\" & "PasteTable.docx")
    wd.Visible = True


'Step 4:  Set focus on the target bookmark
    Set WdRange = wdDoc.Bookmarks("DataTableHere").Range


'Step 5:  Delete the old table and paste new
    On Error Resume Next
    WdRange.Tables(1).Delete
    WdRange.Paste 'paste in the table


'Step 6:  Adjust column widths
    WdRange.Tables(1).Columns.SetWidth _
    (MyRange.Width / MyRange.Columns.Count), wdAdjustSameWidth


'Step 7:  Reinsert the bookmark
    wdDoc.Bookmarks.Add "DataTableHere", WdRange


'Step 8:  Memory cleanup
    Set wd = Nothing
    Set wdDoc = Nothing
    Set WdRange = Nothing


End Sub
```

1. Step 1 declares four variables: `MyRange` contains the target Excel range you want copied; `wd` is an object variable that exposes the `Word Application` object; `wdDoc` is an object variable that exposes the `Word Document` object; and `wdRange` is an object variable that exposes the `Word Range` object.

2. Step 2 copies a range from the Revenue Table worksheet. In this example, the range is hard-coded, but we can always make this range into something more variable.

3. Step 3 opens an existing target Word document that serves as a template. Note that we are setting the `Visible` property of the Word application to `True`. This ensures that we can see the action in Word as the code runs.

4. Step 4 uses Word's `Range` object to set focus on the target bookmark. This essentially selects the bookmark as a range, allowing you to take actions in that range.

5. Step 5 deletes any table that may exist within the bookmark, and then pastes the copied Excel range. If we don't delete any existing tables first, the copied range is appended to the existing data.

6. When you're pasting an Excel range into a Word document, the column widths don't always fit the content in the cells appropriately. Step 6 fixes this issue by adjusting the column widths. Here, each column's width is set to a number that equals the total width of the table divided by the number of columns in the table.

7. When we paste an Excel range to the target bookmark, we essentially overwrite the bookmark. Step 7 re-creates the bookmark to ensure that the next time you run this code, the bookmark is there.

8. Finally, the macro releases the objects assigned to the variables, reducing the chance of any problems caused by rogue objects that may remain open in memory.

How to use it

To implement this macro, you can copy and paste it into a standard module:

1. Activate the Visual Basic Editor by pressing ALT+F11.

2. Right-click the project/workbook name in the Project window.

3. Choose Insert→Module.

4. Type or paste the code in the newly created module.

Macro 98: Simulating Mail Merge with a Word Document

One of the most requested forms of integration with Word is the mail merge. In most cases, *mail merge* refers to the process of creating one letter or document and then combining it with a separate document containing their names and addresses. For example, suppose you had a list of customers and you wanted to compose a letter to each customer. With mail merge, you can write the body of the letter one time, and then run the mail merge feature in Word to automatically create a letter for each customer, affixing the appropriate, address, name and other information to each letter.

For you automation buffs, you can use a macro to simulate the Word mail merge function from Excel.

How it works

The idea is relatively simple. You start with a template that contains bookmarks identifying where each element of contact information should go. After the template is ready, the idea is to simply loop through each contact in your contact list, assigning the component pieces of their contact information to the respective bookmarks.

Tip

One of the sample files for this Part is a document called MailMerge.docx. This document has all the bookmarks needed to run the sample code shown here.

Note that you will need to set a reference to the Microsoft Word Object Library. To do so, open the Visual Basic Editor in Excel and select Tools→References. The Reference dialog box opens. Scroll down until you find the entry Microsoft Word *XX* Object Library, where the *XX* is your version of Word. Select the check box next to the entry.

```
Sub Macro98()

'Step 1:  Declare your variables
    Dim wd As Word.Application
    Dim wdDoc As Word.Document
    Dim MyRange As Excel.Range
    Dim MyCell As Excel.Range
    Dim txtAddress As String
    Dim txtCity As String
    Dim txtState As String
    Dim txtPostalCode As String
    Dim txtFname As String
    Dim txtFullname As String
```

```
'Step 2:  Start Word and add a new document
    Set wd = New Word.Application
    Set wdDoc = wd.Documents.Add
    wd.Visible = True


'Step 3:  Set the range of your contact list
    Set MyRange = Sheets("Contact List").Range("A5:A24")


'Step 4:  Start the loop through each cell
    For Each MyCell In MyRange.Cells


'Step 5:  Assign values to each component of the letter
    txtAddress = MyCell.Value
    txtCity = MyCell.Offset(, 1).Value
    txtState = MyCell.Offset(, 2).Value
    txtPostalCode = MyCell.Offset(, 3).Value
    txtFname = MyCell.Offset(, 5).Value
    txtFullname = MyCell.Offset(, 6).Value



'Step 6:  Insert the structure of template document
    wd.Selection.InsertFile _
    ThisWorkbook.Path & "\" & "MailMerge.docx"


'Step 7:  Fill each relevant bookmark with respective value
    wd.Selection.Goto What:=wdGoToBookmark, Name:="Customer"
    wd.Selection.TypeText Text:=txtFullname

    wd.Selection.Goto What:=wdGoToBookmark, Name:="Address"
    wd.Selection.TypeText Text:=txtAddress

    wd.Selection.Goto What:=wdGoToBookmark, Name:="City"
    wd.Selection.TypeText Text:=txtCity

    wd.Selection.Goto What:=wdGoToBookmark, Name:="State"
    wd.Selection.TypeText Text:=txtState

    wd.Selection.Goto What:=wdGoToBookmark, Name:="Zip"
    wd.Selection.TypeText Text:=txtPostalCode

    wd.Selection.Goto What:=wdGoToBookmark, Name:="FirstName"
    wd.Selection.TypeText Text:=txtFname


'Step 8:  Clear any remaining bookmarks
    On Error Resume Next
```

```
    wdDoc.Bookmarks("Address").Delete
    wdDoc.Bookmarks("Customer").Delete
    wdDoc.Bookmarks("City").Delete
    wdDoc.Bookmarks("State").Delete
    wdDoc.Bookmarks("FirstName").Delete
    wdDoc.Bookmarks("Zip").Delete


'Step 9:  Go to the end, insert new page, and start with the next cell
    wd.Selection.EndKey Unit:=wdStory
    wd.Selection.InsertBreak Type:=wdPageBreak
    Next MyCell


'Step 10:  Set cursor to beginning and clean up memory
    wd.Selection.HomeKey Unit:=wdStory
    wd.Activate
    Set wd = Nothing
    Set wdDoc = Nothing

End Sub
```

1. Step 1 declares four variables: wd is an object variable that exposes the Word Application object, wdDoc is an object variable that exposes the Word Document object, MyRange contains the range defining the contact list, and MyCell is used to pass cell values into the string variables. We also declare six string variables. Each of the string variables holds a component piece of information for each contact in the contact list.

2. This step opens Word with a blank document. Note that we set the Visible property of the Word application to True. This ensures that we can see the action in Word as the code runs.

3. Step 3 defines each contact in the contact list. Note that this range only selects the first column in the contacts table. This is because each cell in the range must be passed individually to string variables. Selecting only the first column gives us one cell per row. From that one cell, we can easily adjust the cursor to the right or left to capture the cells around it. The idea is that if we move to the right one space, we get the value of the next field in that row. If we move to the right two spaces, we get the value of *that* field, and so on.

4. This step starts the loop through each contact as defined in the range set in Step 3.

5. Step 5 uses Excel's Offset method to capture the value of each field in a particular row. We start with the range defined in Step 3 (the first column in the list of contacts). We then use Offset to move the cursor a certain number of columns to the right to capture the data in each relevant field. As each field is covered, we assign their values to the appropriate string variable.

6. In Step 6, we insert the existing template into the empty document in Word. This is tantamount to copying the structure of our template and pasting it into a blank document.

7. Step 7 assigns the value of each string variable to its respective bookmark. As you can see in the code, this step selects the bookmark by name, and then changes the text to equal the value of the assigned string variable.

8. The goal in Step 8 is to remove any stray bookmarks. If any bookmarks linger, we get duplicate bookmarks as the procedure loops through each cell.

9. At this point in the code, we have created a document for one contact in our list of contacts. The idea now is to create a new blank document so that we can perform the same procedure for the next contact. Inserting a page break effectively creates the new blank document. We then loop back to Step 5, where we pick up the contact information for the next row in the list. Then at Step 6, we insert the blank template (complete with bookmarks) into the new page. Finally, we assign values to the bookmarks and clean up. The For…Next loop ensures that this cycle is repeated for each row in the contact list.

10. Step 10 releases the objects assigned to your variables, reducing the chance of any problems caused by rogue objects that may remain open in memory.

How to use it

To implement this macro, you can copy and paste it into a standard module:

1. Activate the Visual Basic Editor by pressing ALT+F11.

2. Right-click the project/workbook name in the Project window.

3. Choose Insert➜Module.

4. Type or paste the code in the newly created module.

Macro 99: Sending Excel Data to a PowerPoint Presentation

It's been said that up to 50 percent of PowerPoint presentations contain data that has been copied straight out of Excel. This is not difficult to believe. It's often much easier to analyze and create charts and data views in Excel than in PowerPoint. After you've created those charts and data views, why wouldn't you simply move them into PowerPoint? The macro in this section allows you to dynamically create PowerPoint slides that contain data from a range you specify.

How it works

In this example, you are copying a range from an Excel file and pasting that range to a slide in a newly created PowerPoint presentation.

Keep in mind that because this code is run from Excel, you need to set a reference to the Microsoft PowerPoint Object Library. Again, you can set the reference by opening the Visual Basic Editor in Excel and selecting Tools➞References. Scroll down until you find the entry Microsoft PowerPoint *XX* Object Library, where the *XX* is your version of PowerPoint. Select the check box next to the entry.

```
Sub CopyRangeToPresentation ()

'Step 1:  Declare your variables
    Dim PP As PowerPoint.Application
    Dim PPPres As PowerPoint.Presentation
    Dim PPSlide As PowerPoint.Slide
    Dim SlideTitle As String


'Step 2:  Open PowerPoint and create new presentation
    Set PP = New PowerPoint.Application
    Set PPPres = PP.Presentations.Add
    PP.Visible = True


'Step 3:  Add new slide as slide 1 and set focus to it
    Set PPSlide = PPPres.Slides.Add(1, ppLayoutTitleOnly)
    PPSlide.Select


'Step 4:  Copy the range as a picture
    Sheets("Slide Data").Range("A1:J28").CopyPicture _
    Appearance:=xlScreen, Format:=xlPicture
```

```
'Step 5:  Paste the picture and adjust its position
    PPSlide.Shapes.Paste.Select
    PP.ActiveWindow.Selection.ShapeRange.Align msoAlignCenters, True
    PP.ActiveWindow.Selection.ShapeRange.Align msoAlignMiddles, True


'Step 6:  Add the title to the slide
    SlideTitle = "My First PowerPoint Slide"
    PPSlide.Shapes.Title.TextFrame.TextRange.Text = SlideTitle


'Step 7:  Memory Cleanup
    PP.Activate
    Set PPSlide = Nothing
    Set PPPres = Nothing
    Set PP = Nothing

End sub
```

1. Step 1 declares four variables: `PP` is an object variable that exposes the PowerPoint Application object; `PPPres` is an object variable that exposes the PowerPoint Presentation object; `PPSlide` is an object variable that exposes the PowerPoint Slide object; and `SlideTitle` is an string variable used to pass the text for the slide title.

2. Step 2 opens PowerPoint with an empty presentation. Note that we are setting the `Visible` property of the PowerPoint application to `True`. This ensures that you can see the action as the code runs.

3. Step 3 adds a new slide to the presentation using the `Add` method of `Slide` object. Note that we are using the `ppLayoutTitleOnly`, ensuring the slide is created with a title text frame. We then take an extra step here and actually set focus on the slide. That is to say, we explicitly tell PowerPoint to select this slide, making it active.

4. Step 4 uses the `CopyPicture` method to copy the target range as a picture. The range being copied here is range A1 to J28 in the Slide Data tab.

5. Step 5 pastes the picture into the active slide and centers the picture both horizontally and vertically.

6. Step 6 stores the text for the title in a string variable, and then passes that variable to PowerPoint to apply text to the title text frame.

7. Step 7 releases the objects assigned to our variables, reducing the chance of any problems caused by rogue objects that may remain open in memory.

How to use it

To implement this macro, you can copy and paste it into a standard module:

1. Activate the Visual Basic Editor by pressing ALT+F11.

2. Right-click the project/workbook name in the Project window.

3. Choose Insert➜Module.

4. Type or paste the code.

Macro 100: Sending All Excel Charts to a PowerPoint Presentation

It's not uncommon to see multiple charts on one worksheet. Many of us occasionally need to copy our charts to PowerPoint presentations. The macro here assists in that task, effectively automating the process of copying each one of these charts into its own slide.

How it works

In this macro, we loop through the `ActiveSheet.ChartObjects` collection to copy each chart as a picture into its own page in a newly created PowerPoint presentation.

Keep in mind that because this code will be run from Excel, you need to set a reference to the Microsoft PowerPoint Object Library. Again, you can set the reference by opening the Visual Basic Editor in Excel and selecting Tools➜References. Scroll down until you find the entry Microsoft PowerPoint *XX* Object Library, where the *XX* is your version of PowerPoint. Select the check box next to the entry.

```
Sub CopyAllChartsToPresentation()

'Step 1:  Declare your variables
    Dim PP As PowerPoint.Application
    Dim PPPres As PowerPoint.Presentation
    Dim PPSlide As PowerPoint.Slide
    Dim i As Integer

'Step 2:  Check for charts; exit if no charts exist
    Sheets("Slide Data").Select
    If ActiveSheet.ChartObjects.Count < 1 Then
    MsgBox "No charts existing the active sheet"
    Exit Sub
    End If

'Step 3:  Open PowerPoint and create new presentation
    Set PP = New PowerPoint.Application
    Set PPPres = PP.Presentations.Add
    PP.Visible = True

'Step 4:  Start the loop based on chart count
    For i = 1 To ActiveSheet.ChartObjects.Count

'Step 5:  Copy the chart as a picture
    ActiveSheet.ChartObjects(i).Chart.CopyPicture _
    Size:=xlScreen, Format:=xlPicture
    Application.Wait (Now + TimeValue("0:00:1"))
```

```
'Step 6:  Count slides and add new slide as next available slide number
   ppSlideCount = PPPres.Slides.Count
   Set PPSlide = PPPres.Slides.Add(SlideCount + 1, ppLayoutBlank)
   PPSlide.Select

'Step 7:  Paste the picture and adjust its position; Go to next chart
   PPSlide.Shapes.Paste.Select
   PP.ActiveWindow.Selection.ShapeRange.Align msoAlignCenters, True
   PP.ActiveWindow.Selection.ShapeRange.Align msoAlignMiddles, True
   Next i

'Step 8:  Memory Cleanup
   Set PPSlide = Nothing
   Set PPPres = Nothing
   Set PP = Nothing

End Sub
```

1. Step 1 declares four variables: `PP` is an object variable that exposes the PowerPoint Application object; `PPPres` is an object variable that exposes the PowerPoint Presentation object; `PPSlide` is an object variable that exposes the PowerPoint Slide object; and `i` is used as a counter to help loop through the charts in the worksheet.

2. Step 2 does an administrative check to ensure that there are actually charts in the specified worksheet. If no charts are found, the macro exits the procedure with no further action.

3. Step 3 opens PowerPoint with an empty presentation. Note that we are setting the `Visible` property of the PowerPoint application to `True`. This ensures that we can see the action as the code runs.

4. Step 4 establishes how many times the macro will go through the procedure by capturing the number of charts in the worksheet. In other words, if the worksheet contains five charts, the code will loop five times. The macro starts the loop with one and keeps looping through the procedure until we hit the number of charts in the worksheet. The variable `i` ultimately represents the chart number we are currently on.

5. Step 5 uses the `CopyPicture` method to copy the chart as a picture. The variable `i` passes the actual chart number we are currently working with. The `Application.Wait` method tells the macro to pause for a second, allowing the clipboard to catch up with all the copying going on.

6. Step 6 adds a new slide to the presentation using the `Add` method of the `Slide` object. Note that we are using `SlideCount+1` to specify the index number of the added slide. Because we are looping through an unknown number of charts, we can't hard-code the index number for each slide. Using `SlideCount+1` allows us to dynamically assign the next available number as the slide index. Note that in Step 6, we are using `ppLayout Blank`, ensuring that the newly created slides start with a blank layout. The macro then

takes an extra step here and actually sets focus on the slide. In other words, the code explicitly tells PowerPoint to select this slide, making it active.

7. Step 7 pastes the picture into the active slide, centers the picture both horizontally and vertically, and then moves to the next chart.

8. Step 8 releases the objects assigned to your variables, reducing the chance of any problems caused by rouge objects that may remain open in memory.

How to use it

To implement this macro, you can copy and paste it into a standard module:

1. Activate the Visual Basic Editor by pressing ALT+F11.

2. Right-click the project/workbook name in the Project window.

3. Choose Insert➜Module.

4. Type or paste the code.

Macro 101: Convert a Workbook into a PowerPoint Presentation

This macro takes the concept of using Excel data in PowerPoint to the extreme. Open the sample workbook called Macro 101 Convert a Workbook into a PowerPoint Presentation.xlsm. In this workbook, notice that each worksheet contains its own data about a region. It's almost like each worksheet is its own separate slide, providing information on a particular region.

The idea here is that you can build a workbook in such a way that it mimics a PowerPoint presentation; the workbook is the presentation itself and each worksheet becomes a slide in the presentation. After you do that, you can easily convert that workbook into an actual PowerPoint presentation using a bit of automation.

With this technique, you can build entire presentations in Excel, where you have better analytical and automation tools. Then you can simply convert the Excel version of your presentation to a PowerPoint presentation.

How it works

Before you implement this macro in your workbook, you need to set a reference to the Microsoft PowerPoint Object Library. Again, you can set the reference by opening the Visual Basic Editor in Excel and selecting Tools➜References. Scroll down until you find the entry Microsoft PowerPoint *XX* Object Library, where the *XX* is your version of PowerPoint. Select a check box next to the entry.

```
Sub Macro101()

'Step 1:  Declare your variables
    Dim pp As PowerPoint.Application
    Dim PPPres As PowerPoint.Presentation
    Dim PPSlide As PowerPoint.Slide
    Dim xlwksht As Excel.Worksheet
    Dim MyRange As String
    Dim MyTitle As String


'Step 2:  Open PowerPoint, add a new presentation and make visible
    Set pp = New PowerPoint.Application
    Set PPPres = pp.Presentations.Add
    pp.Visible = True


'Step 3:  Set the ranges for your data and title
    MyRange = "A1:I27"
```

```
'Step 4:  Start the loop through each worksheet
    For Each xlwksht In ActiveWorkbook.Worksheets
    xlwksht.Select
    Application.Wait (Now + TimeValue("0:00:1"))
    MyTitle = xlwksht.Range("C19").Value

'Step 5:  Copy the range as picture
    xlwksht.Range(MyRange).CopyPicture _
    Appearance:=xlScreen, Format:=xlPicture

'Step 6:  Count slides and add new slide as next available slide number
    SlideCount = PPPres.Slides.Count
    Set PPSlide = PPPres.Slides.Add(SlideCount + 1, ppLayoutTitleOnly)
    PPSlide.Select

'Step 7:  Paste the picture and adjust its position
    PPSlide.Shapes.Paste.Select
    pp.ActiveWindow.Selection.ShapeRange.Align msoAlignCenters, True
    pp.ActiveWindow.Selection.ShapeRange.Top = 100

'Step 8:  Add the title to the slide then move to next worksheet
    PPSlide.Shapes.Title.TextFrame.TextRange.Text = MyTitle
    Next xlwksht

'Step 9:  Memory Cleanup
    pp.Activate
    Set PPSlide = Nothing
    Set PPPres = Nothing
    Set pp = Nothing

End Sub
```

1. Step 1 declares six variables: PP is an object variable that exposes the PowerPoint Application object; PPPres is an object variable that exposes the PowerPoint Presentation object; PPSlide is an object variable that exposes the PowerPoint Slide object; xlwksht is an object variable that exposes the Worksheet object; MyRange is a string variable used to store and pass a range name as a string; and MyTitle is a string variable used to store and pass a title for each slide.

2. Step 2 opens PowerPoint with an empty presentation. Note that we are setting the Visible property of the PowerPoint application to True. This ensures that we can see the action as the code runs.

3. Step 3 fills the MyRange variable with a string representing the range we want to capture as the slide content. We also fill the MyTitle variable with the value of cell C19. The value here becomes the title for the slide.

4. Step 4 starts the loop through each worksheet in the workbook. The loop stops when all worksheets have been looped through. Note that we are using the `Application.Wait` method, telling the macro to pause for a second. This allows the chart to render completely before the range is copied.

5. Step 5 uses the `CopyPicture` method to copy our specified range as a picture.

6. Step 6 adds a new slide to the presentation using the `Add` method of the `Slide` object. Note that we are using `SlideCount+1` to specify the index number of the added slide. Using `SlideCount+1` allows us to dynamically assign the next available number as the slide index. Also note that we are using `ppLayoutTitleOnly`, ensuring our slide is created with a title text frame.

7. Step 7 pastes the picture into the active slide, centers the picture horizontally, and adjusts the picture vertically 100 pixels from the top margin.

8. Step 8 passes the `MyTitle` variable to apply text to the title text frame.

9. Step 9 releases the objects assigned to the variables, reducing the chance of any problems caused by rogue objects that may remain open in memory.

How to use it

To implement this macro, you can copy and paste it into a standard module:

1. Activate the Visual Basic Editor by pressing ALT+F11.

2. Right-click the project/workbook name in the Project window.

3. Choose Insert➜Module.

4. Type or paste the code.

Index

Symbols

& (ampersand), 157, 162

A

absolute references, recording macros with, 11–13

`AC` variable, 278, 280, 282

Access, Microsoft

    compacting database from Excel, 284–285

    opening form from Excel, 282–283

    opening report from Excel, 280–281

    running macro from Excel, 278–279

    running query from Excel, 275–277

Access Object Library, 275

activating VBE, 9, 19

active rows and columns, highlighting, 101–102

active workbook, mailing as attachment, 255–257

active worksheet

    deleting all worksheets except, 75–76

    hiding all worksheets except, 77–78

`ActiveCell.PivotTable.Name` property

    data field titles, adjusting all PivotTable, 203

    PivotTable data items, applying number formatting for all, 208

    PivotTable data items, setting all to Sum, 205

    report filter items, creating new workbook for each, 227

    report filter items, printing PivotTable for each, 224

    restrictions, pivot field, 218

    restrictions, PivotTable, 216

    sorting PivotTable fields in alphabetical order, 212

    subtotals in PivotTable, hiding all, 201

`ActiveChart.Printout` method, 242

`ActiveSheet` object

    AutoFilter, creating new sheet for each item in, 179

    `Name` property, 74

    new workbook, creating from scratch, 40

    `UsedRange` property, 118–119, 120–121, 167

`ActiveSheet.ChartObjects` collection, 296

`ActiveSheet.PrintOut` method, 223

`ActiveWorkbook` object

    deleting all but active worksheet, 75

    hiding all but active worksheet, 77

    refreshing all PivotTables in workbook, 192

    versus `ThisWorkbook`, 59

`ActiveWorkbook.Fullname` syntax, 256

ActiveX controls, 19

`Add` method

    new worksheet, adding, 74

    `Slide` object, 294, 297, 301

    Workbook object, 40

`Address` properties, 102

addresses in contact list, mailing all, 264–265

`AF` variable, 184

`AF.Filters` object, 184–185

`After` argument, `Move` method, 81

aligning chart to specific range, 237–238

alphabetical order

    sorting all PivotTable fields in, 211–212

    sorting worksheets by name, 83–84

alternate color banding, applying, 128–129

ampersand (&), 157, 162

appending text to left or right of cells, 161–162

application flow, 275

`Application` object, 32

`Application.ConvertFormula` function, 209

applications, Office, integrating Excel with. *See also* Outlook, integrating with Excel

    Access database, compacting from Excel, 284–285

    Access form, opening from Excel, 282–283

    Access macro, running from Excel, 278–279

    Access query, running from Excel, 275–277

    Access report, opening from Excel, 280–281

    overview, 4, 275

    PowerPoint presentation, converting workbook into, 299–301

    PowerPoint presentation, sending all Excel charts to, 296–298

    PowerPoint presentation, sending Excel data to, 293–295

    Word document, sending Excel data to, 286–288

    Word document, simulating mail merge with, 289–292

`Application.Wait` method, 297, 301

`ApplyDataLabels` method, 244

area code, appending to cells, 161–162

D

Z

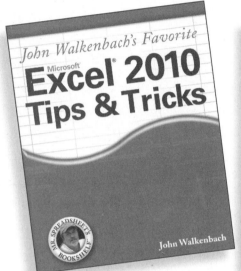
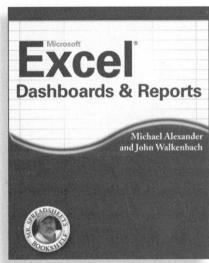
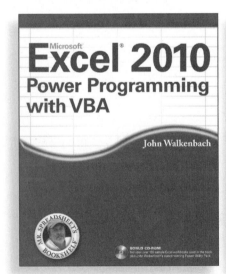
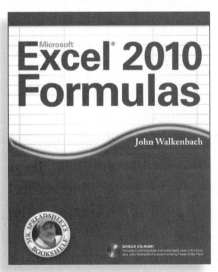